EP Math 6/7

Parent's Guide

Welcome to the EP Math 6/7 Parent's Guide! This was formally called Step 2.

The Math 6/7 Workbook was written with the lesson and examples right on the workbook page so that the students can work independently. This book is set up with a page for each lesson with pictures of the answer pages right on the Parent's Guide instructions for that lesson.

I do suggest you read the Parent's Guide as your child goes through the course. You may find that it helps you remember these topics and keeps you fresh so that you will be able to help when your child is stuck. The Parent's Guide will give some different approaches to problems and shows the set up for word problems, as well as gives a few little notes.

The student workbook is set up differently this year. There is a review section in the beginning. Every Lesson starts with a little review. There are no instructions for that part. You'll find reminders here of how to solve those types of problems if it's needed. Then they will turn to their lesson page.

Each lesson has a "Lesson" page and a "Practice" page. A child who gets all of the lesson page correct can skip the similar type questions on the Practice page and maybe just do the bottom of each page which are typically the more challenging questions. If they got one or two wrong, see if they can find their mistake without you pointing it out. If not, have them complete the similar problems on the practice page.

If they got several wrong or just aren't getting it, use the Parent's Guide with them and have them complete maybe half of the Practice page. Half means half of the problems, not the first half of the page. There may be more than one type of problem on the page, and they should try part of each section. (There are *about* ten problems on the Lesson page and twenty on the Practice page. In the first lesson you'll see this isn't really true, but an approximation.)

If they were getting it the second day, move on to the next lesson and leave the rest of the Practice page blank for review later. However, if they still aren't getting it after using the Lesson and part of the Practice, stay on the lesson. Go over it again, maybe use the lesson EP's Math 6/7 page for that day, and give it another try. Maybe you'll figure out a way they understand best.

If you know your child is struggling at getting math, you may just want to start with the Parent's Guide each day to see if there are helpful tips for introducing or approaching the topic before they try out the Lesson page.

There are review lessons built into the curriculum. On those days it lists for them topics they are supposed to make sure they know. They can work on something in particular, or they can use the practice page to try a little of everything as a refresher. I do recommend they do the practice page for review on those days, even if they are doing well.

And a little note about the guide: To avoid calling all children "he" or the awkward phrasing of "him or her," I've used the plural pronoun when referring to your child, such as, "Today they are comparing fractions."

Have a great year.

Lee

Lesson 1

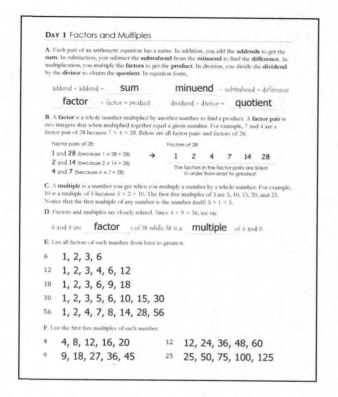

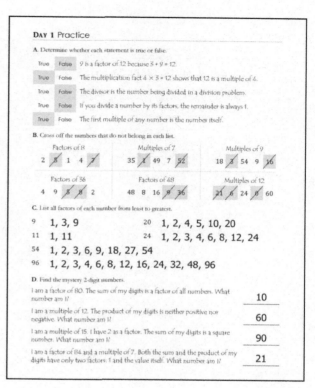

Lesson 1 Lesson – Factors and Multiples

A lot of lessons have new vocabulary in them. Today is no exception. Words like these can sound like a foreign language. It's hard to get comfortable with the math when you aren't comfortable with the English! Try using the formal words when speaking about the questions. You may not really need to know subtrahend, but they should know words like factors and multiples.

They are mostly working on vocabulary in today's lesson, but they will also be finding factors. Factors are all the numbers that you can divide the number by or that you can multiply with to get that number.

Review 1 – Adding single digits

You shouldn't need any extra help with adding single digits. If the students don't know their facts, they should be adept at figuring out the answers and should be working on learning them.

Answers   16   11   18

Lesson 2

DAY 2 Prime Factorization

A. A **prime number** is a positive whole number with exactly two factors: 1 and itself. A number that has more than two factors is called a **composite number**. List the first 10 prime numbers.

2, 3, 5, 7, 11, 13, 17, 19, 23, and 29

B. **Factorization** (also called **factoring** or **to factor**) is writing a number as a product of factors. **Prime factorization** is writing a number as a product of factors that are prime numbers. Here are the steps for using a **factor tree** to break down a number into its prime factors.

```
      1155
      /  \
     3   385
         /  \
        5    77
             /  \
            7    11
```

Therefore, the prime factorization of 1155 =
3 x 5 x 7 x 11

To find the prime factorization of 1155:
1. Start with the smallest prime number, 2. If 2 is a factor of 1155, find the other factor that pair with 2 and write them as branches of the number. 1155 is odd, so 2 is not a factor of 1155.
2. Test the next prime number, 3. In the same way, 1155 ÷ 3 = 385, so 3 is a factor of 1155. Write 3 and 385 as the branches of 1155.
3. Repeat the process with 385. Test 2, 3, 5, and so on until you find a prime number that divides into 385. 385 ÷ 5 = 77, so write 5 and 77 under 385.
4. Continue breaking down factors until all the branches have prime numbers.
5. Multiply all the prime numbers at the end of each branch to find the prime factorization.

C. Find the prime factorization of each number.

8	19	26	42
2 x 2 x 2	prime	2 x 13	2 x 3 x 7

63	78	32	90
3 x 3 x 7	2 x 3 x 13	2 x 2 x 2 x 2 x 2	2 x 3 x 3 x 5

DAY 2 Practice

A. List the prime numbers ending in 3 between 1 and 100.

3, 13, 23, 43, 53, 73, and 83

B. Find the prime factorization of each number.

15	18	23	30
3 x 5	2 x 3 x 3	prime	2 x 3 x 5

52	68	77	45
2 x 2 x 13	2 x 2 x 17	7 x 11	3 x 3 x 5

36	70	95	60
2 x 2 x 3 x 3	2 x 5 x 7	5 x 19	2 x 2 x 3 x 5

48	88	75	92
2 x 2 x 2 x 2 x 3	2 x 2 x 2 x 11	3 x 5 x 5	2 x 2 x 23

Lesson 2 – Prime Factorization

There is some more vocabulary today, prime numbers and prime factorization. A prime number can't be divided by anything (other than 1 and itself).

Every number can be made by multiplying together only prime numbers. That's what they are doing, breaking numbers down to only prime numbers.

They can check their answer with a calculator by multiplying all the factors they found together to see if they equal the original number.

Review 2 – Subtract single digits

You shouldn't need any extra help with subtracting. If students don't know their facts, they should be adept at figuring out the answers and should be working on learning them.

Answers   6   5   7

Lesson 3

DAY 3 Greatest Common Factor (GCF)

A. The **greatest common factor** (GCF) is the largest factor that two or more numbers have in common. One way to find the GCF is to list all the factors of each number and find the greatest one in common. Here is an example. Find the GCF of 24 and 36.

Factors of 24	1, 2, 3, 4, 6, 8, 12, 24	GCF(24, 36) =
Factors of 36	1, 2, 3, 4, 6, 9, 12, 18, 36	12

B. Another method to find the GCF is to use prime factorization. This method works better than the listing method for large numbers. Here are the steps.

$$84 = 2 \times 2 \times 3 \times 7$$
$$98 = 2 \times \quad \times 7 \times 7$$
$$GCF = 2 \times \quad 7$$
$$= 14$$

To find the GCF of 84 and 98:
Write the prime factorization of each number, aligning the common factors vertically.
Bring down the common factors only. The common factors are 2 and 7.
Multiply the common factors to find the GCF.

C. Find the greatest common factor for each number pair.

5 / 7	1	6 / 8	2	2 / 8	2
6 / 10	2	9 / 12	3	8 / 44	4
14 / 49	7	20 / 35	5	12 / 18	6
21 / 35	7	12 / 56	4	25 / 30	5

9

DAY 3 Practice

A. Find the greatest common factor for each number pair.

3 / 9	3	4 / 6	2	7 / 9	1
5 / 20	5	4 / 18	2	6 / 15	3
20 / 30	10	16 / 52	4	24 / 50	2
16 / 27	1	32 / 36	4	42 / 63	21
28 / 70	14	45 / 75	15	84 / 98	14

B. Find the mystery 3-digit numbers.

I am divisible by 5 but not by 10. My first two digits are the greatest common factor of 36 and 54. What number am I?	185
I am divisible by 10. My hundreds digit is the greatest common factor of 15 and 40. My tens digit is the largest prime factor of 210. What number am I?	570
The largest 2-digit prime number makes up my first two digits. My ones digit is the square root of my hundreds digit. What number am I?	973
My tens digit is the only even prime number. The difference between my first two digits is the same as my tens digit. My ones digit is the product of my first two digits. What number am I?	428

Lesson 3 – Greatest Common Factor

When they are comfortable with the lingo, it will help them know what to do. If they know what a factor is, then they should be able to understand what they are looking for if they are trying to find the highest number factor that two numbers have in common.

This will make questions easier in the future, so it's a great thing to learn to do. It will give them smaller numbers to work with.

They are basically looking for what numbers divide into each number. If both numbers end in 0, then they can see easily that they they are both divisible by ten. If both end in 5 or 5 and 0, then they are both divisible by 5. Encourage them to use their brains!

Review 3 – Word problems

These should be simple, but drawing pictures is one way to help figure out how to answer a question.

Answers   13 candies, 17 kids, 8 years old

Lesson 4

DAY 4 Least Common Multiple (LCM)

A. The **least common multiple** (LCM) is the smallest multiple that two or more numbers have in common. One way to find the LCM is to list the multiples of each number until you find the first one in common. Here is an example. Find the LCM of 6 and 8.

Multiples of 6 6, 12, 18, 24, 30, 36, 42, 48, ...   LCM(6, 8) =

Multiples of 8 **8, 16, 24, 32, 40, 48, ...**   **24**

B. You can also use prime factorization to find the LCM. Here are the steps.

$12 = 2 \times 2 \times 3$
$30 = 2 \times \quad 3 \times 5$
$LCM = 2 \times 2 \times 3 \times 5$
$= 60$

To find the LCM of 12 and 30:
1. Write the prime factorization of each number, aligning the common factors vertically.
2. Bring down the factors in each column to combine them. The combined factors are 2, 2, 3, and 5.
3. Multiply the combined factors to find the LCM.

C. Find the least common multiple for each number pair.

5 8	**40**	4 6	**12**	3 9	**9**
10 25	**50**	16 40	**80**	18 24	**72**

D. Solve each problem.

Emily swims every 4 days and Mike every 5 days. They both swam today. In how many days will they swim again together? **20 days**

Sam wants to make a game board using square tiles. The board is 16 inches by 24 inches. If he uses the largest tile possible, how many tiles will he use? **6 tiles**

Mia wants to cut her wires into pieces of all the same length without remainder. One wire is 36 inches long and another is 28 inches long. What is the greatest possible length of the pieces? **4 inches**

A gear with 45 teeth is engaged with another gear with 30 teeth. How many turns must the first gear make for the two gears to return to their original positions? **2 turns**

DAY 4 Practice

A. Find the least common multiple for each number pair.

3 6	**6**	2 9	**18**	5 7	**35**
8 12	**24**	9 15	**45**	4 28	**28**
12 20	**60**	16 22	**176**	14 21	**42**

B. Solve each problem.

Bus A runs every 15 minutes and bus B every 12 minutes. If both buses arrive at the stop at 9 a.m., when will they arrive again at the same time? **10 a.m.**

Jerry is making treat bags for his friends. He has 42 cookies and 36 candies, and he wants to use them all. What is the greatest number of identical bags that Jerry can make? **6 bags**

Matt runs a mile every 8 minutes. Jake runs a mile every 6 minutes. They start running around a 1-mile track. How long will it be before they meet at the starting point? **24 min**

A store had a grand opening event. Every 15th customer received free movie tickets. Every 50th customer received $100. How many customers had to arrive before one of them received both free tickets and $100? **150 cust.**

Dana is making fruit baskets using 28 apples and 21 pears. She wants to make identical baskets with no fruit left over. If she makes the greatest number of fruit baskets possible, how many pears will be in each basket? **3 pears**

The teacher divides 35 boys and 45 girls into groups of the same size, and each group has the same number of boys and the same number of girls. If the teacher makes the greatest number of groups possible, how many boys and how many girls will be in each group? **7 boys 9 girls**

Lesson 4 – Least Common Multiple

This is working in the other direction. They are trying to find the lowest number, not the highest. They are looking not for what they can be divided by, but what they divide into.

They are basically multiplying the numbers this time to see what they have in common. They will always have in common the number that's the product of the two numbers. However, that's not always the least.

They are looking for the least because, again, it's going to make their harder math easier by giving them smaller numbers to work with.

Review 4 – Separate place values

This is showing a mental math trick of finding easier ways to add. Here's the example with an extra step in there. $22 + 18 = 20 + 10 + 2 + 8 = 20 + 10 + 10 = 40$

Answers   60   40   70

Lesson 5

DAY 5 Distributive Property and GCF

A. Consider the array of dots below. You can divide the dots into any two groups and calculate the total number of dots in different ways, and the final result won't change.

The total number of dots
= 4 rows × 11 columns
= 4 rows × (6 + 5) columns
= (4 rows × 6 columns) + (4 rows × 5 columns)

B. The above example shows the **distributive property**, which states that multiplying a sum by a number is the same as multiplying each addend by the number and then adding the products. Symbolically, $a \times (b + c) = (a \times b) + (a \times c)$ and $(b + c) \times a = b \times a + c \times a$. Using the distributive property, you can break difficult multiplication problems into two easy ones.

$29 \times 7 = (20 + 9) \times 7 = (20 \times 7) + (9 \times 7) = 140 + 63 = 203$

Break 29 into 20 + 9, then distribute 7 to 20 and 9. Now it is easier to solve than 29 × 7.

C. You can use the distributive property in reverse. This process is called **factoring** because you are rewriting an expression as a multiplication of factors.

$56 + 24 = (8 \times 7) + (8 \times 3) = 8 \times (7 + 3) = 8 \times 10$

Pull out (or factor out) the GCF 8. Now you have a multiplication of two factors.

D. Circle all statements that show the distributive property.

$6 \times 8 = 6 \times (5 + 3) = (6 \times 5) + (6 \times 3)$ $4 \times 6 = (4 \times 1) \times 6 = (4 \times 6) + (1 \times 6)$

$8 \times 5 = (5 + 3) \times 5 = (5 \times 3) + (3 \times 5)$ $12 \times 5 = (6 + 6) \times 5 = (6 \times 5) + (6 \times 5)$

E. Use the distributive property to rewrite each expression and evaluate.

$4 \times (6 + 8)$ $= (4 \times 6) + (4 \times 8) = 24 + 32 = 56$
$7 \times (7 + 4)$ $= (7 \times 7) + (7 \times 4) = 49 + 28 = 77$
$(4 + 9) \times 4$ $= (4 \times 4) + (9 \times 4) = 16 + 36 = 52$

F. Use the distributive property to factor out the GCF from each expression.

$30 + 42$ $= 6 \times 5 + 6 \times 7 = 6 \times (5 + 7) = 6 \times 12$
$28 + 16$ $= 4 \times 7 + 4 \times 4 = 4 \times (7 + 4) = 4 \times 11$
$81 + 45$ $= 9 \times 9 + 9 \times 5 = 9 \times (9 + 5) = 9 \times 14$

DAY 5 Practice

A. The dots represent 3 × 14. Break 3 × 14 up into two simpler multiplication facts.

$3 \times 14 = 3 \times 7 + 3 \times 7$

B. Use the distributive property to rewrite each expression and evaluate.

$3 \times (7 + 9)$ $= (3 \times 7) + (3 \times 9) = 21 + 27 = 48$
$(6 + 8) \times 5$ $= (6 \times 5) + (8 \times 5) = 30 + 40 = 70$
$8 \times (10 + 7)$ $= (8 \times 10) + (8 \times 7) = 80 + 56 = 136$
$(50 + 4) \times 9$ $= (50 \times 9) + (4 \times 9) = 450 + 36 = 486$
$(30 + 8) \times 6$ $= (30 \times 6) + (8 \times 6) = 180 + 48 = 228$

C. Use the distributive property to factor out the GCF from each expression.

$9 + 15$ $= 3 \times 3 + 3 \times 5 = 3 \times (3 + 5) = 3 \times 8$
$18 + 12$ $= 6 \times 3 + 6 \times 2 = 6 \times (3 + 2) = 6 \times 5$
$28 + 24$ $= 4 \times 7 + 4 \times 6 = 4 \times (7 + 6) = 4 \times 13$
$49 + 35$ $= 7 \times 7 + 7 \times 5 = 7 \times (7 + 5) = 7 \times 12$
$64 + 24$ $= 8 \times 8 + 8 \times 3 = 8 \times (8 + 3) = 8 \times 11$
$80 + 48$ $= 16 \times 5 + 16 \times 3 = 16 \times (5 + 3) = 16 \times 8$

D. Find the mystery 2-digit numbers.

My tens digit is the greatest common factor of 42 and 66. The product of my digits is the least common multiple of 6 and 15. What number am I?   65

I am a common multiple of 8 and 12. I am divisible by 3 but not by 9. The sum of my digits is divisible by 3 but not by 6. What number am I?   96

My ones digit is the largest prime factor of 140. The product of my digits is the same as the total number of dots on a die. What number am I?   37

I am an even number. My tens digit is a common multiple of 2 and 4. My ones digit is a common factor of 18 and 48. The product of my digits is a square number. What number am I?   82

Lesson 5 – Distributive Property and GCF

The distributive property allows you to divide up numbers and add them back together. In the example below, it distributes the 7 to each place value in 123.

$123 \times 7 = 100 \times 7$ and 20×7 and $3 \times 7 = 700 + 140 + 21 = 861$

When they get into algebra, they will be doing the opposite of this often, factoring. It doesn't seem like it makes a lot of sense now, but they are practicing with numbers for when they will be doing it with x and x^2.

Factoring would take the $700 + 140 + 21$ and pull out, factor out, the 7, which is the greatest common factor.

$700 + 140 + 21 = 7 \times (100 + 20 + 3)$

Review 5 – Separate place values

Here's the example a little fuller. $16 + 47 = 10 + 40 + 6 + 7 = 50 + 13 = 63$

Answers   42   67   64

Lesson 6

DAY 6 Adding and Subtracting Fractions

A. Fractions are **equivalent** if they represent the same amount. To find equivalent fractions, multiply or divide the **numerator** and the **denominator** by the same number.

B. You can add or subtract fractions only when they have the same denominator, or **common denominator**. Here are the steps for adding fractions. Subtraction works the same way.

$$\frac{7}{9}+\frac{5}{9}=\frac{5+7}{9}=\frac{12}{9}=\frac{4}{3}=1\frac{1}{3}$$

To add fractions with like denominators:
1. Add the numerators and keep the same denominator.
2. Simplify the answer.

$$\frac{5}{6}+\frac{3}{4}=\frac{10}{12}+\frac{9}{12}=\frac{19}{12}=1\frac{7}{12}$$

To add fractions with unlike denominators:
1. Find equivalent fractions with the same denominator and add their numerators.
2. Simplify the answer.

$$1\frac{1}{2}+2\frac{2}{3}=3+\frac{3+4}{6}=3\frac{7}{6}=4\frac{1}{6}$$

To add mixed numbers:
1. Add the whole number parts and the fraction parts separately.
2. Simplify the fraction part of the answer.

C. Find each sum or difference. Simplify your answers.

$\frac{3}{4}+\frac{3}{4}$ 1 1/2 $\frac{7}{8}-\frac{3}{8}$ 1/2

$\frac{2}{3}+\frac{5}{7}$ 1 8/21 $\frac{4}{5}-\frac{1}{6}$ 19/30

$\frac{1}{2}+3\frac{5}{8}$ 4 1/8 $1\frac{4}{9}-\frac{1}{9}$ 1 1/3

$2\frac{1}{4}+\frac{5}{6}$ 3 1/12 $7\frac{7}{8}-2\frac{1}{6}$ 5 17/24

$2\frac{5}{6}+3\frac{2}{9}$ 6 1/18 $3\frac{9}{10}-2\frac{3}{5}$ 1 3/10

DAY 6 Practice

A. Write three equivalent fractions for each fraction.

$\frac{2}{7}$ Answers will vary. $\frac{9}{12}$

$\frac{5}{8}$ $\frac{24}{36}$

B. Find each sum or difference. Simplify your answers.

$\frac{6}{7}+\frac{5}{7}$ 1 4/7 $\frac{5}{6}-\frac{1}{6}$ 2/3

$\frac{5}{6}+\frac{2}{5}$ 1 7/30 $\frac{6}{7}-\frac{1}{2}$ 5/14

$\frac{3}{8}+5\frac{7}{8}$ 6 1/4 $2\frac{4}{5}-\frac{2}{5}$ 2 2/5

$7\frac{2}{3}+\frac{3}{4}$ 8 5/12 $4\frac{5}{8}-\frac{1}{2}$ 4 1/8

$4\frac{1}{3}+2\frac{5}{6}$ 7 1/6 $5\frac{7}{6}-3\frac{4}{9}$ 2 13/18

$2\frac{4}{8}+7\frac{3}{4}$ 10 1/4 $8\frac{3}{4}-1\frac{1}{6}$ 7 7/12

$3\frac{4}{9}+5\frac{1}{6}$ 8 11/18 $4\frac{4}{5}-2\frac{2}{3}$ 2 2/15

Lesson 6 – Adding and Subtracting Fractions

There is no example in the first part on equivalent fractions. Equivalent fractions are equal. If you have two out of four, that's one half. If you have three out of six, that's one half. One half, two fourths, and three sixths are equivalent fractions. You can get to two fourths by multiplying ½ by two in both the numerator and denominator. You can get three sixths by multiplying ½ by three top and bottom. You can do the reverse and divide to get ½ from three sixths.

This works because any number over itself is 1. Two out of two is one whole. When you multiply or divide by one, the answer is the number you started with. When you divide and multiply a fraction by 1, the fraction stays the same. In these cases the numbers change, but the value of the fraction does not.

Review 6 – Adding double digits

They need to add the ones and the tens and keep the place values in their places.

Answers   39   59   88

Lesson 7

DAY 7 Multiplying and Dividing Fractions

A. The **reciprocal** of a fraction is the fraction turned upside down. A whole number is a fraction whose denominator is 1, so the reciprocal of a whole number (except 0) is 1 over the number.

B. Multiplying fractions is simple: top by top and bottom by bottom. When multiplying mixed numbers, first convert them to improper fractions and then multiply as usual.

$$\frac{5}{6} \times \frac{2}{9} = \frac{5 \times 21}{36 \times 9} = \frac{5}{27}$$

To multiply fractions and mixed numbers:
1. Convert any mixed numbers and whole numbers to improper fractions.
2. Cancel out all common factors.
3. Multiply the numerators and the denominators respectively.
4. Simplify the answer.

$$3 \times 2\frac{1}{4} = \frac{3}{1} \times \frac{9}{4} = \frac{27}{4} = 6\frac{3}{4}$$

C. Dividing fractions is just like multiplying fractions, except that you "flip" the divisor first. When dividing mixed numbers, apply the same rules: convert to improper fractions, then divide.

$$\frac{8}{9} \div \frac{2}{9} = \frac{8}{9} \times \frac{9}{2} = \frac{48 \times 91}{19 \times 21} = \frac{4}{1} = 4$$

To divide fractions and mixed numbers:
1. Convert any mixed numbers and whole numbers to improper fractions.
2. Rewrite division as multiplication by multiplying by the reciprocal of the divisor.
3. Multiply the fractions as usual.
4. Simplify the answer.

$$1\frac{4}{5} \div 6 = \frac{9}{5} \times \frac{1}{6} = \frac{3 9 \times 1}{5 \times 6 2} = \frac{3}{10}$$

D. Find each product or quotient. Simplify your answers.

$\frac{2}{3} \times \frac{1}{4}$ 1/6 $\frac{1}{2} \div \frac{5}{6}$ 3/5

$9 \times \frac{8}{15}$ 4 4/5 $6\frac{2}{3} \div 8$ 5/6

$5\frac{1}{4} \times \frac{2}{9}$ 1 1/6 $9 \div 4\frac{2}{7}$ 2 1/10

$2\frac{5}{8} \times 1\frac{3}{7}$ 3 3/4 $4\frac{2}{3} \div 5\frac{1}{4}$ 8/9

DAY 7 Practice

A. Convert the mixed numbers to improper fractions.

$1\frac{3}{5}$ 8/5 $5\frac{1}{8}$ 41/8 $3\frac{2}{9}$ 29/9 $2\frac{4}{7}$ 18/7

B. Find each product or quotient. Simplify your answers.

$\frac{3}{5} \times \frac{5}{7}$ 3/7 $\frac{5}{6} \div \frac{3}{4}$ 1 1/9

$\frac{4}{9} \times \frac{6}{8}$ 1/3 $\frac{3}{5} \div 9$ 1/15

$16 \times \frac{5}{6}$ 13 1/3 $18 \div \frac{6}{7}$ 21

$\frac{2}{7} \times 5\frac{1}{4}$ 1 1/2 $4\frac{1}{2} \div 5$ 9/10

$3\frac{1}{9} \times 12$ 37 1/3 $\frac{5}{6} \div 3\frac{3}{4}$ 2/9

$1\frac{4}{5} \times 2\frac{2}{9}$ 4 $1\frac{2}{7} \div 1\frac{1}{5}$ 1 1/14

$6\frac{2}{3} \times 3\frac{3}{8}$ 22 1/2 $2\frac{2}{3} \div 1\frac{3}{5}$ 1 2/3

Lesson 7 – Multiplying and Dividing Fractions

They will just multiply straight across to get the answers. To divide, the second number is flipped to get its reciprocal, and then it's just a matter of multiplying.

The trick with these is to look for ways to reduce the fractions. This can be done at the end, but it's simpler and easier to do at the beginning. There are examples in the book. If a number in he tnumerator can be divided by a number in the denominator, or if they can be divided by the same number (for instance if there are two even numbers, they can be divided by two), then divide and simplify so that you have smaller numbers to multiply together.

Review 7 – Adding Double Digits

If the ones add up to more than ten, for instance 12, then the 2 is the ones part of the answer and the 1 is added on as an extra ten in the tens column.

Answers   74   83   82

Lesson 8

DAY 8 Word Problems with Fractions

The table shows how many hours Brian spent studying each subject during this week. Use the table to answer each question. Write your answers in simplest form.

	Mon.	Tue.	Wed.	Thu.	Fri.	
Bible	$2/3$	1	$1/2$	$1 1/4$	$1 1/3$	
Math	$3/4$	$1 1/12$	1	$11/12$	$3/4$	
History	$1 1/6$	$1/4$	$1 5/12$	$1/2$	$5/6$	
Science	1	$1 1/3$	$2/3$	$5/6$	$1/2$	(Unit: hour)

How many minutes did Brian study Bible on Monday?	40 minutes
How many minutes did he study history on Wednesday?	85 minutes
On Tuesday, which subject did he spend the most time on?	Science
On Friday, which subject did he spend the least time on?	Science
How many hours in total did he study on Friday?	3 5/12 hours
How many more hour(s) did he study on Monday than on Friday?	1/6 hour
How many hours in total did he spend on Bible during the week?	4 3/4 hours
How many hour(s) on average did he spend on Bible each day?	19/20 hour
On which subject did he spend the most time in total?	Bible
Brian had set a goal of spending a total of 4 hours on Bible for the week. By how many hour(s) did he exceed his goal?	3/4 hour
On Friday he solved 9 word problems during his math study session. How many minutes on average did he spend on each problem?	5 minutes
Next week Brian plans to study math for $5/6$ of the time he spent on math this week. How many hour(s) will he spend in total?	3 3/4 hours
On Thursday, Brian started studying at 9 a.m. He took three quarter-hour breaks during his study. What time did he finish?	1:15 p.m.

$7 - (7 \div 7) = 7 - 1 = 6$

DAY 8 Practice

Solve each problem.

Sarah had 51 candies. She gave one third of the candies to her sister. How many candies does she have left?	34 candies
Carol picked two thirds of a basket of apples. Chris picked three quarters of a basket of apples. Who picked more apples?	Chris
Kate painted $2/5$ of her room green and $1/4$ of the room ivory. What fraction of the room was not painted yet?	7/20
Tylor had $36 and spent $4/9$ of his money. Kelly had $18 and spent $5/6$ of her money. Who spent more money?	Tylor
Noah drank $1/6$ of a bottle of milk. Now the bottle is $1/3$ full. What fraction of the whole bottle was there at first?	1/2
In a class, $4/5$ of the students have pets. Among those students, $3/4$ have dogs. What fraction of the students in the class have dogs?	3/5
Nathan runs a lap of the track in $1/12$ of an hour. How many laps will he run in 35 minutes?	7 laps
Olivia planted $4 2/3$ rows of roses, 7 rows of violets, and $3/4$ of a row of daisies. How many rows did she plant in total?	12 5/12
Walter ran three-quarters of a mile every day for the past two weeks. How many miles did he run in total?	10 1/2 miles
Mark had $3/8$ of a gallon of milk. He divided the milk evenly into 3 bottles. How much milk did he put in each bottle?	1/8 gallon
Kyle bought $2 5/8$ pounds of beef and used $1 5/8$ pounds to cook dinner. How many pounds of beef did he have left after that?	1 11/24 lbs
Amelia did a total of 3 hours of fitness training, which consisted of one-third-hour sessions. How many sessions did she do?	9 sessions
A restaurant had 12 loaves of bread. They used $7 3/5$ loaves to make sandwiches. How many loaves of bread were left?	4 2/5 loaves
It usually takes Rodney $2 1/2$ minutes to run a lap of the track. Yesterday he ran $7 3/5$ laps. How many minutes did he run?	19 minutes
Emma has a $40 1/2$-inch string. For her science project, she needs to cut it into $3 1/4$-inch pieces. How many whole pieces will she make?	12 pieces

Lesson 8 – Word Problems with Fractions

They might be required to do any of the operations. If they are confused on what to do, they should substitute whole numbers in just for the sake of figuring out how to approach the question.

The last one is different. It's about time. Three quarter hours is ¾ of an hour. That's ¾ around a clock, which is 45 minutes. Each quarter is 15 minutes.

The third from the bottom is about 9 complex algebra problems. That's math. They will divide the time spent on Friday by nine to get the time spent on each.

Review 8 – Subtracting double digits

They need to subtract straight down each place value.

Answers   32   72   15

Lesson 9

DAY 9 Operations with Decimals

A. Decimals are numbers that contain a decimal point. They are a special way of writing fractions whose denominator is a power of 10. Remember that the powers of 10 are 1, 10, 100, and so on.

B. Arithmetic operations with decimals are very similar to those with whole numbers. Here are the steps for adding decimals. Subtraction works the same way. Be sure to align the decimal points!

```
  1 2 . 5 0 0
+   9 . 7 8 3
  2 2 . 2 8 3
```

To add decimals:
1. Line up the decimal points vertically.
2. Add zeros so the decimal parts have the same length.
3. Add the numbers as you would whole numbers.
4. Carry the decimal point directly down into the answer.

C. When multiplying decimals, just be careful with placing the decimal point in your answer!

```
    1  2 . 5
×   0 . 5  3
    3  7  5
  6  2  5
  6 . 6  2  5
```

To multiply a decimal by a decimal:
1. Ignore the decimal point and multiply as usual.
2. Count the total number of decimal places in the factors. The two factors 12.5 and 0.53 have a total of 3 decimal places.
3. Place a decimal point in the answer so that the answer has the same number of decimal places that you counted. Place a decimal point in 6625 so that it has 3 decimal places.

D. When dividing decimals, remember to make the divisor a whole number before dividing!

```
                     1 5
0.06 ) 0.09  ⇒  6 ) 9.0
                     6
Move both            3 0
decimal points       3 0
2 places               0
to the right.
```

To divide a decimal by a decimal:
1. Move the decimal points in the divisor and dividend the same number of places to the right to make the divisor a whole number.
2. Ignore the decimal points and divide as usual.
3. If there is a remainder, keep adding zeros to the right of the dividend and continue to divide.
4. Place a decimal point in the quotient directly above the decimal point in the dividend.

E. Find each sum, difference, product, or quotient.

9.4 + 0.253   **9.653**   0.25 × 30.6   **7.65**

43.7 − 3.72   **39.98**   6.624 ÷ 3.2   **2.07**

12.3 − 8.705   **3.595**   29.16 ÷ 0.72   **40.5**

DAY 9 Practice

Find each sum, difference, product, or quotient.

1.4 + 2.38	**3.78**	7.7 − 5.809	**1.891**
5.3 − 2.07	**3.23**	2.718 + 3.5	**6.218**
0.7 × 8.9	**6.23**	46.35 ÷ 0.45	**103**
36 ÷ 80	**0.45**	0.706 × 13.5	**9.531**
0.75 + 0.95	**1.7**	0.32 + 0.192	**0.512**
0.15 ÷ 0.6	**0.25**	0.159 ÷ 0.02	**7.95**
5.3 × 2.7	**14.31**	8.103 − 3.86	**4.243**
4.06 − 1.6	**2.46**	532 × 0.504	**268.128**
31.2 ÷ 1.2	**26**	25.9 × 0.367	**9.5053**

Lesson 9 – Operations with Decimals

To add and subtract decimals, the important thing is to line up the decimal points so that the same place values are being added together. The operation is carried out as usual. The decimal point drops straight down into the answer in the same place.

To multiply decimals you can just ignore the decimals until the answer. 0.53 x 0.275 is just 275 x 53 with five decimal places in the answer because there are a total of five decimal places in the question.   275 x 53 = 14,575   0.53 x 0.275 = 0.14575
                                                    12   345   12345 number of decimal places

They will divide normally after they take the first step of making sure they are dividing by a whole number. To do that you move the decimal point over in the divisor (the one you are dividing by) until it's a whole number and move the decimal point in the dividend the same amount.

$$0.4 \overline{)16} \quad \text{becomes} \quad 4 \overline{)160}^{\,40}$$

Review 9 – Subtracting Double Digits

If the bottom number in the ones column is more than the top number, borrow ten from the top number in the tens column. 54 is the same as 40 + 14. That's what you are doing when you are borrowing.
Answers   12   25   44

Lesson 10

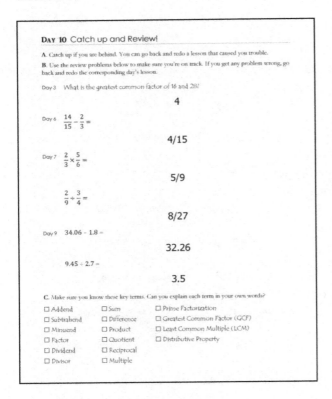

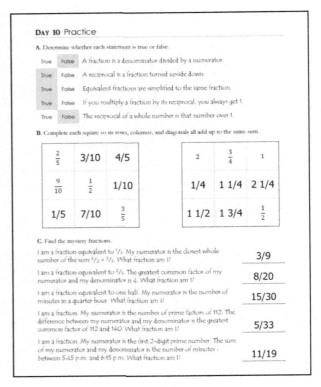

Lesson 10 Catch Up and Review

You can go back to a previous lesson if you know there was one you should try again and use the practice page. You could also use the first page to check if there's an area you need to spend time on today. If you are on top of things, turn the page and use the practice page to keep sharp.

No Review

Lesson 11

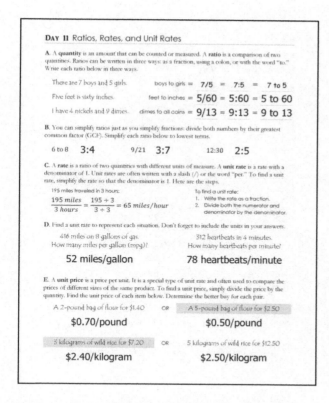

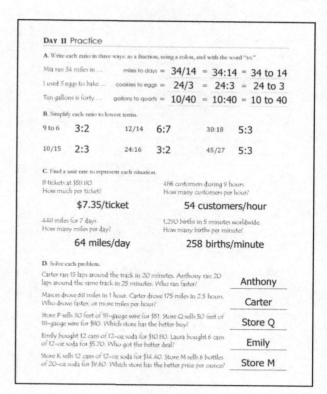

Lesson 11 – Ratios, Rates, and Unit Rates

A ratio compares two numbers. If there are 10 boys and 5 girls, then the ratio of boys to girls is 10 to 5, 10:5, 10/5. That means that for every five girls there are ten boys.

A rate is how many "per." To do that you divide. If "of" means multiply, "per" means divide.

If you had 6 people and 12 cookies to share, how many cookies per person do you have? You take the cookies and divide it by the number of people (per person). That gives you 2. You have two cookies for one person, per person.

To find the unit rate all they will be doing is dividing. If it's "per day," then they divide by the number of days to find the answer for just one day.

Review 11 – Word Problems

Another tip for solving word problems is to use smaller numbers. For instance, change 62, 15, and 19 in the first question to 6, 1, 1, to figure out what you are supposed to do to solve. Once you know what to do, plug back in the original numbers.

Answers   28 markers, $18, 16 flowers

Lesson 12

DAY 12 Ratio Tables

A. Ratios are **equivalent** if they can be simplified to the same ratio. To find equivalent ratios, multiply or divide both numbers by the same number. Write three equivalent ratios for each ratio.

2:5   Answers will vary.   70/30

B. Suppose a recipe calls for 2 eggs to bake a dozen cookies. If you have 5 eggs, how many cookies can you bake? If you need 4 dozen cookies, how many eggs will you need to buy? You can answer these questions by making a table of equivalent ratios called a **ratio table**, as shown on the right. Notice that all of the ratios in the ratio table are equivalent (simplified to the same ratio):

2:12 = 5:30 = 8:48 = 1:6

Eggs	Cookies
2	12
5	30
8	48

C. Complete each table using equivalent ratios.

Ana bought 4 tickets at $28.

Tickets	Cost ($)
4	28
3	21
8	56

Sam runs 35 miles every 7 days.

Miles	Days
35	7
25	5
50	10

Jake can type 675 words in 15 minutes.

Words	Minutes
675	15
450	10
225	5

Ben bought 3 kilograms of rice for $6.15.

Rice (kg)	Cost ($)
3	6.15
5	10.25
10	20.50

D. Complete the ratio tables to find the unit prices of pears. Which store has the better buy?

Store T sells 5 pears for $4.60.

Price ($)	Pears
4.6	5
9.20	10
0.92	1

Store K sells 16 pears for $14.08.

Price ($)	Pears
14.08	16
3.52	4
0.88	1

Better buy

DAY 12 Practice

A. Write three equivalent ratios for each ratio.

3/5   Answers will vary.   28:49

B. Complete each table using equivalent ratios.

Max ran 4 laps in 16 minutes.

Minutes	Laps
16	4
20	5
40	10

Karen solved 120 problems over 5 days.

Problems	Days
120	5
192	8
72	3

Emily bought 8 pairs of socks at $52.

Cost ($)	Pairs
52	8
39	6
6.5	1

Mike's team scored 432 points in 6 games.

Points	Games
432	6
144	2
72	1

Carl bought a dozen eggs for $1.80.

Cost ($)	Eggs
1.80	12
0.60	4
0.15	1

Joe earned $820 for 40 hours of work.

Wage ($)	Hours
820	40
82	4
20.50	1

C. Find the mystery ratios. Write your answers using a colon.

I am equivalent to the ratio of the number of nickels to the number of quarters in a dollar. The product of my two numbers is the greatest common factor of 25 and 40. What ratio am I?   5:1

I am equivalent to the ratio of the smallest prime number to the smallest two-digit prime number. The sum of my two numbers is the least common multiple of 5 and 15. What ratio am I?   6:33

Lesson 12 – Ratio Tables

A ratio is a comparison of two amounts. The example from Day 11 had ten boys for every five girls.

We can reduce that. The ratio of boys to girls is 2 to 1, 2:1, 2/1. You can reduce it just like a fraction. This means that for every girl there are two boys. So, for every two girls there are four boys, for every three girls there are six boys, for every four girls there are eight boys, and for every five girls there are ten boys, and there is the ratio we started with. Those are all equivalent (fractions) ratios.

Review 12 – Addition with Three Digits

The important thing in adding larger numbers is to make sure you are always adding the same place values together, ones with ones, tens with tens. Ten ones equals one ten. Ten tens equals one hundred. The "one" gets added to the next place value column.

Answers   1,230   1,511   1,144

Lesson 13

DAY 13 Proportions

A. A **proportion** is a statement that two ratios are equal. When two ratios are equal, we say they are **proportional** or **in proportion**. A proportion is written as $a:b = c:d$ or $a/b = c/d$ and is read as "a is to b as c is to d." For example, $2:3 = 4:6$ and $3/4 = 9/12$ are proportions.

B. Solving a proportion means finding an unknown value in the proportion. One way to solve a proportion is to find the appropriate equivalent ratio, as shown in the example below.

9 pears at $15; how many pears at $5?   Set up a proportion → $\frac{9}{15} = \frac{x}{5}$ Find the equivalent ratio. → $\frac{9 \div 3}{15 \div 3} = \frac{3}{5}$ $x = 3$

C. You can set up your proportions in several ways. Below are the proportions you can set up from the example above. Notice that the two ratios in each proportion compare corresponding quantities in the same order.

$\frac{9 \text{ pears}}{\$15} = \frac{x \text{ pears}}{\$5}$ $\frac{\$15}{9 \text{ pears}} = \frac{\$5}{x \text{ pears}}$ $\frac{9 \text{ pears}}{x \text{ pears}} = \frac{\$15}{\$5}$ $\frac{x \text{ pears}}{9 \text{ pears}} = \frac{\$5}{\$15}$

D. Solve each proportion using equivalent ratios.

$\frac{3}{4} = \frac{x}{20}$ x = 15 $\frac{x}{10} = \frac{27}{45}$ x = 6

$\frac{x}{4} = \frac{25}{10}$ x = 10 $\frac{21}{28} = \frac{15}{x}$ x = 20

In a grocery, apples and pears are sold in the ratio of 6:7. If the grocery sells 49 pears, how many apples are sold?

42 apples

At a farmer's market, 6 tomatoes were being sold for $3.80. Peter bought 30 tomatoes. How much money did he spend in all?

$19

A recipe calls for 4 cups of beans to make 6 servings of chili. How many cups of beans will you need to make 15 servings?

10 cups

Sandy can solve 24 division problems every 15 minutes. How many problems can she solve in 10 minutes?

16 problems

DAY 13 Practice

Solve each proportion using equivalent ratios.

$\frac{6}{7} = \frac{x}{35}$ x = 30 $\frac{x}{40} = \frac{20}{25}$ x = 32

$\frac{8}{x} = \frac{24}{18}$ x = 6 $\frac{14}{18} = \frac{35}{x}$ x = 45

$\frac{15}{10} = \frac{6}{x}$ x = 4 $\frac{x}{21} = \frac{35}{49}$ x = 15

Six apples are sold at $7.15. How much do 18 apples cost?

$21.45

A pack of 12 cans of soda weighs 144 ounces. How much do 8 cans of soda weigh?

96 ounces

There are 12 grams of protein in two eggs. How many grams of protein are there in a carton of 12 eggs?

72 grams

Sam drew a rectangle whose length to width ratio was 3 to 2. If the width of the rectangle was 10 inches, what was its length?

15 inches

A recipe calls for 6 bananas to make 4 servings of banana pudding. How many bananas will be used to make 10 servings?

15 bananas

In a zoo, the ratio of adults to children is 5 to 7. If there are 125 adults in the zoo, how many children are there?

175 children

Ella planted 15 violets, 24 daisies, and 30 roses. For every 5 roses, how many daisies did Ella plant?

4 daisies

A book club has 28 members, and the ratio of boys to girls is 3:4. How many boys are in the book club?

12 boys

Lesson 13 – Proportions

Proportions are like the ratios and rates. Proportions are two equal ratios. They are to set up the ratios being careful to compare the same things. The first word problem uses apples and pears. They need to have apples on top of both fractions, both ratios. They need to have the pears on the bottom of both fractions, both ratios. Or the other way around, but the point is to match apples to apples and pears to pears.

To find the missing number in the proportion, find an equivalent fraction. Reduce the known fraction. Make the known numbers match. Then the X, the unknown number, matches as well.

Here's the first example. $3/4 = x/20$ You can multiply 4 x 5 to make the denominators both 20. Then we have to, at the same time, multiply 3 by 5 to make them equivalent fractions. Then it is clear that x = 15. If you can't just take that step, reduce the fraction first.

Review 13 – Multi-digit Subtraction

When subtracting and borrowing, they are taking one from the next place value and splitting it into ten to add to the number they are subtracting from. To borrow from 0, an easy thing to do is to combine it with the next digit that's not a zero. In their review they subtract from 500. They can cross out 50 and turn it into 49. The zero on the right gets 10. Then they just have to subtract straight down from 10, 9, and 4.

Answers   234   216   228

Lesson 14

DAY 14 Proportions

A. You can solve a proportion using **cross multiplication**. If you cross multiply two ratios in proportion, their **cross products** must be equal. Symbolically, if $a/b = c/d$, then $a \times d = b \times c$. After cross multiplying, you divide both sides of the equation by the number in front of the unknown to find its value. Here is an example.

$$\frac{x}{8} \times \frac{9}{12} \quad \text{Cross multiply.} \quad x \times 12 = 8 \times 9 \quad \text{Divide by 12.} \quad \frac{12 \times x}{12} = \frac{8 \times 9}{12} \quad x = 6$$

B. Solve each proportion using cross multiplication.

$\frac{6}{9} = \frac{x}{30}$ x = 20 $\frac{24}{x} = \frac{10}{25}$ x = 60

$\frac{15}{10} = \frac{3}{x}$ x = 2 $\frac{18}{21} = \frac{42}{x}$ x = 49

$\frac{9}{x} = \frac{36}{24}$ x = 6 $\frac{55}{44} = \frac{x}{36}$ x = 45

A recipe calls for 3 cups of milk for every 2 cups of flour. Sarah used 6 cups of flour. How many cups of milk did she use?

9 cups

Adam can solve 15 fraction problems every 18 minutes. How many problems can he solve in 12 minutes?

10 problems

A restaurant makes cakes to pies in the ratio of 4 to 5. If the restaurant makes 35 pies, how many cakes does it make?

28 cakes

Larry's car uses 5 gallons of gas to travel 110 miles. How many miles can Larry drive on 2 gallons of gas?

44 miles

DAY 14 Practice

Solve each proportion using cross multiplication.

$\frac{5}{8} = \frac{x}{24}$ x = 15 $\frac{x}{20} = \frac{27}{30}$ x = 18

$\frac{8}{5} = \frac{x}{70}$ x = 112 $\frac{40}{x} = \frac{96}{12}$ x = 5

$\frac{x}{6} = \frac{25}{15}$ x = 10 $\frac{21}{35} = \frac{15}{x}$ x = 25

$\frac{3}{x} = \frac{12}{32}$ x = 8 $\frac{x}{10} = \frac{24}{40}$ x = 6

$\frac{x}{9} = \frac{49}{63}$ x = 7 $\frac{20}{28} = \frac{x}{21}$ x = 15

Angie drove 58 miles per hour for 4 hours. How many miles did she drive?

232 miles

Six cans of soda cost $2.50. How many cans of soda can you buy for $20?

48 cans

Eight candies are sold at $2. Brian bought 30 candies and paid with $20. How much change did he receive?

$12.50

Ana can type 135 words every 3 minutes. If she types 20 minutes each day, how many words will she type in 5 days?

4,500 words

Lesson 14 – Proportions

They will be using the ratio to solve cross multiplication problems. Multiply the opposite denominators and numerators together and then solve. Here are examples.

$$^9/_x \text{ as } ^3/_4 \quad 9 \times 4 = 3x \quad 36 \div 3 = x \quad 12 = x$$

$$^y/_{20} \text{ as } ^3/_4 \quad 4y = 3 \times 20 \quad y = 60 \div 4 \quad y = 15$$

This is the same as:

9:x as 3:4 To find x we multiply nine times the ratio 4:3. $9(^4/_3) = 36 \div 3 = 12$

y:20 as 3:4 To find y we multiply 20 times the ration 3:4 since we're looking for the length on the smaller triangle this time. $20(^3/_4) = 60 \div 4 = 15$

Review 14 – Multi-digit Subtraction

This is the same as Lesson 13 review.

Answers   556   426   164

Lesson 15

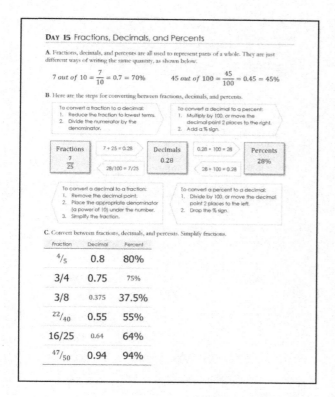

DAY 15 Fractions, Decimals, and Percents

A. Fractions, decimals, and percents are all used to represent parts of a whole. They are just different ways of writing the same quantity, as shown below.

$$7 \text{ out of } 10 = \frac{7}{10} = 0.7 = 70\% \qquad 45 \text{ out of } 100 = \frac{45}{100} = 0.45 = 45\%$$

B. Here are the steps for converting between fractions, decimals, and percents.

To convert a fraction to a decimal:
1. Reduce the fraction to lowest terms.
2. Divide the numerator by the denominator.

To convert a decimal to a percent:
1. Multiply by 100, or move the decimal point 2 places to the right.
2. Add a % sign.

To convert a decimal to a fraction:
1. Remove the decimal point.
2. Place the appropriate denominator (a power of 10) under the number.
3. Simplify the fraction.

To convert a percent to a decimal:
1. Divide by 100, or move the decimal point 2 places to the left.
2. Drop the % sign.

C. Convert between fractions, decimals, and percents. Simplify fractions.

Fraction	Decimal	Percent
$^4/_5$	0.8	80%
3/4	0.75	75%
3/8	0.375	37.5%
$^{22}/_{40}$	0.55	55%
16/25	0.64	64%
$^{47}/_{50}$	0.94	94%

DAY 15 Practice

A. Convert between fractions, decimals, and percents. Simplify fractions.

Fraction	Decimal	Percent
5/8	0.625	62.5%
3/5	0.6	60%
$^6/_{16}$	0.375	37.5%
7/20	0.35	35%
$^{18}/_{24}$	0.75	75%
21/25	0.84	84%
23/50	0.46	46%
$^9/_{75}$	0.12	12%

B. Find the mystery numbers.

I am a decimal. As a fraction, my denominator is twice my numerator. What number am I?	0.5
I am a percent. In fraction form, I am equivalent to five eighths times four tenths. What number am I?	25%
I am a decimal between 3 and 4. I have two digits in total and my tenths digit is the square of 3. What number am I?	3.9
I am a fraction equivalent to three fourths. My denominator is the sum of all prime factors of 66. What number am I?	12/16
I am a fraction. My numerator and denominator are both prime. In percent form, I can be written as 40%. What number am I?	2/5
I am a percent. In decimal form, my whole number part is the greatest common factor of 18 and 24. My decimal part is the least common multiple of 21 and 28. What number am I?	684%

Lesson 15 – Fractions, Decimals, and Percents

They are going to be converting both ways. To turn a decimal into a fraction, you take the digits in the decimal and put it over one with the same number of zeros as there were decimal places. The decimal 0.05 would be 5 over 100, two zeros because there are two decimal places in 0.05.

To go the other way, they divide the denominator into the numerator. They will know if they are going the correct way if they get answer that is smaller than one, if the denominator was a larger number than the numerator.

I'm okay with kids using a calculator to do this part. That's up to you. If they can do the division without trouble, let them do it. They will place a decimal point in the dividend and then add as many zeros as necessary. The decimal point goes straight up into the quotient.

To find percent, they are really just multiplying by 100 because a percent is a part of a hundred. To find a decimal from a percent, they just divide by 100. This means they will move the decimal point over two places.

Review 15 – Multi-digit Subtraction

This is the same as Lesson 13 review.

Answers   453   268   264

Lesson 16

DAY 16 Percent of a Number

A. Percent means "per 100" or "out of 100" and the symbol % is used to represent it. A percent is a special way of writing a fraction with a denominator of 100. Convert each percent to a decimal and a fraction. Simplify fractions. Review Day 15 if needed.

Percent	Decimal	Fraction
125%	1.25	1 1/4
45%	0.45	9/20
240%	2.4	2 2/5

B. Finding the percent of a number is easy. Just remember "of" means multiplication! For example, you buy a shirt for $24 and the sales tax is 6%. How much sales tax will you pay?

6% of 24 = 6% × 24 = 0.06 × 24 = 1.44

To find the percent of a number:
1. Convert the percent to a decimal.
2. Multiply as usual.

C. You can also use a proportion to find the percent of a number. Since a percent is the ratio of a part to a whole with 100 as the whole, all percent problems can be set up as the proportion *part/whole = percent/100*. Here's how you solve the example above using a proportion.

$\frac{x}{24} = \frac{6}{100}$ Cross multiply and solve. $x \times 100 = 24 \times 6$
$x = \frac{144}{100} = 1.44$

To find the percent of a number:
1. Set up a proportion as follows: part/whole = percent/100
2. Solve using cross multiplication.

D. Solve each problem.

A math quiz had 25 problems and Laura scored 80% on the quiz. How many problems did she get correct?	20 problems
A TV originally cost $420, but it is now on sale for 80% of its regular price. What is the sale price?	$336
Levi's soccer team won 13 out of 20 games. Mike's soccer team won 55% of 20 games. Which team had the greater winning percentage?	Levi's team
Store W sells a $20 sweater at 85% of its regular price. Store M offers a $4 discount on the same sweater. Which store offers the better deal?	Store M
A pair of socks sells for $8. The sales tax is 5%. Sophia bought 10 pairs of socks. How much did she pay in total?	$84

DAY 16 Practice

A. Convert each percent to a decimal and a fraction. Simplify fractions.

Percent	Decimal	Fraction
15%	0.15	3/20
175%	1.75	1 3/4
64%	0.64	16/25
260%	2.6	2 3/5

B. Find the percent of each number.

What is 5% of 48?	2.4
What is 8% of 110?	8.8
What is 65% of 23?	14.95
What is 31% of 700?	217
What is 120% of 55?	66
What is 250% of 460?	1,150

C. Solve each problem.

Ryan has 28 crayons, and 25% of the crayons are broken. How many crayons are broken?	7 crayons
There are 20 children in Josh's book club. Seven of them wear glasses. What percent of the book club wear glasses?	35%
The dinner bill was $36, and Julian left a 20% tip. How much did he pay for the dinner?	$43.20
Ariana bought a pair of shoes at 90% of its regular price of $36. She paid $55. How much change did she receive?	$2.60
Sandra saved $80. Her sister Lucy saved 70% of Sandra's amount. How much money did they save all together?	$136

Lesson 16 – Percent of a Number

If the sale price is 80% of the regular price, then you would find the sale price by multiplying the regular price by 80%. "Of" is a key word for multiplication. You multiply by a percent by using the decimal value. If the regular price was $10.00, we'd multiply it by .8. The sale price would be 10 x 0.8 = $8.00.

Their page also has the same thing set up as a proportion. My example would be x/10 = 80/100. 80/100 would reduce to 8/10 and then you could see straight away that x = 8.

Review 16 – Adding Large Numbers

They need to be more careful to keep their place values line up, especially when the two numbers have a different number of digits.

Answers   26,418   41,839   372,732

Lesson 17

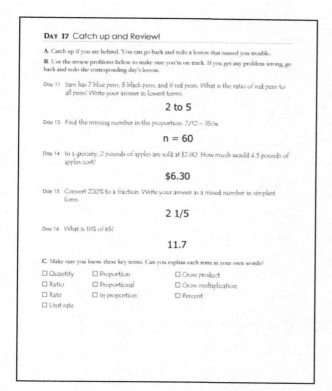

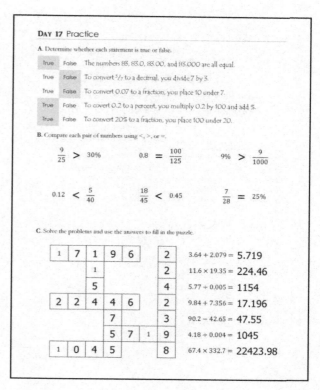

Lesson 17 Catch Up and Review

Have your child check themselves using the lesson page and go back to work on problem areas. See if your child can explain the terms on the page. If they are doing well, have them use the practice page today to stay sharp.

No Review

Lesson 18

DAY 18 Exponents and Order of Operations

A. An **exponent** is a way to represent how many times a number is multiplied by itself. The expression b^n means the number b is multiplied n times. The repeated number b is called the **base**, and the number n is called the **exponent**, or **power**. In words, the expression b^n is read "b raised to the n-th power" or simply "b to the n." Special cases are b^2, which is read "b squared," and b^3, which is read "b cubed." Write each expression below in expanded form and evaluate.

$1^5 = 1 \times 1 \times 1 \times 1 \times 1 = 1$ $5^3 = 5 \times 5 \times 5 = 125$

$2^3 = 2 \times 2 \times 2 = 8$ $3^4 = 3 \times 3 \times 3 \times 3 = 81$

B. Evaluating an expression means finding its value. When evaluating expressions, you must pay attention to the **order of operations**. To get correct answers, you must perform operations in the proper order: Parentheses, Exponents, Multiplication and Division in order from left to right, then Addition and Subtraction in order from left to right. These order-of-operations rules are often referred to as **PEMDAS**, which you can remember as "Please Excuse My Dear Aunt Sally."

$9 + 3 \times 3 - 4^2$	Exponents	$8 \div (5 - 3)^2 \times 5$	Parentheses
$= 9 + 3 \times 3 - 16$	Multiplication	$= 8 \div 2^2 \times 5$	Exponents
$= 9 + 9 - 16$	Addition	$= 8 \div 4 \times 5$	Division
$= 18 - 16$	Subtraction	$= 2 \times 5$	Multiplication
$= 2$		$= 10$	

C. Evaluate each expression using the order of operations.

$17 - 2 \times 6$ 5 $9 + 5 \times (5 \div 5)^4$ 14

$42 \div 6 - 3$ 4 $(3^3 - 7) \times 4 + 3^2$ 89

$5^2 + 3 \times 2$ 31 $10 + 2^5 \div 2^3 \div 4$ 11

$4 \times (5 + 2)$ 28 $4 + 2^4 \div 8 \times (7 - 2)^2$ 54

$(8 + 2)^2 \div 2^2$ 25 $(9 - 4)^3 - (9 - 4)^2 \div 5^2$ 124

DAY 18 Practice

A. Rewrite each expression using an exponent.

$9 \times 9 \times 9$ 9^3 $8 \times 8 \times 8 \times 8 \times 8 \times 8$ 8^7

$4 \times 4 \times 4 \times 4$ 4^4 $35 \times 35 \times 35 \times 35 \times 35 \times 35$ 35^6

B. Evaluate each expression.

1^7 1 12^2 144

5^2 25 10^3 1000

C. Evaluate each expression using the order of operations.

$8 + 12 \div 4$ 11 $9^2 - (6 - 4) \times 3^2$ 63

$4^2 + 6 \times 3$ 34 $30 - 3^4 \div (5 - 2)^3$ 27

$2 \times (4 + 7)$ 22 $2^3 + 7 \times 6 \div (5 - 3)$ 29

$(10 - 3 \times 2)^2$ 16 $4 \times (7 - 2)^2 \div 2 + 6^2$ 86

$15 \div 3 \times 5 + 2^5$ 57 $5^2 \times 2^2 - 4 \times (8 - 3)$ 80

$3^4 + 6 \times (7 - 5)$ 93 $36 \div (6^2 - 7 \times 5)^4 + 2$ 38

$(5^2 - 5) \div 2 + 4$ 14 $(5 + 6)^2 - (8 - 4)^2 \times 5$ 41

$9 + 8 \times (3 - 3)^4$ 9 $8 + (4 \times 2^3 - 8 + 2) \div 4$ 15

Lesson 18 – Exponents and Order of Operations

Exponents are shortcuts to writing that we're multiplying the same number over and over again. The example is one to the fifth power. That's one multiplied by itself five times, five ones.

The rest of the page is about order of operations. That's the order that you solve a problem. If you just work left to right, you might get a totally different answer. Solve anything in parentheses first, then exponents are done, then multiply and divide, and finally add and subtract. This is the trick to remember the order.

Please   Excuse   My Dear   Aunt Sally
parentheses, exponents, multiplication/division, addition/subtraction

This year we'll talk about how subtracting is just adding a negative and dividing is just multiplying the reciprocal, which enables us to multiply and divide and add and subtract in any order. However, when working with order of operations with division and subtraction, you work left to right if there is any question about which to do first, like when there are multiple things to add and subtract.

Review 18 – Subtracting Large Numbers

You can use the zero trick even in the middle of a number. In their questions, they need to borrow from 40 and 90. Those become 39 and 89. They will also subtract from 900,000, which can just all at once become 899,99(10) when you borrow 1 from 90,000.
Answers   32,869   54,542   392,095

Lesson 19

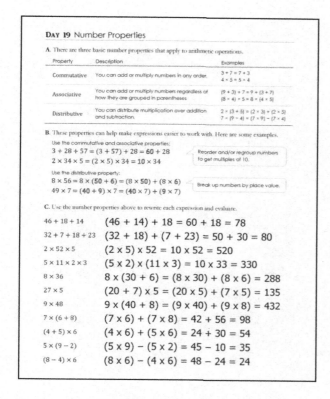

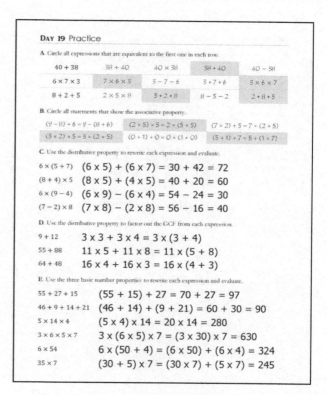

Lesson 19 – Number Properties

They are shown three of what we call properties today. They have seen all these before.

Commutative just means that you can move the numbers around if they are being added or multiplied. (Subtraction is adding the negative. $3 - 2 = -2 + 3$ And division is multiplying the reciprocal. $3 \div 2 = 3 / 2 = 3 \times \frac{1}{2}$ They don't need to know this today.)

Associative just means that you can combine any two things together when you're dealing with addition and multiplication.

Distributive means that you can split apart a number. This is a mental math trick, to break apart the place value.

Here's an example from the lesson. $2 \times 52 \times 5$. $(2 \times 5) \times 52 = 10 \times 52 = 520$
Here's another example. $8 \times 36 = 8 \times 30 + 8 \times 6 = 240 + 48 = 288$

Review 19 – Multi-Step Word Problems

They need to make sure they are answering the question being asked. The answer is not going to be the first thing they figure out.

Answers   28 stickers, 252 bags, 132 cups

Lesson 20

DAY 20 Algebraic Expressions

A. An expression is a mathematical statement that does not contain an equal sign. An expression that contains only numbers and operations is called a **numerical expression**.

$4 - 1 + 2$	$2^2 \times 5 + 10$	$(6 + 8) \div 4$
Four minus one plus two	Two squared times five plus ten	Six plus eight, divided by four

B. While a numerical expression contains only numbers and operations, an **algebraic expression** contains numbers, variables, and operations. A **variable** is a letter that represents a value that can vary. Any letter can be a variable. The most common variables are x, y, and z.

$x - 3$	$y \div 8$	$2z + 10$
Three less than a number	A number divided by eight	Ten more than twice a number

C. The value of an algebraic expression changes as the values of the variables change. To evaluate an algebraic expression, replace the variables with the given values and evaluate using the order of operations. Evaluate each expression below when $x = 3$, $y = 4$, and $z = 8$.

$2x$ $2 \times 3 = 6$	$4x + 3$ **15**	$z^2 - 20$ **44**
$3y$ **12**	$5z - 9$ **31**	$8(x + 5)/4$ **16**
$z/2$ **4**	$12 - 2y$ **4**	$y^2 + 2y - 3$ **21**

D. Write an expression that answers each question.

Gasoline costs $3 per gallon. What's the cost of g gallons?   **3g**

An electrician charges a $35 flat fee plus $40 per hour. How much does the electrician charge for an h-hour job?   **35 + 40h**

Larry has a 185-page reading assignment. He read 20 pages per day for d days. How many pages does he have left to read?   **185 − 20d**

E. Evaluate your expression to answer each question above.

The cost of 4 gallons of gasoline	The total charge for a 2-hour job	The number of pages left after 6 days
$12	**$115**	**65 pages**

DAY 20 Practice

A. Evaluate each expression when $x = 5$, $y = 3$, and $z = 9$.

$4x$ **20**	$7 - y$ **4**	$xyz/3^2$ **15**
$5y$ **15**	$2x + z$ **19**	$x + 3y - z$ **5**
$z/3$ **3**	$3y - 6$ **3**	$4x(y - 2)^4$ **20**
$2xy$ **30**	$x^2 - 2x$ **15**	$x^2 - (y + z)$ **13**

B. Write an expression that answers each question.

Ava bought c cookies at $0.50 each. What's the total cost?   **0.5c**

Lisa bought p pears at $12. What's the price of one pear?   **12/p**

A plumber charges a $50 flat fee plus $35 per hour. How much will the plumber charge for a job that takes h hours?   **50 + 35h**

Carter bought b comic books at $3 each. He paid with a $20 bill. How much change did he get back?   **20 − 3b**

Hannah drove for h hours at an average speed of 60 miles per hour. How far did she drive?   **60h**

Lucas has n dollars. Ryan has 5 dollars less than Lucas. Levi has twice as much money as Ryan. How much money does Levi have?   **2(n − 5)**

C. Evaluate your expression to answer each question above.

The total cost if Ava bought 8 cookies	The price of a pear if Lisa bought 8 pears	The total charge if the plumber took 2 hours
$4	**$1.50**	**$120**
The amount of change if Carter bought 5 books	The number of miles Hannah drove in 1.5 hours	The amount of Levi's money if Lucas has 14 dollars
$5	**90 miles**	**$18**

Lesson 20 – Algebraic Expressions

There's some vocabulary on their page. An expression is basically an equation without the equal sign. A variable is what we use in place of a number. In the expressions in part C, they are given values to substitute in. For instance if $X = 5$ and the expression was $X - 3$, then the answer is, the expression is evaluated by saying $5 - 3 = 2$.

In part D, they will be writing expressions. The first one is about gasoline that costs $3 per gallon. $3 times the number of gallons would be the cost of the total number of gallons. That would be 3g$. If their brain won't wrap around that, have them think of how they would find the cost of two gallons and then substitute the variable for the two.

Review 20 – Multiplying Single Digits

You shouldn't need any extra help with that.

Answers   0   48   49

Lesson 21

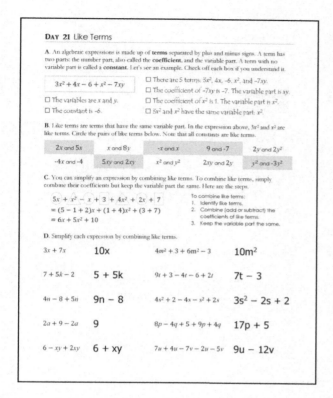

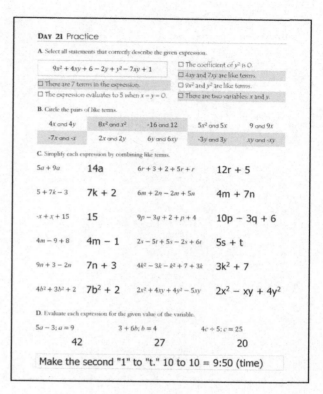

Lesson 21 – Like Terms

Working with like terms means adding together, combining the things that are the same. Think of it as coming home from the store with bags of fruit that you put on the table. Then you put all the apples together in one bowl and all the oranges together in another bowl, all the pears in another. They will be piling together, so to speak, all the Xs together, and then separately all the Ys. X^2 is different than X. They need to keep them separate.

2 apples + 3 oranges – 1 apple – 1 orange = 1 apple + 2 oranges
2x   + 3y   - 1x   - 1y   = 1x + 2y = x + 2y

That's simplifying, by combining all you can.

Review 21 – Multiplying by Multiples of Ten

They are just adding the zeros onto the number they are multiplying by, but why? When you multiply, you are multiplying together each place value. 8 x 10 is 8 x 0 ones plus 8 x 1 ten which is 0 ones + 8 tens = 80.

Answers   80   500   3,000

Lesson 22

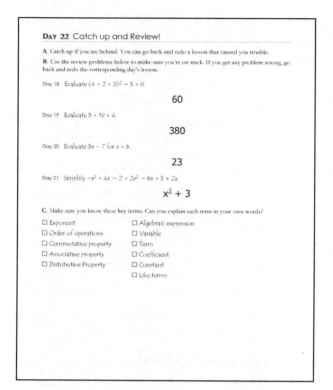

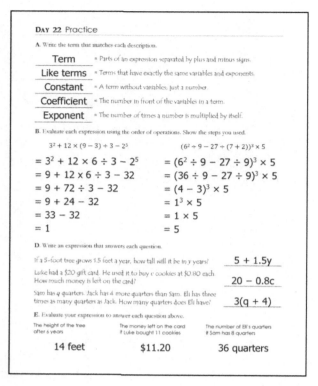

DAY 22 Catch up and Review!

A. Catch up if you are behind. You can go back and redo a lesson that caused you trouble.

B. Use the review problems below to make sure you're on track. If you get any problem wrong, go back and redo the corresponding day's lesson.

Day 18 Evaluate $(4 + 2 \times 5)^2 - 5 \times 8$.

60

Day 19 Evaluate $5 \times 19 \times 4$.

380

Day 20 Evaluate $5x - 7$ for $x = 6$.

23

Day 21 Simplify $-x^2 + 4x - 2 + 2x^2 - 6x + 5 + 2x$.

$x^2 + 3$

C. Make sure you know these key terms. Can you explain each term in your own words?

☐ Exponent   ☐ Algebraic expression
☐ Order of operations ☐ Variable
☐ Commutative property ☐ Term
☐ Associative property ☐ Coefficient
☐ Distributive Property ☐ Constant
                      ☐ Like terms

DAY 22 Practice

A. Write the term that matches each description.

Term = Parts of an expression separated by plus and minus signs.

Like terms = Terms that have exactly the same variables and exponents.

Constant = A term without variables; just a number.

Coefficient = The number in front of the variables in a term.

Exponent = The number of times a number is multiplied by itself.

B. Evaluate each expression using the order of operations. Show the steps you used.

$3^2 + 12 \times (9 - 3) \div 3 - 2^5$ $(6^2 \div 9 - 27 \div (7 + 2))^3 \times 5$

$= 3^2 + 12 \times 6 \div 3 - 2^5$ $= (6^2 \div 9 - 27 \div 9)^3 \times 5$
$= 9 + 12 \times 6 \div 3 - 32$ $= (36 \div 9 - 27 \div 9)^3 \times 5$
$= 9 + 72 \div 3 - 32$ $= (4 - 3)^3 \times 5$
$= 9 + 24 - 32$ $= 1^3 \times 5$
$= 33 - 32$ $= 1 \times 5$
$= 1$ $= 5$

D. Write an expression that answers each question.

If a 5-foot tree grows 1.5 feet a year, how tall will it be in y years? $5 + 1.5y$

Luke had a $20 gift card. He used it to buy c cookies at $0.80 each. How much money is left on the card? $20 - 0.8c$

Sam has q quarters. Jack has 4 more quarters than Sam. Eli has three times as many quarters as Jack. How many quarters does Eli have? $3(q + 4)$

E. Evaluate your expression to answer each question above.

The height of the tree after 6 years	The money left on the card if Luke bought 11 cookies	The number of Eli's quarters if Sam has 8 quarters
14 feet	$11.20	36 quarters

Lesson 22 Catch Up and Review

Have your child check themselves using the lesson page and go back to work on problem areas. See if your child can explain the terms on the page. If they are doing well, have them use the practice page today to stay sharp.

No Review

Lesson 23

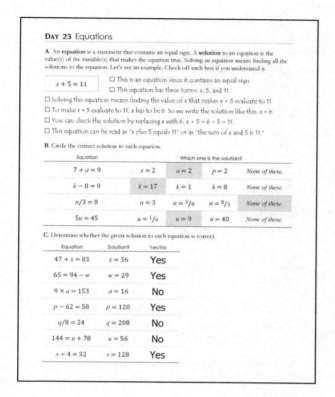

DAY 23 Equations

A. An **equation** is a statement that contains an equal sign. A **solution** to an equation is the value(s) of the variable(s) that makes the equation true. Solving an equation means finding all the solutions to the equation. Let's see an example. Check off each box if you understand it.

$x + 5 = 11$
☐ This is an equation since it contains an equal sign.
☐ This equation has three terms: x, 5, and 11.
☐ Solving this equation means finding the value of x that makes $x + 5$ evaluate to 11.
☐ To make $x + 5$ evaluate to 11, x has to be 6. So we write the solution like this: $x = 6$.
☐ You can check the solution by replacing x with 6: $x + 5 = 6 + 5 = 11$.
☐ This equation can be read as "x plus 5 equals 11" or as "the sum of x and 5 is 11."

B. Circle the correct solution to each equation.

Equation	Which one is the solution?			
$7 + a = 9$	$x = 2$	$a = 2$	$p = 2$	None of these.
$k - 8 = 9$	$k = 17$	$k = 1$	$k = 8$	None of these.
$n/3 = 8$	$n = 3$	$n = {}^3/_8$	$n = {}^8/_3$	None of these.
$5u = 45$	$u = {}^1/_9$	$u = 9$	$u = 40$	None of these.

C. Determine whether the given solution to each equation is correct.

Equation	Solution?	Yes/No
$47 + x = 83$	$x = 36$	Yes
$65 = 94 - w$	$w = 29$	Yes
$9 \times a = 153$	$a = 16$	No
$p - 62 = 58$	$p = 120$	Yes
$q/8 = 24$	$q = 208$	No
$144 = u + 78$	$u = 56$	No
$x \div 4 = 32$	$x = 128$	Yes

DAY 23 Practice

A. Determine whether the given solution to each equation is correct.

Equation	Solution?	Yes/No
$x + 57 = 103$	$x = 36$	No
$15 = n/8$	$n = 120$	Yes
$84 - r = 59$	$r = 25$	Yes
$u \times 7 = 77$	$u = 11$	Yes
$132 - y = 84$	$y = 48$	Yes
$q \div 7 = 14$	$q = 90$	No
$153 = 94 + v$	$v = 79$	No
$6 = s - 57$	$s = 63$	Yes
$15z = 80$	$z = 6$	No
$k + 43 = 62$	$k = 19$	Yes
$9m = 108$	$m = 12$	Yes
$8 = 64/p$	$p = 16$	No

B. Write an equation that represents each situation.

Daniel is m years old. In 5 years, he will be 19.	$m + 5 = 19$
Jacob drove at 60 mph for k hours. He traveled 150 miles in total.	$60k = 150$
Apples cost $0.90 each. Sandra bought x apples and paid $18.	$0.9x = 18$
Sam had p. He spent half of his money to buy a book at $15.	$p/2 = 15$
Max bought a jacket at $11. It was $5 off the regular price of w.	$w - 5 = 11$
Last night 1.4 inches of snow fell. This morning n inches of more snow fell. Now there are 3 inches of snow on the ground.	$1.4 + n = 3$

Lesson 23 – Equations

Equations are expressions that are equal to something. They have an equals sign. We use an equation to find the value of the variable, the part we don't know.

Today they aren't solving equations like that. They are going to be evaluating answers. On Day 20 we plugged in values for variables to evaluate expressions. $x - 3$ when $x = 5$ is 2. They will be doing the same thing today, substituting values into the equation to see if it works.

Here's a simple example.

$1 + x = 3$, $x = 2$
Does $x = 2$? Yes, $1 + 2 = 3$

Review 23 – Multiplying with Zeros

This is just like Lesson 12, but they will have numbers other than 1 to multiply with. $4 \times 30 = 4 \times$ 0 ones and 4×3 tens $= 0 + 12$ tens $= 120$, which is just 4×3 with the zero tagged on.

Answers   120   7,200   42,000

Lesson 24

DAY 24 Addition and Subtraction Equations

A. Suppose you have two piles of coins that are the same amount. You add 5 cents to each pile. Which pile has more money? Add 10 more cents to each pile. Now which pile has more money? As you see, both piles will have the same amount of money as long as you add equal amounts to each pile. In other words, adding the same number to both sides of an equation does not change the equality. This property is called the **addition property of equality**, which can be expressed symbolically as follows: if $a = b$, then $a + c = b + c$.

B. The same goes for subtraction. The **subtraction property of equality** states that subtracting the same number from both sides of an equation does not change the equality. Symbolically expressed, if $a = b$, then $a - c = b - c$.

C. Now consider an addition equation $x + 3 = 5$. Solving the equation means you end up with "$x = ...$" That is, you must get the variable x by itself on one side without changing the equality. To leave the variable x alone, you must undo adding 3 by subtracting 3. To keep the equality, you must subtract 3 from both sides. Subtraction equations work the same way. Here are the steps.

$x + 3 = 5$	$x - 3 = 5$
$-3\ -3$	$+3\ +3$
$x = 2$	$x = 8$

Check: $2 + 3 = 5$ Check: $8 - 3 = 5$

To solve an addition or subtraction equation:
1. Subtract or add the same number on each side of the equation to get the variable alone on one side of the equation and the answer on the other side.
2. Check your solution by substituting it for the variable in the original equation.

D. Solve each equation. Check your solution.

$a + 5 = 8$	$u - 2 = 8$	$5 = x - 9$
a = 3	u = 10	x = 14
$y - 27 = 45$	$38 + h = 84$	$52 = c + 16$
y = 72	h = 46	c = 36
$39 = k - 15$	$45 = 18 + m$	$f - 19 = 24$
k = 54	m = 27	f = 43

DAY 24 Practice

Solve each equation. Check your solution.

$x + 6 = 8$	$n - 4 = 4$	$g + 7 = 11$
x = 2	n = 8	g = 4
$12 = b - 9$	$14 = 6 + v$	$3 = w - 5$
b = 21	v = 8	w = 8
$q - 23 = 35$	$32 = u + 26$	$15 = r - 48$
q = 58	u = 6	r = 63
$27 + c = 63$	$m - 58 = 29$	$80 = 24 + h$
c = 36	m = 87	h = 56
$95 = d - 36$	$j - 42 = 12$	$15 + p = 32$
d = 131	j = 54	p = 17
$k + 26 = 75$	$54 = t + 49$	$z - 87 = 46$
k = 49	t = 5	z = 133

Did you know? Zero is the only number that can't be represented in Roman numerals.

Lesson 24 – Addition and Subtraction Equations

When our equation says, x = 5 (or whatever), then we know what X is, we've solved the equation. So that's going to be the goal, to get the variable alone so that they know what it equals.

To get the X by itself, we get rid of whatever is with the variable to get it alone. To do that, we do the opposite. If a number is added to x, then we subtract it off. If a number is subtracted with X, then we add it to X. There's an example below. The properties at the top are saying that if $1 = 1$ then $1 + 2 = 1 + 2$ and if $5 = 5$ then $5 - 1 = 5 - 1$.

3 + x minus three leaves us with just X.   x – 5 plus five leaves us with just X.

The first one on the page is   a + 5 = 8.
$$\begin{array}{r} - 5\ \ -5 \\ \hline a + 0 = 3 \\ a = 3 \end{array}$$

Review 24 – Multiplying with Zeros

This time there are zeros in each number. 30 x 60 = 3 x 6 with two zeros tagged on because there are two zeros in the question. This is 30 x 0 ones and 30 x 6 tens = 0 + 180 tens = 1800.

However many zeros there are in the question, there will be that many in the answer. 8000 x 8 = 8 x 8 with 3 zeros tagged on.   Answers   2,100   3,000   36,000

Lesson 25

DAY 25 Addition and Subtraction Equations

DAY 25 Addition and Subtraction Equations

A. Complete each sentence in your own words. Give examples. Review Day 24 if needed.

To solve an addition equation,

Examples will vary. See Day 24, Part C.

To solve a subtraction equation,

Examples will vary. See Day 24, Part C.

B. Solve each equation. Check your solution.

$a + 15 = 23$	$f - 17 = 31$	$12 + h = 70$
a = 8	f = 48	h = 58

$m - 27 = 6$	$u - 22 = 7$	$18 = k - 46$
m = 33	u = 29	k = 64

$25 = 16 + w$	$31 + x = 53$	$23 = c - 19$
w = 9	x = 22	c = 42

$15 = k - 26$	$45 = b + 17$	$u + 28 = 54$
k = 41	b = 28	u = 26

$y - 25 = 50$	$9 = p - 36$	$70 = 29 + n$
y = 75	p = 45	n = 41

DAY 25 Practice

A. Solve each equation. Check your solution.

$m - 51 = 19$	$c + 9 = 12$	$24 = 8 + r$
m = 70	c = 3	r = 16

$h + 11 = 60$	$34 = a - 27$	$17 = x - 46$
h = 49	a = 61	x = 63

$p - 25 = 29$	$73 = w + 16$	$29 = y - 52$
p = 54	w = 57	y = 81

$16 = b - 36$	$n - 44 = 28$	$39 + q = 92$
b = 52	n = 72	q = 53

$17 + d = 33$	$s - 28 = 15$	$82 = 34 + h$
d = 16	s = 43	h = 48

B. Here is a tricky equation puzzle. Can you find the value of each shape? (Hint: Add each side of the equations to find the sum of the three shapes.)

○ + ⬡ = 10   ○ = 3
☆ + ○ = 8   ⬡ = 7
⬠ + ☆ = 12   ☆ = 5

Lesson 25 – Addition and Subtraction Equations

They will doing the same as Lesson 24. They will add and subtract, doing the opposite, in order to get a 0 with the variable so that it is left alone.

You'll know that the answer is correct if you can plug it back in and it gives you the correct answer.

Review 25 – Multiplying by Larger Numbers

To multiply they will just need to multiply the single digit by each place value. 34 x 2 is 30 x 2 and 4 x 2 added together.

Answers   88   68   930

Lesson 26

DAY 26 Multiplication and Division Equations

A. There are two more properties of equality useful in solving equations. The **multiplication property of equality** states that multiplying both sides of an equation by the same number does not change the equality. Symbolically expressed, if $a = b$, then $a \times c = b \times c$.

B. The same goes for division. The **division property of equality** states that dividing both sides of an equation by the same number does not change the equality. Symbolically expressed, if $a = b$, then $a \div c = b \div c$.

C. Using the properties above, you can solve equations involving multiplication and division.

$$3x = 6 \qquad x/3 = 6$$
$$\div 3 \quad \div 3 \qquad \times 3 \quad \times 3$$
$$x = 2 \qquad x = 18$$

Check:
$$3 \cdot 2 = 6$$

Check:
$$18/3 = 6$$

To solve a multiplication or division equation:
1. Divide or multiply each side of the equation by the same number to get the variable alone on one side of the equation and the answer on the other side.
2. Check your solution by substituting it for the variable in the original equation.

D. Solve each equation. Check your solution.

$7x = 49$ $\frac{a}{3} = 8$ $45 = 9q$

x = 7   a = 24   q = 5

$9 = \frac{c}{4}$ $35 = 5d$ $\frac{y}{8} = 40$

c = 36   d = 7   y = 320

$14p = 70$ $11 = \frac{n}{11}$ $45 = 15g$

p = 5   n = 121   g = 3

$\frac{m}{7} = 16$ $15 = \frac{s}{10}$ $24k = 72$

m = 112   s = 150   k = 3

DAY 26 Practice

Solve each equation. Check your solution.

$3b = 15$ $54 = 6m$ $\frac{x}{4} = 5$

b = 5   m = 9   x = 20

$\frac{y}{2} = 18$ $8x = 72$ $6 = \frac{k}{7}$

y = 36   x = 9   k = 42

$10h = 80$ $\frac{c}{25} = 8$ $77 = 11q$

h = 8   c = 200   q = 7

$\frac{x}{30} = 9$ $12p = 84$ $4 = \frac{t}{45}$

x = 270   p = 7   t = 180

$27 = \frac{d}{8}$ $168 = 21s$ $31 = \frac{u}{12}$

d = 216   s = 8   u = 372

$160 = 32n$ $\frac{w}{102} = 9$ $16g = 128$

n = 5   w = 918   g = 8

You took two apples, so you have two.

Lesson 26 – Multiplication and Division Equations

This is a continuation of the same idea, getting the variable alone so that we know what it equals. We're still going to do the opposite. If it was divided, we'll multiply. If it was multiplied, then we divide. When we do that, we're getting a one instead of a zero.

$3 - 3 + x = 0 + x = x$
$3x/3 = 1x = x$

This works because $3/3 = 1$. Three out of three is one whole.

The first one in the book is $7x = 49$. Divide each side by 7 to get X alone. That give us $1x = 7$ or $x = 7$.

Review 26 – Multiplying by Larger Numbers

This is just like the review from Lesson 26.

Answers   348   846   413

Lesson 27

DAY 27 Multiplication and Division Equations

A. Complete each sentence in your own words. Give examples. Review Day 26 if needed.

To solve a multiplication equation,

Examples will vary. See Day 26, Part C.

To solve a division equation,

Examples will vary. See Day 26, Part C.

B. Solve each equation. Check your solution.

$4k = 28$	$\frac{c}{8} = 8$	$63 = 7h$
k = 7	c = 64	h = 9
$9 = \frac{d}{6}$	$12y = 60$	$\frac{y}{3} = 13$
d = 54	y = 5	y = 39
$56 = 8b$	$11 = \frac{n}{4}$	$52 = 13q$
b = 7	n = 44	q = 4
$\frac{m}{7} = 21$	$8 = \frac{s}{10}$	$15x = 45$
m = 147	s = 80	x = 3
$11m = 66$	$\frac{g}{6} = 12$	$19 = \frac{r}{20}$
m = 6	g = 72	r = 380

DAY 27 Practice

A. Solve each equation. Check your solution.

$4x = 96$	$99 = 9m$	$\frac{y}{8} = 5$
x = 24	m = 11	y = 40
$\frac{x}{3} = 17$	$44 = 22q$	$6 = \frac{s}{11}$
x = 51	q = 2	s = 66
$14p = 70$	$\frac{k}{12} = 8$	$16b = 64$
p = 5	k = 96	b = 4
$\frac{x}{20} = 7$	$15h = 90$	$5 = \frac{t}{13}$
x = 140	h = 6	t = 65
$12 = \frac{u}{12}$	$125 = 25h$	$30 = \frac{w}{11}$
u = 144	h = 5	w = 330

B. Here is a tricky equation puzzle. Can you find the value of each shape? (Hint: Add or subtract the equations to get an equation in one shape.)

☆ + ⬠ + ○ = 14
⬠ + ○ + ○ = 13
○ + ☆ + ☆ = 11

○ = 3
⬠ = 7
☆ = 4

Lesson 27 – Multiplication and Division Equations

This is a practice of what they learned in Lesson 26. They will be multiplying and dividing to get the variable alone. That will show them its value. It's a mystery that they get to solve.

They can plug in their answer to see if it's correct.

The first one:

$\frac{4k}{4} = \frac{28}{4}$

1k = 7

k = 7

4 x 7 = 28 YES

Review 27 – Multiplying by Larger Numbers

To multiply they will just need to multiply the single digit by each place value. 314 x 2 is 300 x 2 and 10 x 2 and 4 x 2 all added together.

Answers   5,103   3,438   2,574

Lesson 28

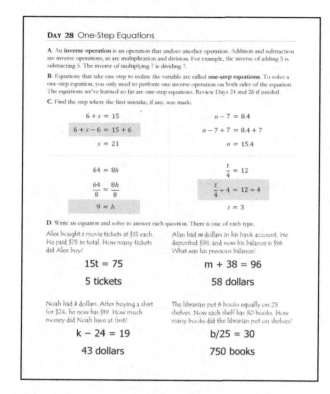

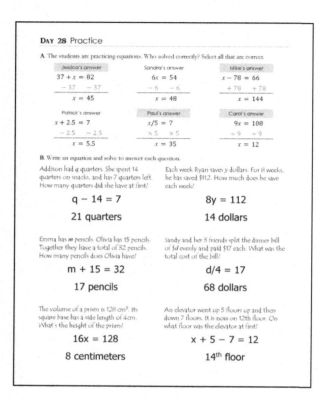

Lesson 28 – One-Step Equations

They are going to be applying what they learned today. There are four word problems. They will write the equations, similar to how they wrote expressions in Lesson 20.

They will write the questions as equations. One will be an addition equation. One will be a subtraction equation. One will be a multiplication equation. One will be a division equation. If they aren't sure, they can substitute a number for the unknown value and see how they'd figure it out. Then they would just substitute in the variable.

Then they will solve. These are word problems, so they need to find the answer, not just a number. They are finding tickets, books, etc. They need to label their answers.

Review 28 – Multiplying Double Digits

The first question is 43 times 27. That's 43 x 7 and 43 x 20 added together. Of course, 43 x 20 is just 43 x 2 with a zero tagged on. That's why traditionally you add a zero to the first column and then multiply by the tens digit. You can do those in any order because you can multiply and add in any order and get the same answer.

Answers   1,161   3,072   4,161

Lesson 29

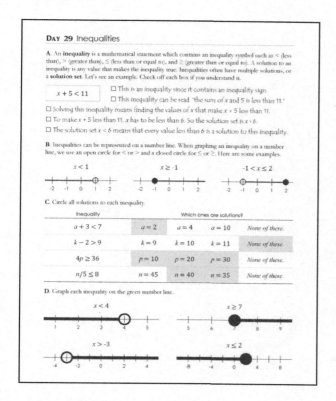

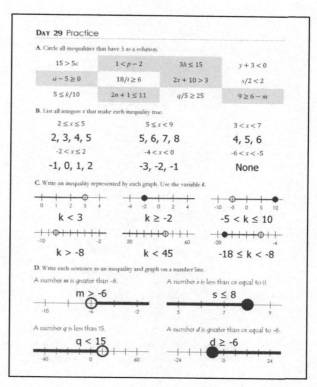

Lesson 29 – Inequalities

An inequality is an equation without the equals sign. x < 4 means that x could be 3, 2, 1, 0, -1, -2, etc. There are graphs on the page. Have your child explain what the graphs show. Anything touched is part of the solution, any of those answers would make the inequality true.

In part C, there could be more than one answer.

They are going to draw a graph of inequalities today.

Review 29 – Multiplying Hundreds

Multiply by each place value. 283 x 56 is 283 x 50 and 283 x 6 added together. 283 x 50 is 283 x 5 with one zero tagged on. Traditionally, you'd write one zero in the answer and then multiply by the tens digit.

Answers   15,848   12,626   21,385

Lesson 30

DAY 30 One-Step Inequalities

A. Compare each pair of numbers when $a < b$. Notice when the inequality sign changes.

$$a + 2 \; < \; b + 2 \qquad 2a \; < \; 2b \qquad -2a \; > \; -2b \qquad \frac{a}{2} \; > \; \frac{b}{2}$$

B. Solving inequalities is just like solving equations, except for one thing: when multiplying or dividing by a negative number, you have to flip the inequality sign. Here are the steps.

$$\begin{array}{ccc} x + 3 &>& 5 \\ -3 & & -3 \\ \hline x &>& 2 \end{array} \qquad \begin{array}{ccc} x - 3 &\le& 5 \\ +3 & & +3 \\ \hline x &\le& 8 \end{array}$$

To solve an addition or subtraction inequality:
1. Subtract or add the same number on each side of the inequality.
2. Keep the inequality sign as is.

$$\begin{array}{ccc} -3x &<& 6 \\ \div -3 & & \div -3 \\ \hline x &>& -2 \end{array} \qquad \begin{array}{ccc} x/3 &\ge& 6 \\ \times 3 & & \times 3 \\ \hline x &\ge& 18 \end{array}$$

To solve a multiplication or division inequality:
1. Divide or multiply each side of the inequality by the same number.
2. Flip the inequality sign if a negative number is multiplied or divided.

C. Solve each inequality.

$x + 19 > 50$	$x - 29 \le 18$	$17 + x \le 23$
x > 31	x ≤ 47	x ≤ 6

$7x \le 49$	$-5x > 15$	$8x < -64$
x ≤ 7	x < -3	x < -8

$\frac{x}{4} > 9$	$\frac{x}{7} \ge -8$	$\frac{x}{3} \le 9$
x < -36	x ≥ -56	x ≤ 27

D. Write an inequality that represents each situation. Use the variable x.

Nighttime temperatures on Mars can drop below -148 °F	x < -148
The ocean covers more than 70 percent of the surface of Earth.	x > 0.7
Biologists found that at least 473 genes are needed to sustain life.	x ≥ 473

DAY 30 Practice

A. Solve each inequality.

$x + 5 > 11$	$x - 4 \le 18$	$x - 19 > 5$
x > 6	x ≤ 22	x > 24

$29 + x \le 46$	$x - 25 \ge 39$	$x + 37 \le 60$
x ≤ 17	x ≥ 64	x ≤ 23

$5x > 40$	$-9x < 54$	$\frac{x}{4} > 7$
x > 8	x > -6	x > 28

$\frac{x}{6} \le -9$	$-3x \ge -27$	$-\frac{x}{3} \le -9$
x ≤ -54	x ≤ 9	x ≥ 27

$\frac{x}{9} < 11$	$-\frac{x}{12} \ge 7$	$11x > -55$
x < 99	x ≤ -84	x > -5

B. Write an inequality that represents each situation. Use the variable x.

Last year we had at most 10 inches of snow.	x ≤ 10
Tomorrow the temperature will drop below 40 °F.	x < 40
In the U.S. Senate, if everyone is present, it takes a minimum of 51 votes to pass a bill.	x ≥ 51
The American Heart Association recommends no more than 1,500 milligrams of sodium a day.	x ≤ 1,500
According to the Saffir-Simpson Hurricane Wind Scale (SSHS), a Category 5 hurricane has winds of at least 157 miles per hour.	x ≥ 157

Lesson 30 – One-Step Inequalities

They are going to solve these just like solving equations. They are going to do the same thing. The only difference is that instead of an equals sign, they will write the inequality sign.

Part A is going to require some thinking. If they can't figure it out, they can substitute 1 for A and 2 for B (since a < b and 1 < 2) and see what the answer will be. That answer will be true no matter what A and B equal. They need to pay attention to the negatives!

Review 30 – Multiplying by Hundreds

This is the same concept as Lesson 33. Multiply by each place value. 283 x 576 is 283 x 500 and 283 x 70 and 283 x 6 all added together. 283 x 500 is 283 x 5 with two zeros tagged on. Traditionally, you'd write two zeros and then multiply by the hundreds digit.

Answers   34,692   159,408   126,588

Lesson 31

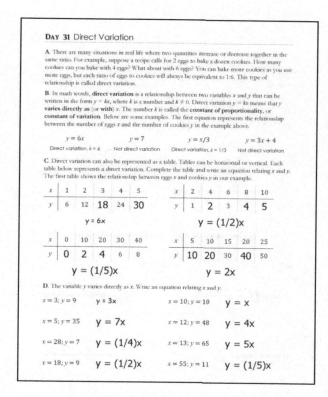

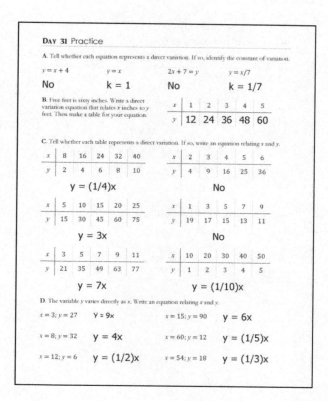

Lesson 31 – Direct Variation

There is more vocabulary today. Work on learning and using the vocabulary, but don't let it shut down your student when they first face it. You can turn them back to the example of a recipe needing two eggs, so if you are making two batches, then you'll need four eggs. That's all this lesson is talking about, things that vary directly. The one increases, the other is impacted in an expected way, such as doubling or tripling, or dividing in half.

If something has direct variation, then X is mutiplied to find Y. $y = 2x$ means that when $x = 1$ then $y = 2$ and when $x = 5$ then $y = 10$. If $y = \frac{1}{2}x$, it means that when $x = 2$ then $y = 1$ and if $x = 24$ then $y = 12$. Those are examples of direct variation.

When you add or subtract, it's not direct variation. They wil be looking at X and thinking about what they need to multiply or divide by to get the Y. Their equation will always be $y = ?x$. The ? will always be something they multiply by. The last one on the page is $x = 55$ and $y = 11$. They need to divide 55 by 5 to get to 11. $y = (1/5)x$. That's how they show division, by using a fraction.

Review 31 – Multiplying by Thousands

This is, again, the same concept. Multiply the smaller number by each place value in the larger.

Answers   212,625   67,648   273,325

Lesson 32

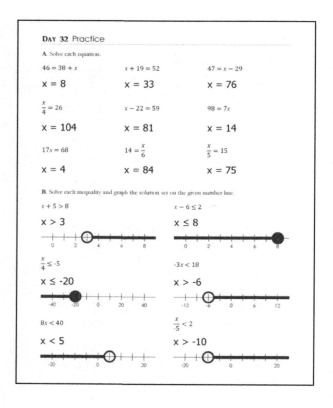

DAY 32 Catch up and Review!

A. Catch up if you are behind. You can go back and redo a lesson that caused you trouble.

B. Use the review problems below to make sure you're on track. If you get any problem wrong, go back and redo the corresponding day's lesson. Solve for x.

Day 26 $x + 25 = 42$ $x - 16 = 38$

x = 17   x = 54

Day 27 $8x = 48$ $x/4 = 13$

x = 6   x = 52

Day 30 $x + 7 > 15$ $-5x \le 20$

x > 8   x ≥ -4

Day 26   Write a direct variation equation when $x = 28$ and $y = 84$.

y = 3x

C. Make sure you know these key terms. Can you explain each term in your own words?

☐ Equation   ☐ Addition Property of Equality
☐ Inequality   ☐ Subtraction Property of Equality
☐ Inverse Operation   ☐ Multiplication Property of Equality
☐ Direct Variation   ☐ Division Property of Equality
☐ Constant of Proportionality

DAY 32 Practice

A. Solve each equation.

$46 = 38 + x$ $x + 19 = 52$ $47 = x - 29$

x = 8   x = 33   x = 76

$\frac{x}{4} = 26$ $x - 22 = 59$ $98 = 7x$

x = 104   x = 81   x = 14

$17x = 68$ $14 = \frac{x}{6}$ $\frac{x}{5} = 15$

x = 4   x = 84   x = 75

B. Solve each inequality and graph the solution set on the given number line.

$x + 5 > 8$ $x - 6 \le 2$

x > 3   x ≤ 8

$\frac{x}{4} \le -5$ $-3x < 18$

x ≤ -20   x > -6

$8x < 40$ $\frac{x}{-5} < 2$

x < 5   x > -10

Lesson 32 Catch Up and Review

Have your child check themselves using the lesson page and go back to work on problem areas. See if your child can explain the terms on the page. If they are doing well, have them use the practice page today to stay sharp.

No Review

Lesson 33

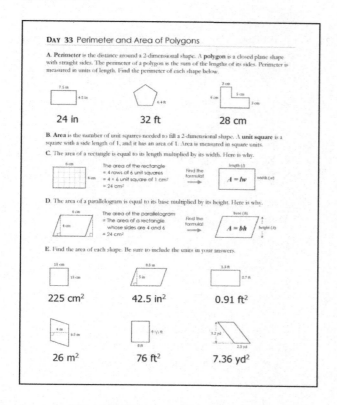

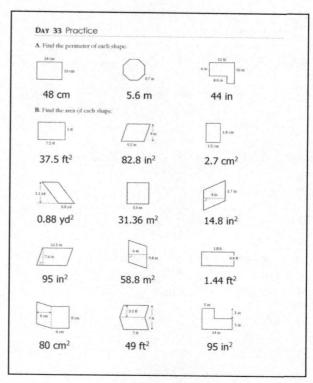

Lesson 33 – Perimeter and Area of Polygons

They are figuring out perimeter and area today.

The perimeter is the measure around a shape. If there isn't a measurement listed, you are supposed to know it. In a regular shape, like a square, only one side has the measurement because all the sides are the same length. In an irregular shape (like on the right on their page), they are to assume the top and bottom lines are parallel and that each side is 8 inches high.

To find area they are just multiplying length times width, which is called base times height in a parallelogram. To find the area of an irregular shape, like on the bottom right, they should draw a line to divide it into two rectangles and then add together the area of each.

Review 33 – Multiplying with Thousands

This is the same as the review in Lesson 31.

Answers   321,057   204,850   171,675

Lesson 34

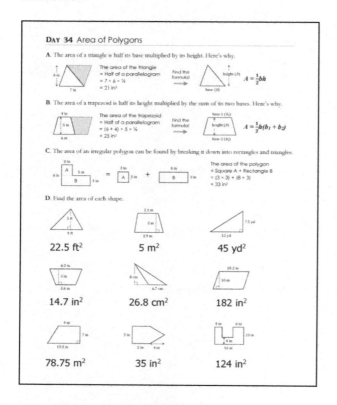

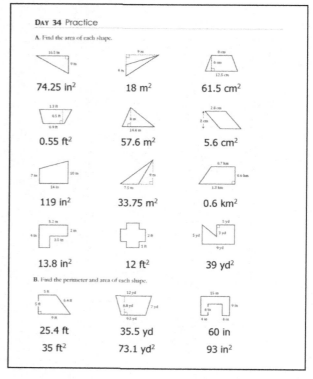

Lesson 34 – Area of Polygons

This time they are finding the area of triangles and trapezoids and different types of shapes. The examples show that a parallelogram is just two trapezoids put together, so the area of a trapezoid is half the area of a parallelogram.

For triangles they can think about how they can draw a diagonal line from one corner of a square or rectangle to divide it in half, into two triangles. The triangle is half the shape, half a parallelogram.

A parallelogram's area is found by multiplying base times height, so these will be one half of the base times the height. If either measurement is even, they can divide that in two before they multiply. Dividing by two is multiplying by one half, and you can multiply in any order, so they should do it in the order that makes it easiest for them!

Review 34 – Missing Numbers

They are to figure out what's in the blanks. For instance, the first one is ? x 5 = 40. They can think what times five equals forty. They could also find the answer by dividing 40 by 5.

Answers   8   9   7

Lesson 35

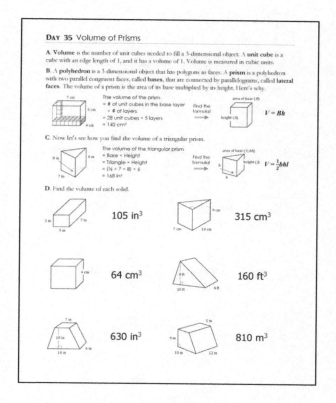

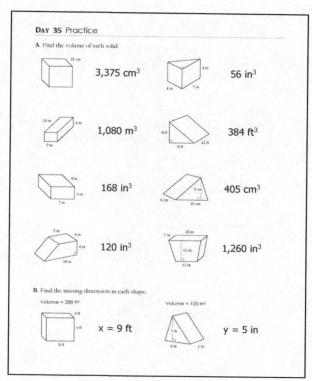

Lesson 35 – Volume of Prisms

For part C there is no written work, but they should explain to you the principles behind each formula. The volume of a cube is the area of the base times the height except that the height is the same as the length and width, so you are just multiplying that measurement three times (length x width x height = side x side x side). The cuboid is listed as volume = length x width x height, which is just the area of the base (length x width) x height, just like in the example. And just like the area of a triangle is half the area of a rectangle, the volume of a 3D triangle is half the volume of a 3D rectangle.

Getting comfortable plugging numbers into formulas will be important.

Review 35 – Missing Number

This time they are set up as division problems ? divided by 8 = 9 is the first one. This is the oppostite of Lesson 34. They can think what divided by 8 equals 9, or ask themselves what 9 x 8 equals.

Answers   72   9   8

Lesson 36

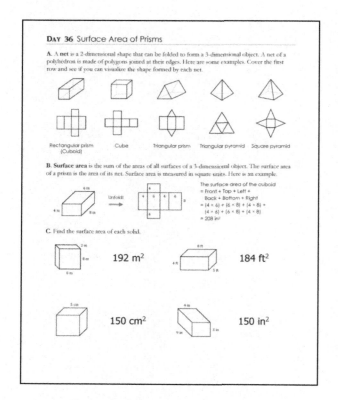

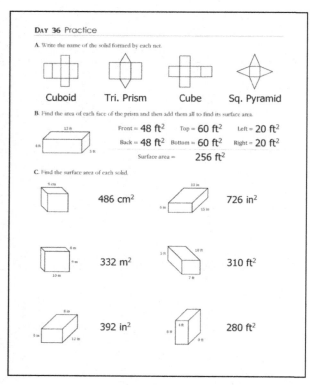

Lesson 36 – Surface Area of Prisms

They are finding the surface area today which means they need to find the area of each surface. They can pick up any book, tissue box, etc. around them and look at the surfaces and what measurements would give them the area of each side.

In part C they are again to think through, and explain to you, the surface area formulas. The cube has six sides that are all equal, so you need to find the area of just one side and then multiply that by six to get the total for all six sides. There are six sides of a cuboid as well, so that formula is finding the area for each of the three different sides and then doubling it for the other three sides. For the prism, they can think of finding the perimeter of the base being like adding together the bases of the trapezoid.

Review 36 – Division

They need to know their facts for this. If they don't know, they could subtract over and over or think the opposite, "What times six equals forty-two?"

Answers   7   7   8

Lesson 37

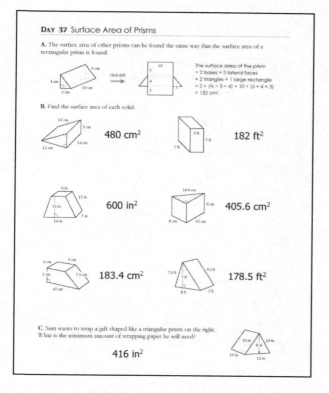

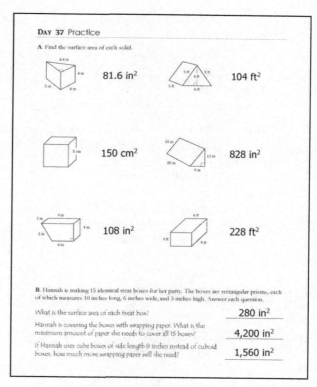

Lesson 37 – Surface Area of Prisms

They will be finding surface area again. There are trapezoids and triangles used this time. They can look back to Lesson 34 for reminders about how to find the area of triangles and trapezoids.

Review 37 – Long Division

They first see how many times the number, the divisor, goes into the first digit in the dividend, the number under the line. If it's bigger than that digit, then they look at the first two digits. Above the last digit they are looking at, they write the answer. Then they multiply it by the divisor, subtract the total, add on the next digit and keep going. Dividing is repeated subtraction. What they are doing is seeing how many they can subtract off. If they don't subtract off enough, they just subtract off another. The answer is how many times you can subtract the number to get to zero.

Answers   113   49   71

Lesson 38

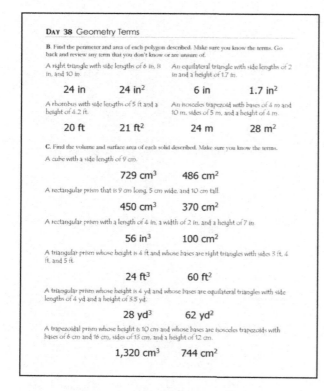

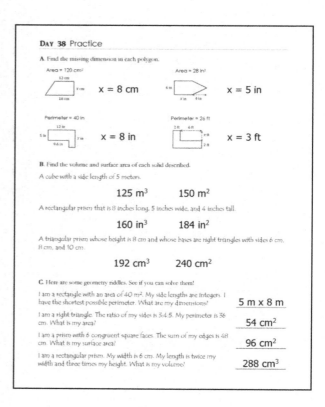

Lesson 38 – Geometry Terms

They should read through the list. Ideally, they'd read the word and then try to define it before reading the definition. They could fold over the page to cover the definitions or you could talk through the page with your child.

They need to turn the page. That's not all. There is work to do. This is review work dealing with all these geometry terms.

Review 38 – Long Division

This is similar to the review in Lesson 37.

Answers   3,874   493   534

Lesson 39

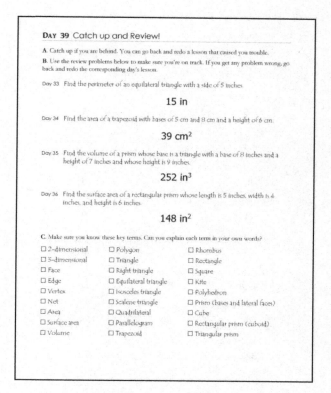

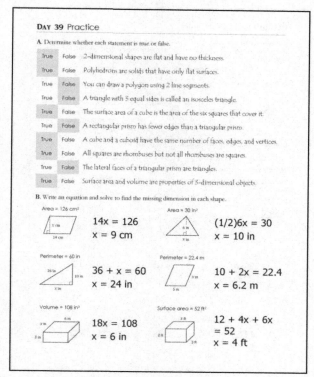

Lesson 39 Catch Up and Review

Have your child check themselves using the lesson page and go back to work on problem areas. See if your child can explain the terms on the page. If they are doing well, have them use the practice page today to stay sharp.

No Review

Lesson 40

DAY 40 Measures of Center

A. **Statistics** is the study of collecting, organizing, analyzing, and interpreting numerical data. A **measure of center** is a value used in statistics to represent the center of a numerical data set with a single number. The common measures of center are the **mean, median,** and **mode.**

Measure	Definition	How to find	Examples
Mean	Average	Divide the sum of the numbers by the number of numbers.	2, 5, 8, 3 Mean = (2 + 5 + 8 + 3)/4 = 4.5
Median	Middle number	Order the numbers and find the middle number. If there are two middle numbers, add them and divide by 2.	5, 7, 3, 6, 9 → 3, 5, 6, 7, 9 Median = 6 4, 8, 3, 7 → 3, 4, 7, 8 Median = (4 + 7)/2 = 5.5
Mode	Most frequent number(s)	Find the number that occurs most frequently. A data set can have no mode, one mode, or multiple modes.	4, 5, 2, 2, 6, 2, 9 Mode = 2 5, 7, 4, 3, 3, 7, 9, 3, 7 Mode = 3, 7

B. Find the mean, median, and mode(s) of each data set.

6, 5, 8, 2, 6, 2, 6, 3, 6, 2

4.6   5.5   6

7, 6, 8, 5, 7, 9, 8, 7, 8, 4, 9, 9, 5, 8, 5

7   7   8

10, 16, 12, 11, 15, 14, 10, 18, 7, 9, 18, 10

12.5   11.5   10

48, 58, 30, 44, 43, 32, 30, 25, 29, 34, 45

38   34   30

312, 327, 345, 313, 339, 330, 364, 330

332.5   330   330

DAY 40 Practice

Find the mean, median, and mode(s) of each data set.

7, 2, 6, 8, 7, 5, 7

6   7   7

4, 9, 4, 8, 5, 9, 4, 1

5.5   4.5   4

3, 5, 2, 7, 4, 2, 1, 6, 8, 5, 5, 4, 3, 2, 9

4.4   4   5, 2

8, 6, 4, 7, 3, 9, 11, 10, 8, 7, 2, 5, 1, 1, 8

6   7   8

14, 18, 16, 9, 9, 7, 16, 12, 9, 11, 8, 3

11   10   9

24, 21, 20, 29, 22, 20, 28, 25, 27

24   24   20

52, 56, 62, 48, 22, 14, 56, 43, 42, 33

42.8   45.5   56

102, 85, 42, 93, 106, 90, 35

79   90   None

532, 517, 526, 413, 526, 618

522   526   526

Lesson 40 – Measures of Center

They are going to be finding the average of a set of numbers. I wouldn't mind them using a calculator on these.

The mode just means which number is there the most. There can be more than one.

The median is the number in the middle when you line them up smallest to largest. If there is an even number, so that there is no middle number in the list, then you find the number between the two middle numbers. 1 2 3 4 → the middle would be 2½ .

The mean is when you add them all up and divide by how many numbers there are.

Review 40 – Remainders

The remainder is what's left over after you've subtracted all you can and there are still some remaining. 9 divided by 4 is 2 with a remainder of 1. 9 – 4 = 5 – 4 = 1 I subtracted 4 two times and there was 1 left over. I couldn't subtract four again. To work faster you should think 4 x 2 = 8 and then 9 – 8 = 1.

Answers   4 R 3   5 R 6   7 R 1

Lesson 41

DAY 41 Measures of Variability

A. While measures of center such as mean, median, and mode describe the center of a data set, **measures of variability** describe the spread of a data set. The common measures of variability are the **range** and **mean absolute deviation** (MAD).

Measure	Definition	Example
Range	The difference between the highest and lowest values in a data set.	5, 9, 8, 8, 3, 9, 7 Range = 9 − 3 = 6
Mean absolute deviation (MAD)	The mean (average) distance between each data value and the mean.	See the example below.

B. The mean absolute deviation describes how far, on average, each data value is from the mean.

Given: 5, 8, 2, 9, 5, 7

Absolute deviations:

To find the mean absolute deviation:
1. Find the mean.
   (5 + 8 + 2 + 9 + 5 + 7)/6 = 6
2. Find the absolute deviations, the distances between the data values and the mean.
   |5 − 6| = 1, |8 − 6| = 2, |2 − 6| = 4, |9 − 6| = 3, |5 − 6| = 1, |7 − 6| = 1
3. Find the mean (average) of these distances.
   (1 + 2 + 4 + 3 + 1 + 1)/6 = 2

C. Find the range and mean absolute deviation of each data set.

6, 4, 9, 10, 2, 5, 7, 9, 6, 12, 8, 12, 10, 1, 4

| 11 | 2.8 |

10, 28, 18, 16, 27, 23, 17, 13, 19, 29

| 19 | 5.4 |

15, 32, 56, 24, 55, 26, 19, 20, 15, 18

| 41 | 11.8 |

74, 88, 98, 76, 60, 76, 89, 95

| 38 | 10.5 |

DAY 41 Practice

Find the range and mean absolute deviation of each data set.

3, 5, 4, 11, 6, 9, 8, 10

| 8 | 2.5 |

13, 6, 3, 2, 4, 6, 1, 9

| 12 | 3 |

18, 7, 12, 3, 9, 5, 9, 5, 9, 23

| 20 | 4.6 |

1, 12, 8, 9, 6, 18, 7, 20, 6, 14, 4, 10, 2, 2, 16

| 19 | 4.8 |

20, 45, 20, 37, 23, 45, 20, 10, 8, 12

| 37 | 11 |

42, 35, 18, 27, 55, 56, 12, 15

| 44 | 14.5 |

44, 50, 83, 65, 39, 87, 45, 83

| 48 | 17.5 |

115, 96, 132, 144, 123

| 48 | 13.2 |

425, 260, 718, 418, 459

| 458 | 106 |

Lesson 41 – Measures of Variability

This sounds all fancy, but this page is just about how accurate the average is. It gives a little more information about the average informaion given. If the data numbers were 1, 50, and 100, then the mean would be 50, the median would be 50. But that doesn't actually tell us a lot. Today's lesson shows us a bigger picture of what the data points include.

The range is the distance between the highest and lowest numbers in the data. In my little example, it would be 100 − 1, which would be 99. The absolute deviation is the average of the difference between the mean and each number in the data.

Let's walk through the first one in Part C. The range would be 12 − 1, or 11, because 12 is the highest number in the list and 1 is the lowest. To find the absolute deviation, we start with finding the mean. The total of the numbers all added together is 105. We divide that by how many values there are, 15. The mean is 7, 105/15. Then we find all the distances from the mean to each number. For instance, the distance, or difference, between 6 and 7 is 1. All the distances are: 1, 3, 2, 3, 5, 2, 0, 2, 1, 5, 1, 5, 3, 6, 3. Now, we find the mean again. We add those together and divide by 15. Their total is 42. 42/15 = 2.8 The absolute deviation is 2.8.

Review 41 – Dividing with Remainders

This is similar to Lessons 37 and 40.
Answers   52 R 4   92 R 3   84 R 8

Lesson 42

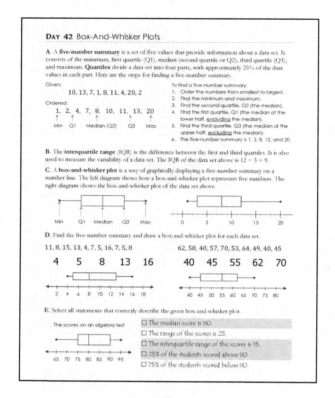

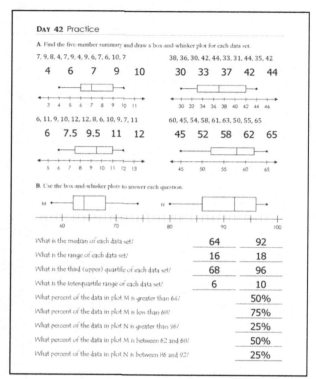

Lesson 42 – Box-and-Whisper Plots

They are still looking at averages here. There's a big word used, quartile. A quarter is a fourth. They are dividing the data numbers into four parts. Each part is a quarter of the whole, a quartile.

They mark the lowest and highest numbers and the median. That median marks the second quartile, Q2. Then they find the median of the data points below the Q2; that is the first quartile, Q1. Then they find the median of the data above Q2. That median is the Q3. The interquartile range is the difference between Q3 and Q1. These numbers Q1, Q2, and Q3 divide the data into four parts. This is show below.

> data data Q1 data data Q2 data data Q3 data data

The box-and-whisper plot shows visually what these numbers are. It shows if more numbers are in a certain area of the data.

Review 42 – Dividing with Remainders

This is similar to Lessons 37 and 40.

Answers   528 R 4   441 R 2   727 R 3

Lesson 43

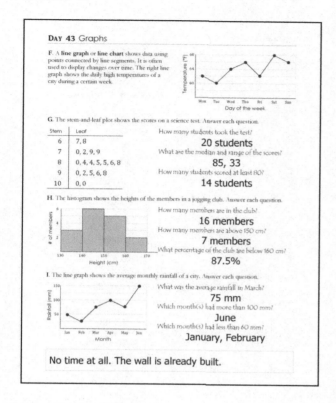

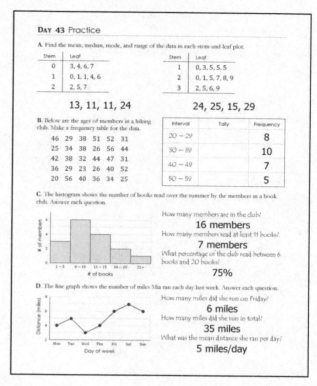

Lesson 43 – Graphs

They should be familiar with a bar graph. There is a second page with questions to practice reading graphs.

A bar graph they should be familiar with. A histogram is just a bar graph with no gaps between the values at the bottom.

A frequency table is just counting. A dot plot is the same type of thing, counting using X or a dot instead of the tally marks of a frequency table.

The stem-and-leaf plot is just separating out the tens values and ones values.

The line graph is similar to a bar graph, marking the top number, but those numbers are connected by lines, showing clearly the changing value.

Review 43 – Dividing with Multiple Digits

This is just like dividing with one digit in the divisor. It won't go into the first digit. You'll automatically start with checking to see if it goes into the first two digits in the dividend.

Answers   28   21   16

Lesson 44

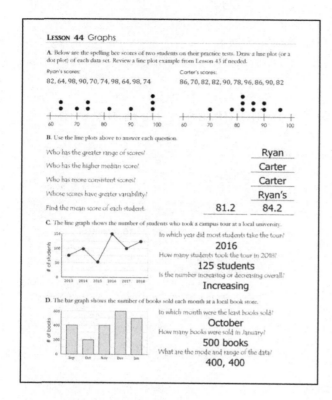

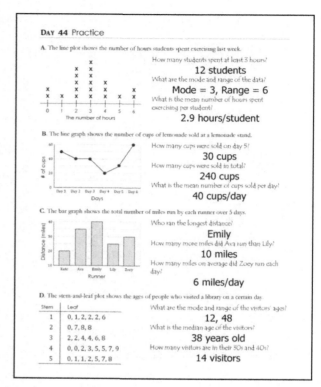

Lesson 44 – Graphs

They will be making and reading graphs today. You can turn back to Lesson 43 for a reminder.

Review 44 – Dividing with Multiple Digits

This is like the review in Lesson 43.

Answers   29   62   36

Lesson 45

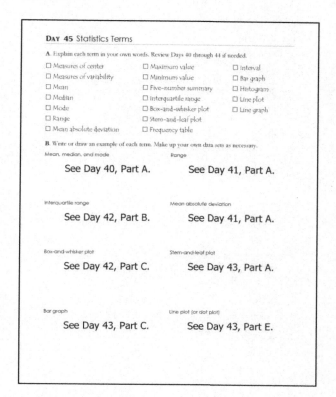

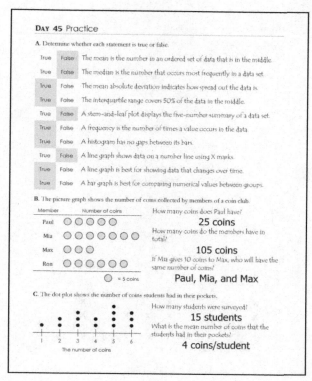

Lesson 45 – Statistics Terms

This is a review of all the terms from this statistics unit, talking about data.

You'll need to sit with your child while they work through explaining the terms.

Review 45 – Dividing with Multiple Digits

Another way to think about division is to take out multiples of ten. For instance, 27 divided into 4968. You can take out one hundred 27s. That would be 2700. You take those away and are left with 2268. You can take out ten 27s. That would be 270. You can do that eight times, subtracting it off each time, to be left with 108. Then you can subtract off one 27 four times. So you divided into groups of 100, 80, and 4. The answer is 184.

Answers   16   28   37

Lesson 46

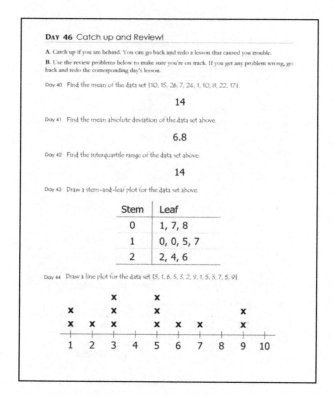

DAY 46 Catch up and Review!

A. Catch up if you are behind. You can go back and redo a lesson that caused you trouble.

B. Use the review problems below to make sure you're on track. If you get any problem wrong, go back and redo the corresponding day's lesson.

Day 40   Find the mean of the data set {10, 15, 26, 7, 24, 1, 10, 8, 22, 17}.

14

Day 41   Find the mean absolute deviation of the data set above.

6.8

Day 42   Find the interquartile range of the data set above.

14

Day 43   Draw a stem-and-leaf plot for the data set above.

Stem	Leaf
0	1, 7, 8
1	0, 0, 5, 7
2	2, 4, 6

Day 44   Draw a line plot for the data set {3, 1, 6, 5, 3, 2, 9, 1, 5, 3, 7, 5, 9}.

DAY 46 Practice

A. Solve each equation.

$65 = 29 + x$ $25 = \frac{x}{6}$ $32 = x - 17$

x = 36   x = 150   x = 49

$\frac{x}{4} = 12$ $x - 38 = 25$ $13x = 91$

x = 48   x = 63   x = 7

B. Evaluate each expression using the order of operations.

$7 + 52 \div 4$ 20 $9^2 - (5 - 4) \times 3^4$ 0

$3^2 + 7 \times 5$ 44 $62 - 6^2 \div (5 - 4)^2$ 26

$2^3 \times (3^2 - 2^2)$ 40 $1^3 + 9 \times 5 \div (7 - 2)$ 10

C. Find the mean, median, mode, and range of each data set.

5, 7, 5, 2, 6

5   5   5   5

10, 3, 7, 9, 7, 12

8   8   7   9

4, 6, 2, 6, 5, 7

5   5.5   6   5

13, 3, 9, 13, 4, 12, 16

10   12   13   13

7, 9, 4, 9, 3, 7, 8, 9

7   7.5   9   6

3, 9, 16, 6, 7, 3, 18, 14

9.5   8   3   15

Lesson 46 Catch Up and Review

Have your child check themselves using the lesson page and go back to work on problem areas. See if your child can explain the terms on the page. If they are doing well, have them use the practice page today to stay sharp.

No Review

Lesson 47

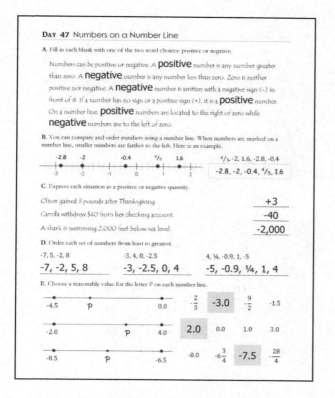

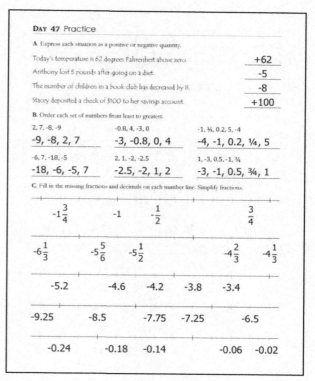

Lesson 47 – Numbers on a Number Line

They are looking at positive and negative numbers. The larger the positive number the farther to the right on the number line. The larger the negative number, the smaller the number actually is, and it shows up farther to the left on the number line.

They are going to be thinking about numbers being positive or negative. When something gains, we use a positive number. When something is lost, a negative number is used.

The other part is ordering fractions and decimals. They don't need to think too hard about these. They need to think a little about where each number would fall on the number line. They are estimating.

Review 47 – Dividing with Multiple Digits

This is like the review in Lesson 43.

Answers   42   23   31

Lesson 48

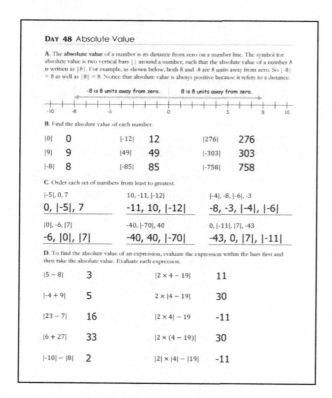

DAY 48 Absolute Value

A. The **absolute value** of a number is its distance from zero on a number line. The symbol for absolute value is two vertical bars | | around a number, such that the absolute value of a number *b* is written as |*b*|. For example, as shown below, both 8 and -8 are 8 units away from zero. So |-8| = 8 as well as |8| = 8. Notice that absolute value is always positive because it refers to a distance.

-8 is 8 units away from zero.   8 is 8 units away from zero.

B. Find the absolute value of each number.

	0		0		-12		12		276		276
	9		9		49		49		-303		303
	-8		8		-85		85		-758		758

C. Order each set of numbers from least to greatest.

|-5|, 0, 7 → 0, |-5|, 7
10, -11, |-12| → -11, 10, |-12|
|-4|, -8, |-6|, -3 → -8, -3, |-4|, |-6|

|0|, -6, |7| → -6, |0|, |7|
-40, |-70|, 40 → -40, 40, |-70|
0, |-11|, |7|, -43 → -43, 0, |7|, |-11|

D. To find the absolute value of an expression, evaluate the expression within the bars first and then take the absolute value. Evaluate each expression.

	5 − 8		3		2 × 4 − 19		11
	-4 + 9		5	2 ×	4 − 19		30
	23 − 7		16		2 × 4	− 19	-11
	6 + 27		33		2 × (4 − 19)		30
|-10| − |8|	2	|2| × |4| − |19|	-11

DAY 48 Practice

A. Find the absolute value of each number.

	1		1		50		50		-176		176
	-5		5		-37		37		-418		418
	-7		7		-92		92		630		630

B. Order each set of numbers from least to greatest.

|-7|, 1, 4 → 1, 4, |-7|
13, -31, |-15| → -31, 13, |-15|
-3, -7, |-5|, |-2| → -7, -3, |-2|, |-5|

|3|, -6, |1| → -6, |1|, |3|
-24, |-62|, 45 → -24, 45, |-62|
-9, |-7|, |6|, -8 → -9, -8, |6|, |-7|

C. Circle all expressions that have an absolute value of 25.

5 × (4 − 9)	5 × (2 + 3)	5 × 5 × 0	10 + 5² ÷ 5
-5 × 5 ÷ -5	0² − 5²	5² − 10 × 10	5 + (2 × 5)
125 ÷ 25 × (-125)	-10 ÷ 10 + -5	5 − 5 × 5	5⁴ ÷ 5²

D. Evaluate each expression.

	8 + -8		0		5 × 6 − 8 ÷ 2		26
	-7 − 3		10	5 ×	6 − 8	÷ 2	5
	8 + 33		41		5 × 6	−	8 ÷ 2		26
	5 − 28		23		9 + 4 × 7 − 7		30
	42	−	-5		37	9 +	4 × 7	− 7	30
|-46| + |6|	52	|9 + 4| × |7 − 7|	0

Lesson 48 – Absolute Value

Absolute value is technically the distance between zero and a number. It's basically the positive value of a number. The absolute value of 3 is 3. The absolute value of -3 is also 3.

In part D they will be using absolute value and order of operation. They have to solve the expression inside the absolute value before they can find the absolute value.

$$|-19| - |9| = 19 - 9 = 10$$
$$|-19 - 9| = |-28| = 28$$

Review 48 – Word Problems

These are word problems using arithmetic. They can use techniques such as drawing a picture and using smaller numbers to figure out what they need to do in order to find the answer.

Answers   336 cans, 16 books, 12 pages

Lesson 49

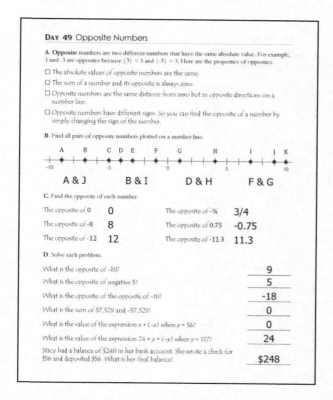

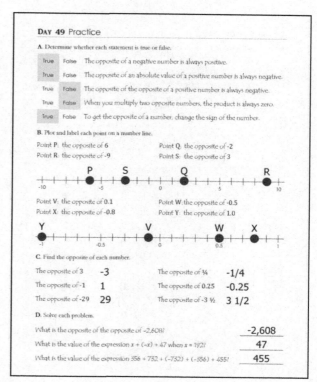

Lesson 49 – Opposite Numbers

This is a simple lesson, so don't let them get in their head. 2 and -2 are opposite numbers. Oppostie numbers are the positive and negative values of a number.

Zero has no opposite.

There are some variables used. The point to learn is that a number and its opposite equal zero when added together. This is how we solved equations. We subtracted off the same number to get zero. It works with variables as well. X – X = 0 no matter what X is. They should be able to understand that is true. They can substitute any number in there to check that it's true.

Review 49 – Multi-Step Word Problems

When there are multiple steps in a word problem, the trick is to make sure you finish and answer the question being asked and not just give as the answer the first thing you figure out.

Answers   4 pieces, 9 stamps, 8 bags

Lesson 50

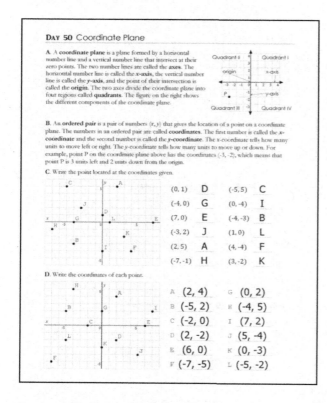

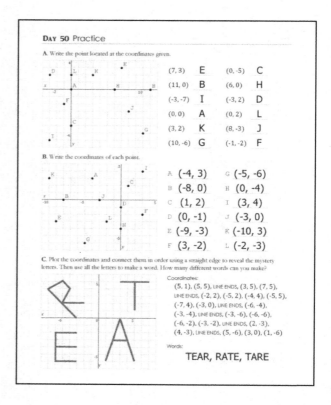

Lesson 50 – Coordinate Plane

They are plotting points on a graph today, a coordinate plane. Each block is 1 unit. The origin, the starting point is the center, where the horizontal and vertical lines intersect. We label that as (0,0). One over from there to the right is (1, 0). One up from the origin is (0,1).

The coordinates are labeled (x, y). X is the horizontal axis. Y is the vertical axis. The coordinates are labeled showing how far right and left from the origin and then how far above and below from the origin.

Review 50 – Word Problems

This is similar to Lesson 49.

Answers   3 peaches, $11, 79 coins

Lesson 51

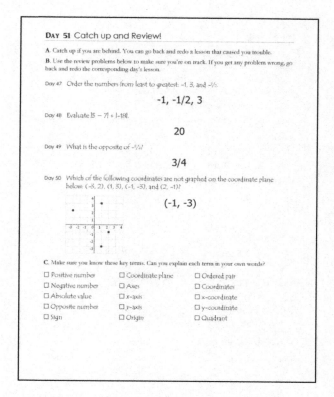

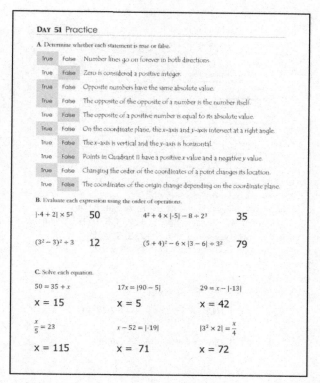

Lesson 51 Catch Up and Review

Have your child check themselves using the lesson page and go back to work on problem areas. See if your child can explain the terms on the page. If they are doing well, have them use the practice page today to stay sharp.

No Review

Lesson 52

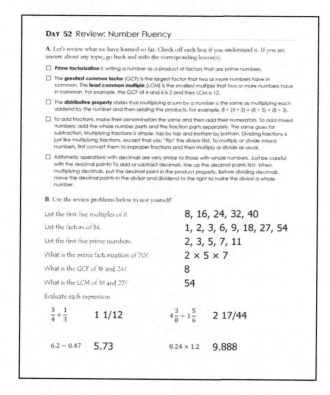

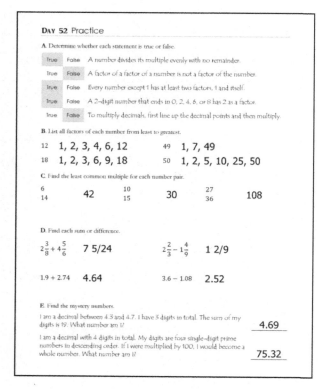

Lesson 52 – Review: Number Fluency

This is a review. They should carefully read through the top and make sure they understand, looking back as necessary.

They should complete part B. Check their work.

There's a practice page if they get through quickly, or if there's something specific they need to try again, or if you want to take a second day for this review.

No Review

Lesson 53

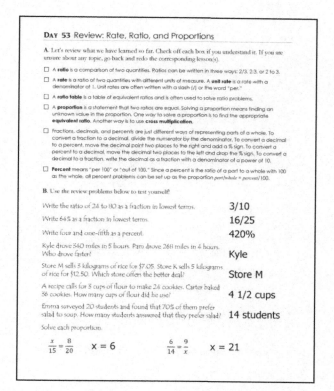

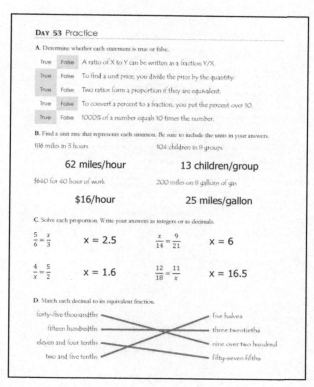

Lesson 53 – Review: Rates, Ratio, and Proportions

This is a review. They should carefully read through the top and make sure they understand, looking back as necessary.

They should complete part B. Check their work.

There's a practice page if they get through quickly, or if there's something specific they need to try again, or if you want to take a second day for this review.

No Review

Lesson 54

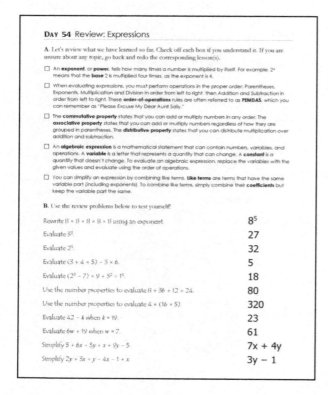

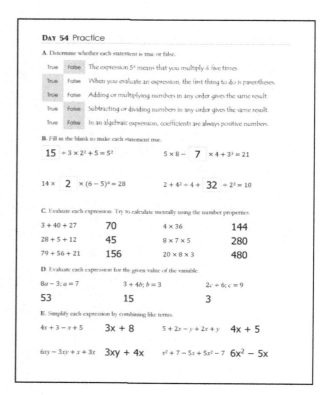

Lesson 54 – Review: Expressions

This is a review. They should carefully read through the top and make sure they understand, looking back as necessary.

They should complete part B. Check their work.

There's a practice page if they get through quickly, or if there's something specific they need to try again, or if you want to take a second day for this review.

No Review

Lesson 55

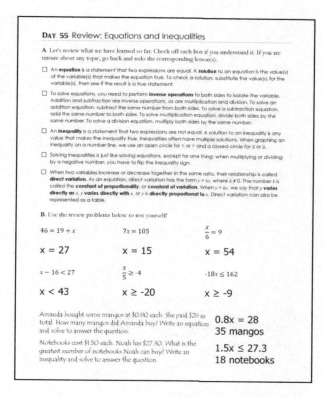

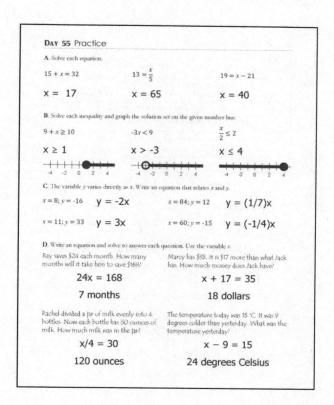

Lesson 55 – Review: Equations and Inequalities

This is a review. They should carefully read through the top and make sure they understand, looking back as necessary.

They should complete part B. Check their work.

There's a practice page if they get through quickly, or if there's something specific they need to try again, or if you want to take a second day for this review.

No Review

Lesson 56

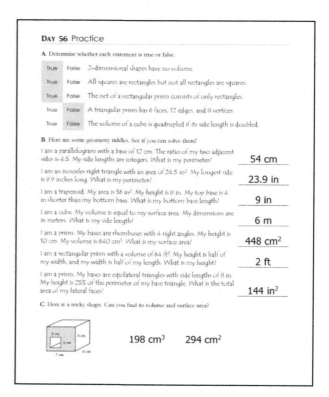

Lesson 56 – Review: Area and Volume

This is a review. They should carefully read through the top and make sure they understand, looking back as necessary.

They should complete part B. Check their work.

There's a practice page if they get through quickly, or if there's something specific they need to try again, or if you want to take a second day for this review.

No Review

Lesson 57

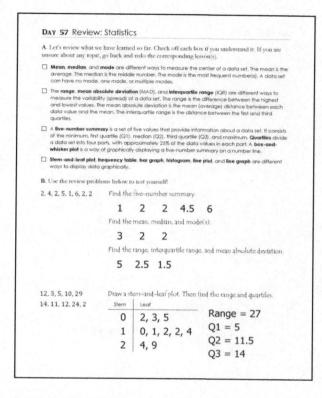

DAY 57 Review: Statistics

A. Let's review what we have learned so far. Check off each box if you understand it. If you are unsure about any topic, go back and redo the corresponding lesson(s).

☐ **Mean, median,** and **mode** are different ways to measure the center of a data set. The mean is the average. The median is the middle number. The mode is the most frequent number(s). A data set can have no mode, one mode, or multiple modes.

☐ The **range, mean absolute deviation** (MAD), and **interquartile range** (IQR) are different ways to measure the variability (spread) of a data set. The range is the difference between the highest and lowest values. The mean absolute deviation is the mean (average) distance between each data value and the mean. The interquartile range is the distance between the first and third quartiles.

☐ A **five-number summary** is a set of five values that provide information about a data set. It consists of the minimum, first quartile (Q1), median (Q2), third quartile (Q3), and maximum. **Quartiles** divide a data set into four parts, with approximately 25% of the data values in each part. A **box-and-whisker plot** is a way of graphically displaying a five-number summary on a number line.

☐ **Stem-and-leaf plot, frequency table, bar graph, histogram, line plot,** and **line graph** are different ways to display data graphically.

B. Use the review problems below to test yourself!

2, 4, 2, 5, 1, 6, 2, 2   Find the five-number summary.

1   2   2   4.5   6

Find the mean, median, and mode(s).

3   2   2

Find the range, interquartile range, and mean absolute deviation.

5   2.5   1.5

12, 3, 5, 10, 29   Draw a stem-and-leaf plot. Then find the range and quartiles.
14, 11, 12, 24, 2

Stem	Leaf
0	2, 3, 5
1	0, 1, 2, 2, 4
2	4, 9

Range = 27
Q1 = 5
Q2 = 11.5
Q3 = 14

DAY 57 Practice

A. Find the five-number summary for each data set.

Data set	Min	Q1	Q2	Q3	Max
3, 5, 2, 7, 9, 4, 5	2	3	5	7	9
7, 13, 18, 12, 10, 15, 8	7	8	12	15	18
2, 7, 4, 2, 1, 3, 4, 6, 5, 4	1	2	4	5	7
4, 15, 6, 8, 19, 15, 7, 22	4	6.5	11.5	17	22

B. Find the mean, median, and mode(s) for each data set.

Data set	Mean	Median	Mode
5, 5, 2, 7, 4	4.6	5	5
6, 10, 12, 6, 9, 5	8	7.5	6
16, 24, 8, 12, 16, 9, 5, 6	12	10.5	16
6, 4, 3, 1, 2, 9, 7, 9, 5, 8	5.4	5.5	9

C. Find the range and mean absolute deviation (MAD) for each data set.

Data set	Range	MAD
4, 3, 2, 7, 9	7	2.4
8, 6, 1, 6, 4, 8	7	2
14, 12, 6, 15, 2, 8, 6, 9	13	3.5
2, 1, 8, 2, 7, 2, 5, 9, 2, 6	8	2.6

D. The stem-and-leaf plot shows the ages of people at a restaurant. Answer each question.

Stem	Leaf
2	2, 4, 6, 6
3	0, 3, 4, 6, 7, 9
4	5, 5, 6, 6, 6
5	3, 6, 7
6	1, 8

How many people were at the restaurant? 20

What was the age of the oldest person? 68

Find the range and quartiles.

R: 46, Q1: 31.5, Q2: 42, Q3: 49.5

Lesson 57 – Review: Statistics

This is a review. They should carefully read through the top and make sure they understand, looking back as necessary.

They should complete part B. Check their work.

There's a practice page if they get through quickly, or if there's something specific they need to try again, or if you want to take a second day for this review.

No Review

Lesson 58

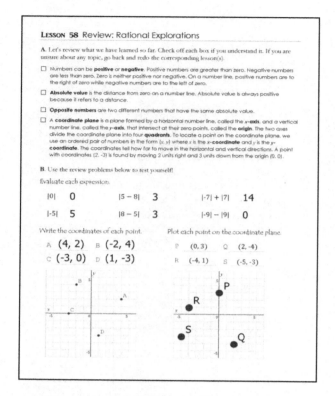

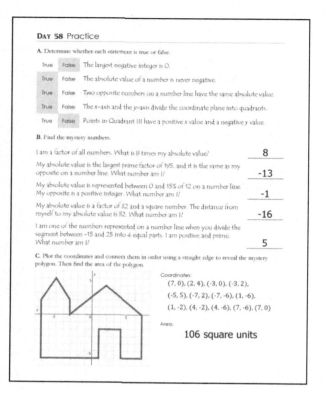

Lesson 58 – Review: Rational Explorations

This is a review. They should carefully read through the top and make sure they understand, looking back as necessary.

They should complete part B. Check their work.

There's a practice page if they get through quickly, or if there's something specific they need to try again, or if you want to take a second day for this review.

No Review

Lesson 59

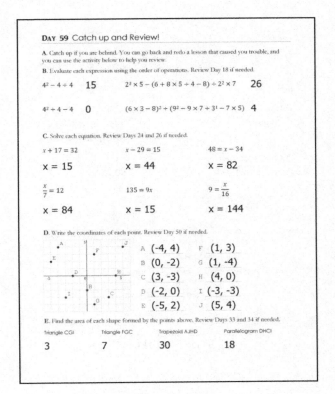

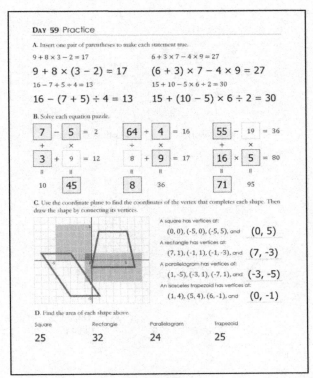

Lesson 59 Catch Up and Review

Have your child check themselves using the lesson page and go back to work on problem areas. See if your child can explain the terms on the page. If they are doing well, have them use the practice page today to stay sharp.

No Review

Lesson 60

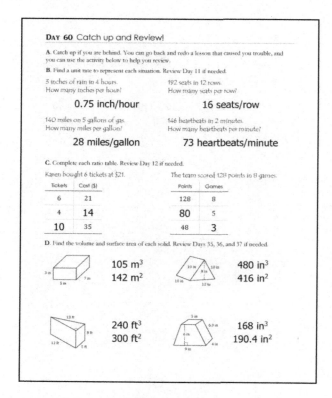

Lesson 60 Catch Up and Review

Have your child check themselves using the lesson page and go back to work on problem areas. See if your child can explain the terms on the page. If they are doing well, have them use the practice page today to stay sharp.

No Review

Lesson 61

DAY 61 Number Properties

A. The number properties listed below are true for any numbers *a*, *b*, and *c*. Check off each property if you can come up with an example.

Property	Addition	Multiplication
☐ Commutative	$a + b = b + a$	$ab = ba$
☐ Associative	$(a + b) + c = a + (b + c)$	$(ab)c = a(bc)$
☐ Identity	$a + 0 = 0 + a = a$	$a \cdot 1 = 1 \cdot a = a$
☐ Inverse	$a + (-a) = (-a) + a = 0$	$a \cdot \frac{1}{a} = \frac{1}{a} \cdot a = 1, a \neq 0$
☐ Distributive	$a(b + c) = ab + ac$ and $a(b - c) = ab - ac$	

B. Match the number property and its description.

a. Commutative property of addition
b. Commutative property of multiplication
c. Associative property of addition
d. Associative property of multiplication
e. Identity property of addition
f. Identity property of multiplication
g. Inverse property of addition
h. Inverse property of multiplication
i. Distributive property

e The sum of zero and any number is the number.
b Changing the order of factors does not change the product.
d Changing the grouping of factors does not change the product.
g The sum of any number and its inverse is 0.
i The product of the sum of two numbers is the same as the sum of their products.
a Changing the order of addends does not change the sum.
h The product of any number and its inverse is 1.
f The product of 1 and any number is the number.
c Changing the grouping of addends does not change the sum.
h The number property you use to solve 2x = 6.
g The number property you use to solve 4 + x = 9.

DAY 61 Practice

A. Write an example for each number property.

Property	Addition	Multiplication
Commutative		
Associative	Answers will vary.	
Identity		
Inverse		
Distributive		

B. Circle the number property that each equation illustrates.

$7(m + 2) = 7m + 14$	commutative	associative	**distributive**	identity
$x \cdot 5 = 5 \cdot x$	**commutative**	distributive	identity	inverse
$w \cdot 1 = w$	associative	distributive	**identity**	inverse
$(9x) \cdot y = 9 \cdot (xy)$	commutative	**associative**	distributive	identity
$3 + (-3) = 0$	associative	distributive	identity	**inverse**
$6 + p = p + 6$	**commutative**	associative	identity	inverse
$(k + 9) + 8 = k + (9 + 8)$	commutative	**associative**	distributive	identity

C. Circle all statements that show the distributive property.

$4 \times 8 = (4 \times 8) \times (4 \times 8)$	**$7 \times 9 = (7 \times 5) + (7 \times 4)$**	$7 \times 6 = (2 \times 3) + (5 \times 3)$
$11 \times 4 = (5 \times 4) + (6 \times 4)$	**$8 \times 6 = (5 \times 6) + (3 \times 6)$**	$5 \times 7 = (5 \times 5) \times (5 \times 2)$

D. Use the distributive property to factor out the GCF from each expression.

24 + 42   = 6 x 4 + 6 x 7 = 6 x (4 + 7) = 6 x 11
21 + 28   = 7 x 3 + 7 x 4 = 7 x (3 + 4) = 7 x 7
81 + 54   = 27 x 3 + 27 x 2 = 27 x (3 + 2) = 27 x 5

Lesson 61 – Number Properties

These are the rules of arithmetic, like the laws of physics, things that are just always true, except even more so. Sometimes we find a law of science really wasn't true, and God just breaks those sometimes, anyway. Math laws are ALWAYS true.

They've seen these already. They can substitute numbers in for the variables to convince themselve the rules are true. They know that a + b = b + a. That means that 1 + 3 = 3 + 1. And they know that a + 0 = a. That means that 5 + 0 = 5. Now they just have to relax into describing it with variables and work on being familiar with the terminology.

Commutative is about moving, like your commute to work.
Associative is about grouping, like who you associate with.
Identity is about staying the same, like keeping true to who you are, maintaining your identity.
Inverse is about the opposite, like something inverted or upside down.
Distributive is about passing out a number, distributing it to each piece.

Review 61 – Positive and Negative Numbers

They are just going to write the number and add a negative sign if it represents a value less than zero.

Answers   +78   -1,000   +1,500

Lesson 62

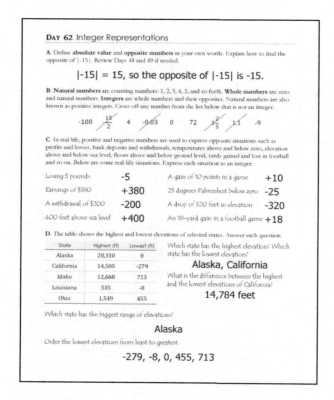

Lesson 62 – Integer Representations

This is again looking at positive and negative numbers, integers, and numbers in general. There is vocabulary on the page. Have your child explain them to you. There's no trick here. There are the numbers you count with, those along with zero, and those and their opposites. They each have a math name: natural numbers, whole numbers, integers.

Review 62 – Number Line

They need to figure out how much each line is worth. The first one has each line being five away from the next. The second line jumps by eights. The numbers will be the same on each side of zero, but the numbers on the left will be negative.

Answers   -25, -15, 0, 10, 20   -48, -32, 8, 24, 48

Lesson 63

DAY 63 Operations with Integers

A. Here are the rules for integer operations. Study the examples carefully!

Operation	Rules	Examples
Addition	If the signs are alike, add the absolute values and keep the sign. If the signs are unlike, find the difference and take the sign of the larger absolute value.	$3 + (-5) = -(5 - 3) = -2$ $(-3) + 5 = +(5 - 3) = 2$ $(-3) + (-5) = -(3 + 5) = -8$
Subtraction	Change to add the opposite, then use the addition rules. (Remember that subtraction is the same as addition of the opposite.)	$2 - 7 = 2 + (-7) = -5$ $2 - (-7) = 2 + 7 = 9$ $(-2) - 7 = (-2) + (-7) = -9$
Multiplication & Division	Multiply or divide as usual, then determine the sign of the product or quotient. Two like signs become a positive sign. Two unlike signs become a negative sign.	$4 \times (-8) = -32$ $(-4) \times 8 = -32$ $(-4) \times (-8) = 32$

B. Use the rules above to evaluate each expression.

$(-2) + 7$ **5** $(-2) - 4$ **-6** $(-5) + (-48)$ **-53**

$(-7) \times 9$ **-63** $(-6) \div 6$ **-1** $(-5) - (-48)$ **43**

$6 - (-8)$ **14** $4 \times (-5)$ **-20** $(-12) \div (-3)$ **4**

C. Evaluate each expression using the order of operations. Review Day 18 if needed.

$4 - 8 \times (-5)$ **44** $5^2 + (-2)^3$ **17**

$7 \times (-3) + 5 \times (-2)$ **-31** $27 - (-10 + 4) \div (-3)$ **25**

D. Solve each problem.

A plane is 12 km above the ground. Write an integer to represent the distance that the plane needs to descend to reach the ground.   **-12**

The temperature in the morning was 8 °C, but it dropped to -2 °C in the evening. How much did it drop during the day?   **10 °C**

Mia had $235 in her bank account. She withdrew $25 each week for the past 5 weeks. What is her final balance?   **$110**

On a hike, Abigail descended 90 feet in 15 minutes. Write an integer to represent her average elevation change per minute.   **-6**

DAY 63 Practice

A. Determine whether each statement is true or false.

True **False** If you add two negative numbers, you get a positive answer.

True False Subtracting a negative number is the same as adding its absolute value.

True False Multiplying three negative numbers results in a positive product.

True False If either the dividend or divisor is negative, the quotient is negative.

B. Use the integer rules to evaluate each expression.

$5 - (-3)$ **8** $8 + (-7)$ **1** $(-52) \times (-7)$ **364**

$(-8) \div 1$ **-8** $9 \times (-5)$ **-45** $(-37) - (-9)$ **-28**

$(-4) + 9$ **5** $(-1) \div 1$ **-1** $(-36) \div (-8)$ **-44**

$(-7) \times 7$ **-49** $(-9) - 4$ **-13** $(-84) \div (-7)$ **12**

C. Evaluate each expression using the order of operations.

$6^2 + 7 \times (-4)$ **8** $(-5) + 2 \times (-5)^2$ **45**

$\dfrac{3^2 - (-3)}{-3}$ **-4** $4^2 - 6 \times \dfrac{(-5) - 4}{-9}$ **10**

D. Solve each problem.

A submarine is 320 feet below the surface of the water. How far does it need to ascend to get back to the surface of the water?   **320 feet**

It is -15 °C in Cleveland and -6 °C in Lexington. What is the difference in temperature between the two cities?   **9 °C**

A company's stock price dropped 8 points every day for 9 days. Write an integer to represent the change in the company's stock price after 9 days.   **-72**

Greg had $186 in his bank account. He withdrew the same amount of money each week for the past 6 weeks. His current balance is $60. Write an integer to represent the weekly change in his bank account.   **-21**

Lesson 63 – Operations with Integers

They should know how to do these operations with integers. They need to think about the sign and they need to think about order of operation. PEMDAS

Review 63 – Ordering Numbers

They will put the numbers in order from least to greatest, remembering that a large negative number is going to be the least in the order.

Answers   -7, -3, 0, 2   -16, -2, 8, 14   -80, -16, 45, 74

Lesson 64

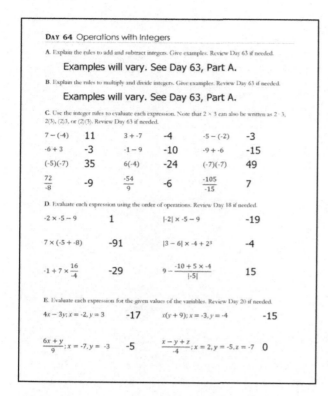

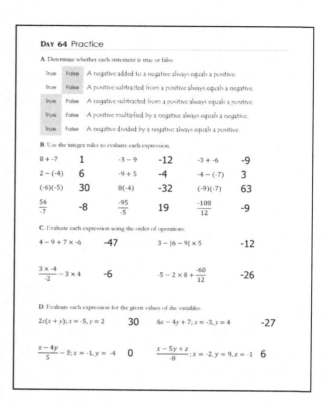

Lesson 64 – Operations with Integers

This is the same thing as Lesson 63.

(-7)(-7) means (-7) x (-7)

They will be using expressions as well. They are given four expressions in Part E. They are to substitute in the values of X and Y and Z into the expression and then solve it.

Here's the first one. 4x – 3y where x = -2 and y = 3 That becomes 4(-2) – (3x3)= -8 – 9 = -17

Review 64 – Opposite

This is a simple review of choosing the inverse, the opposite number to add together to make zero.

Answers   0   4   -18

Lesson 65

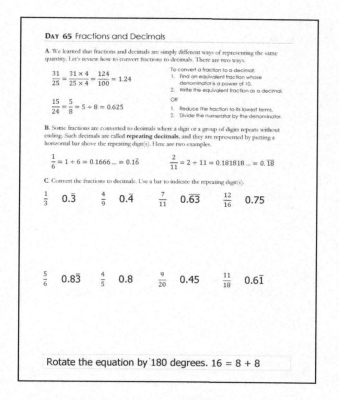

DAY 65 Fractions and Decimals

A. We learned that fractions and decimals are simply different ways of representing the same quantity. Let's review how to convert fractions to decimals. There are two ways.

$$\frac{31}{25} = \frac{31 \times 4}{25 \times 4} = \frac{124}{100} = 1.24$$

To convert a fraction to a decimal:
1. Find an equivalent fraction whose denominator is a power of 10.
2. Write the equivalent fraction as a decimal.

OR

$$\frac{15}{24} = \frac{5}{8} = 5 \div 8 = 0.625$$

1. Reduce the fraction to its lowest terms.
2. Divide the numerator by the denominator.

B. Some fractions are converted to decimals where a digit or a group of digits repeats without ending. Such decimals are called **repeating decimals**, and they are represented by putting a horizontal bar above the repeating digit(s). Here are two examples.

$$\frac{1}{6} = 1 \div 6 = 0.1666\ldots = 0.1\bar{6}$$
$$\frac{2}{11} = 2 \div 11 = 0.181818\ldots = 0.\overline{18}$$

C. Convert the fractions to decimals. Use a bar to indicate the repeating digit(s).

$\frac{1}{3}$ 0.$\bar{3}$ $\frac{4}{9}$ 0.$\bar{4}$ $\frac{7}{11}$ 0.$\overline{63}$ $\frac{12}{16}$ 0.75

$\frac{5}{6}$ 0.8$\bar{3}$ $\frac{4}{5}$ 0.8 $\frac{9}{20}$ 0.45 $\frac{11}{18}$ 0.6$\bar{1}$

Rotate the equation by 180 degrees. 16 = 8 + 8

DAY 65 Practice

A. Write each number as a fraction and a decimal.

three fourths   3/4   0.75
two ninths   2/9   0.$\bar{2}$
five and two thirds   5 2/3   5.$\bar{6}$
two and one eighth   2 1/8   2.125

B. Convert the fractions to decimals. Use a bar to indicate the repeating digit(s).

$\frac{7}{9}$ 0.$\bar{7}$ $\frac{5}{3}$ 1.$\bar{6}$ $\frac{3}{20}$ 0.15 $\frac{13}{18}$ 0.7$\bar{2}$

$\frac{3}{5}$ 0.6 $\frac{4}{3}$ 1.$\bar{3}$ $\frac{7}{15}$ 0.4$\bar{6}$ $\frac{11}{50}$ 0.22

$\frac{5}{8}$ 0.625 $\frac{1}{6}$ 0.1$\bar{6}$ $\frac{9}{25}$ 0.36 $\frac{16}{33}$ 0.$\overline{48}$

Lesson 65 – Fractions and Decimals

One way to turn a fraction into a decimal is to find the equivalent fraction with a 10 or 100 in the denominator. 0.1 is one tenth, one over ten. 0.01 is one hundredth or 1 over 100.

However, that's not always going to be possible. They will, however, always be able to divide the fraction to get the equivalent decimal. They will be dividing the numerator by the denominator. They will know that they are going the correct way if the answer is smaller than one.

I'm okay with kids using a calculator to do this part. They will place a decimal point in the dividend and then add as many zeros as necessary. The decimal point goes straight up into the quotient.

Some of the answers are going to be repeating decimals and some won't. When they are dividing, they will have to keep adding a zero until they figure out the answer. Here's an example: one eighth, 1/8 You divide eight into one. It can't go in, so you add a decimal and a 0 and continue.

```
    0.125
8 | 1.000
    8
    20
    16
    40
```

Review 65 – Absolute Value

The absolute value is the distance to zero, basically just the number given with no sign.

Answers   0   7   13

Lesson 66

DAY 66 Fractions and Decimals

A. Decimals with digits that end are called **terminating** decimals. Terminating decimals represent fractions whose denominator is a power of 10, so converting terminating decimals to fractions is simply a matter of using appropriate denominators. Let's review with some examples.

$0.025 = \frac{25}{1000} = \frac{1}{40}$

$7.48 = 7\frac{48}{100} = 7\frac{12}{25}$

To convert a decimal to a fraction:
1. Leave the whole number part as is.
2. Convert the decimal part to a fraction where the numerator is the number after the decimal point and the denominator is a power of 10 with as many zeros as the number of decimal places.
3. Simplify the fraction.

B. Convert the decimals to fractions. Simplify the fractions.

0.5   1/2   0.32   8/25

3.4   3 2/5   4.125   4 1/8

0.06   3/50   7.098   7 49/500

1.35   1 7/20   3.225   3 9/40

C. Convert the fractions to decimals. Use a bar to indicate the repeating digit(s).

$\frac{4}{5}$ 0.8 $\frac{3}{8}$ 0.375 $\frac{14}{12}$ 1.1$\bar{6}$ $\frac{49}{35}$ 1.4

DAY 66 Practice

A. Convert the decimals to fractions. Simplify the fractions.

0.2   1/5   6.75   6 3/4

1.6   1 3/5   0.004   1/250

0.05   1/20   7.048   7 6/125

2.12   2 3/25   5.625   5 5/8

B. Convert the fractions to decimals. Use a bar to indicate the repeating digit(s).

$\frac{1}{9}$ 0.$\bar{1}$ $\frac{7}{4}$ 1.75 $\frac{31}{50}$ 0.62 $\frac{54}{30}$ 1.8

$\frac{3}{8}$ 0.375 $\frac{5}{9}$ 0.$\bar{5}$ $\frac{28}{16}$ 1.75 $\frac{30}{48}$ 0.625

Lesson 66 – Fractions and Decimals

They are going to be converting decimals into fractions today. They just have to read the decimal and write that as a fraction. The last step is to simplify the fraction.

They make a fraction by putting the digits in the decimal as the numerator and in the denominator placing a one and the same number of zeros as decimal places.

0.05 would be 5 over 100, two zeros because there are two decimal places in 0.05. The you could divide the numerator and denominator by 5 and end up with 1/20.

This works with terminating decimals, ones that have an end.

Review 66 – Absolute Value

This is a true or false activity for absolute value. They need to find the absolute value and then compare the numbers.

Answers   True   True   False

Lesson 67

DAY 67 Operations with Decimals

A. We learned that arithmetic operations with positive decimals are very similar to those with whole numbers. You just have to be careful with the decimal point. Review Day 9 if needed.

B. The rules for adding, subtracting, multiplying, and dividing integers apply to decimals as well. Let's see with examples. Review Day 63 if needed.

0.25 + -5.9	0.25 − (-5.9)	5.9 × -0.25	-5.9 ÷ -0.25
Find 5.9 − 0.25. Add the negative sign.	Just find 0.25 + 5.9. The answer is positive.	Find 5.9 × 0.25. Add the negative sign.	Just find 5.9 ÷ 0.25. The answer is positive.

C. Find each sum, difference, product, or quotient.

16 + -2.75	**13.25**	0.48 − 5.284	**-4.804**
32.7 × -9.8	**-320.46**	-92.72 ÷ 7.6	**-12.2**
-5.95 ÷ -1.7	**3.5**	-12.2 + -7.95	**-20.15**
-1.3 − (-0.921)	**-0.379**	35.4 × -17.2	**-608.88**
-0.073 × -2.8	**0.2044**	10.08 ÷ -12.6	**-0.8**

A video game costs $35.80. Now it's on sale for $24.99. How much less is the sale price than the original price?   **$10.81**

The temperature at 9 a.m. was 5 °C. Since then, it has been dropping 1.25 degrees every hour. What will be the temperature at 3 p.m.?   **-2.5 °C**

Carter filled his car with 8.2 gallons of gas. He paid $30 and received $9.50 as change. What's the price of gas per gallon?   **$2.50/gallon**

DAY 67 Practice

Find each sum, difference, product, or quotient.

-0.9 + -16.74	**-17.64**	0.08 − 2.103	**-2.023**
15.8 × -0.09	**-1.422**	-30.45 ÷ -5.8	**5.25**
-0.2 − (-1.158)	**0.958**	-4.27 × -15.2	**64.904**
0.578 ÷ -1.7	**-0.34**	2.095 + -1.28	**0.815**
1.08 − (-0.953)	**2.033**	29.3 × -1.36	**-39.848**
-2.964 ÷ -3.8	**0.78**	-8.85 + 4.29	**-4.56**
-8.7 × -0.247	**2.1489**	52.08 ÷ -2.1	**-24.8**

At a store, Jessica paid her groceries with two $20 bills and received $4.86 as change. What was the cost of her groceries?   **$35.14**

One foot is 12 inches and one inch is 2.54 centimeters. Aubrey is 4 feet 11 inches tall. How tall is Aubrey in centimeters?   **149.86 cm**

A box of 100 pencils sells at $11.00. Jason bought 25 pencils and paid $10. What was his change?   **$7.25**

Lesson 67 – Operations with Decimals

They will be doing arithmetic with decimals today. They know how to do this. They just need to pay attention to the signs.

Adding and subtracting: line up the decimal points; when the signs are the same, they add the numbers and the answer will have that sign; otherwise, they will find the difference and the answer will have the sign of the largest number

Multiplying: the answer has the total number of decimal places as the question

Dividing: remove the decimal point from the divisor by moving it to the right until you have only an integer, move the decimal point in the dividend the same number of places

Multiplying and dividing: if the signs are the same, the answer is positive, if opposite, then negative

Review 67 – Absolute Value

They need to find the absolute value where marked and then compare the numbers to put them in order. They aren't finding the absolute value of every number.

Answers   2, |-5|, 8   -5, 10, |-12| -8, -2, |-1|, |-6|

Lesson 68

DAY 68 Operations with Decimals

A. Circle all expressions that give the same product as 6.74 × 0.8. Explain how you know.

674 × 0.008   674 × 0.08   67.4 × 800   67.4 × 0.08   0.674 × 8

See Day 9 for placing the decimal point in the product.

B. Find each sum, difference, product, or quotient.

-3 + 16.2 + 15.9	29.1	-5.7 + -6.23 + -2.048	-13.978
7.24 + -16.3 + -9.14	-18.2	-0.238 + -5.17 + 4.82	-0.588
11.6 − 9.08 − 25	-22.48	15.3 − (-7.4) − 18.903	3.797
-2.94 − (-3.85) − (-16)	16.91	8.92 − 20 − (-16.274)	5.194
2.36 × -3.7	-8.732	9.35 × -28	-261.8
-1.82 × -5.4	9.828	-0.04 × 12.6	-0.504
-7 ÷ -87.5	0.08	13.63 ÷ -47	-0.29
5.04 ÷ 12.6	0.4	-1.292 ÷ 0.34	-3.8

DAY 68 Practice

Find each sum, difference, product, or quotient.

-12 + 0.75 + 3.1	-8.15	-3.5 + 2.7 + -15.7	-16.5
16 + -5.24 + -2.78	7.98	9.34 + -21.27 + -3.42	-15.35
4.28 − 2.74 − 18.3	-16.76	5.28 − (-6.152) − 3.3	8.132
-18.5 − 7.32 − (-24)	-1.82	40.25 − (-7.39) − 21.99	25.65
8.7 × -6.3	-54.81	0.025 × -25.6	-0.64
-7.2 × -3.4	24.48	-12.4 × -8.02	99.448
-1.53 ÷ 1.7	-0.9	4.998 ÷ -3.57	-1.4
-0.81 ÷ -4.5	0.18	-64.97 ÷ 7.3	-8.9
12.6 ÷ -0.63	-20	-0.576 ÷ -0.12	4.8

Lesson 68 – Operations with Decimals

This is more practice with decimals and negative signs. You can look back to Lesson 67 for help.

Review 68 – Adding Negative Numbers

If the numbers have the same sign, you just add them up and keep the sign. If they have opposite signs, you find the difference and give the answer the sign of the largest number.

Answers   2   6   -13

Lesson 69

DAY 69 Adding and Subtracting Fractions

A. We learned that fractions can be added or subtracted only when they have the same denominator. When they do not, you must make their denominators same using a common denominator. Once the denominators are same, you can just add or subtract the numerators and keep the same denominator. Review Day 6 if needed.

B. The integer rules we learned on Day 63 also apply to fractions. Just be careful when you subtract mixed numbers. You may need to regroup. Study the examples carefully!

$\frac{1}{2} + -\frac{2}{3} = \frac{3}{6} + -\frac{4}{6} = -\left(\frac{4}{6} - \frac{3}{6}\right) = -\frac{1}{6}$ — The signs are unlike, so find the difference and and take the sign of the larger absolute value.

$2\frac{1}{2} - 4\frac{2}{3} = 2\frac{3}{6} + -4\frac{4}{6} = -\left(4\frac{4}{6} - 2\frac{3}{6}\right) = -2\frac{1}{6}$ — Subtract the whole numbers and fractions separately.

$2\frac{2}{3} - 4\frac{1}{2} = 2\frac{4}{6} + -4\frac{3}{6} = -\left(4\frac{3}{6} - 2\frac{4}{6}\right) = -\left(3\frac{9}{6} - 2\frac{4}{6}\right) = -1\frac{5}{6}$ — Regroup before subtracting.

C. Find each sum or difference. Simplify your answers.

$-\frac{5}{6} + \frac{1}{6}$	-2/3		$\frac{7}{9} - \frac{5}{9}$	-1 1/3
$-\frac{3}{5} + -\frac{3}{4}$	-1 7/20		$-\frac{5}{6} - -\frac{3}{4}$	-1/12
$-2\frac{1}{4} + 8$	5 3/4		$6 - 2\frac{4}{7}$	3 3/7
$-3\frac{4}{5} + 2\frac{3}{5}$	-1 1/5		$2\frac{1}{3} - 5\frac{2}{3}$	-3 1/3
$6\frac{3}{8} + -3\frac{3}{4}$	2 5/8		$7\frac{4}{9} - 2\frac{5}{6}$	4 11/18

DAY 69 Practice

A. Compare the mixed numbers.

$2\frac{3}{8} > 2\frac{1}{3}$ $1\frac{3}{5} < 2\frac{5}{9}$ $3\frac{5}{7} < 3\frac{4}{5}$ $1\frac{6}{7} < 5\frac{1}{2}$

B. Find each sum or difference. Simplify your answers.

$-\frac{3}{7} + \frac{5}{7}$	2/7		$-\frac{3}{8} - \frac{7}{8}$	-1 1/4
$\frac{3}{4} + -\frac{5}{6}$	-1/12		$\frac{3}{5} - \frac{7}{9}$	-8/45
$-\frac{2}{3} + \frac{5}{8}$	-1 7/24		$\frac{1}{2} - \frac{3}{4}$	-1 1/4
$5 + -\frac{2}{7}$	4 5/7		$3\frac{1}{6} - 4$	-5/6
$-1\frac{2}{9} + 4$	2 7/9		$6 - 2\frac{5}{8}$	3 3/8
$-2\frac{2}{5} + 3\frac{3}{5}$	1 1/5		$6\frac{2}{7} - 2\frac{6}{7}$	3 3/7
$3\frac{1}{3} + -2\frac{1}{4}$	1 1/12		$-5\frac{3}{4} - 2\frac{2}{3}$	-8 5/12
$-1\frac{1}{6} + -2\frac{3}{8}$	-3 13/24		$-4\frac{5}{6} - 2\frac{2}{9}$	-2 11/18

Lesson 69 – Adding and Subtracting Fractions

To add and subtract fractions they must have a common denominator. To get common denominators they need to find an equivalent fraction with that denominator. One way that always works is to multiply each fraction (top and bottom) by the other denominator. This won't always give you the least common denominator, but it will give you something to work with.

They will be using positive and negative numbers this time, so they will have to be thinking about signs. It may say add, but it may be adding an negative number, so they will really be subtracting.

When there is a mixed number, they can separate out the whole numberor turn it into an improper fraction. 1 ½ + 3 ½ = 1 + 3 + ½ + ½ = 5   1 ½ - ¾ = 1 – ¼ = ¾ OR ³/₂ – ¾ = ⁶/₄ – ¾ = ¾

Review 69 – Subtracting Negative Numbers

Subtraction of a positive number is the same as adding a negative. $0 – 8 = 0 + (-8)$ Subtracting a negative number is adding its opposite, which means just adding the number. $0 – (-8) = 0 + 8 = 8$ They can think of the two minus signs coming together and making a plus sign.

They are only being asked to rewrite the expressions, not solve them.

Answers $9 + (-6) + (-5)$ $4 + 9 + (-5)$ $(-5) + (-3) + 2$

Lesson 70

DAY 70 Adding and Subtracting Fractions

A. Let's review how to regroup a mixed number by borrowing a 1 from the whole number.

$5\frac{2}{3} = 5 + \frac{2}{3} = 4 + 1 + \frac{2}{3} = 4 + \frac{3}{3} + \frac{2}{3} = 4 + \frac{5}{3} = 4\frac{5}{3}$

B. Regroup each mixed number by borrowing a 1 from the whole number.

$4\frac{1}{2}$ 3 3/2 $5\frac{2}{7}$ 4 9/7 $2\frac{3}{5}$ 1 8/5 $3\frac{5}{9}$ 2 14/9

C. Find each sum or difference. Simplify your answers.

$-\frac{4}{9} + \frac{2}{9}$	-2/9	$-\frac{7}{8} - \frac{3}{8}$	-1 1/4
$\frac{2}{3} + -\frac{5}{9}$	1/9	$\frac{1}{2} - -\frac{6}{7}$	1 5/14
$-\frac{1}{4} + \frac{2}{3}$	5/12	$-\frac{1}{3} - \frac{3}{8}$	-17/24
$-6 + 1\frac{5}{6}$	-4 1/6	$2\frac{2}{5} - 7$	-4 3/5
$-3\frac{5}{7} + 5$	1 2/7	$8 - 2\frac{2}{9}$	5 7/9
$2\frac{5}{8} + -1\frac{7}{8}$	3/4	$6\frac{1}{3} - 1\frac{2}{3}$	4 2/3
$-1\frac{1}{2} + 2\frac{5}{6}$	1 1/3	$2\frac{5}{8} - -3\frac{5}{6}$	6 11/24

DAY 70 Practice

Find each sum or difference. Simplify your answers.

$\frac{3}{5} + -\frac{2}{5}$	1/5	$\frac{3}{4} - -\frac{1}{4}$	1
$-\frac{1}{2} + \frac{6}{7}$	5/14	$-\frac{2}{3} - \frac{4}{5}$	-1 7/15
$-\frac{2}{9} + -\frac{5}{6}$	-1 1/18	$-\frac{3}{4} - \frac{5}{8}$	-1 3/8
$-\frac{1}{3} + 4$	3 2/3	$6 - \frac{2}{7}$	5 5/7
$-8 + 2\frac{4}{7}$	-5 3/7	$3\frac{2}{5} - 9$	-5 3/5
$-1\frac{2}{5} + 4\frac{4}{5}$	3 2/5	$3\frac{2}{9} - 2\frac{7}{9}$	4/9
$2\frac{2}{3} + -4\frac{3}{4}$	-2 1/12	$1\frac{4}{7} - 2\frac{1}{2}$	-13/14
$-1\frac{2}{5} + 2\frac{2}{3}$	1 4/15	$4\frac{5}{6} - -3\frac{4}{5}$	8 19/30
$-1\frac{1}{2} + -4\frac{7}{8}$	-6 3/8	$-2\frac{3}{7} - 5\frac{2}{3}$	-8 2/21

Lesson 70 – Adding and Subtracting Fractions

They are adding and subtracting fractions again. The top of the page talks about regrouping. Just like they can borrow a ten from 21 to subtract 5, making it 10 and 11-5 to get 16, they can borrow from a whole number. One is just any number over itself. If the numerator and denominator are equal, that fraction equals one. It's one whole. Picture a shape completely colored in. It's all the parts.

3 ¼ = 2 ⁴/₄ and ¼   That way you could subtract something like ¾ from 3 ¼ .

They can decide what makes sense to them. Here's an example.

2 ¼ - 4 = 2 + ¼ - 4 = -2 + ¼ = -1 ¾

⁹/₄ - ¹⁶/₄ = ⁻⁷/₄ = -1 ¾

Review 70 – Subtract

They will be combining what they did for review in Lessons 68 and 69. They will change the signs and then add. If they are both the same sign, they combine them and keep the sign. If the numbers have opposite signs, they find the difference and keep the sign of the larger number.

Answers   -11   9   -2

Lesson 71

DAY 71 Multiplying Fractions

A. Multiplying fractions is simple: top by top and bottom by bottom. Just remember to convert any mixed and whole numbers to improper fractions before multiplying! Review Day 7 if needed.

B. The sign rules for multiplying integers apply to fractions as well: two like signs become a positive sign and two unlike signs become a negative sign. Review Day 63 if needed.

C. Find each product. Simplify your answers.

$\frac{1}{2} \times -\frac{4}{5}$	-2/5	$\frac{8}{15} \times -\frac{5}{12}$	-2/9
$-\frac{5}{8} \times -4$	2 1/2	$-14 \times -\frac{5}{21}$	3 1/3
$-2\frac{6}{7} \times \frac{7}{9}$	-2 2/9	$4\frac{5}{8} \times -\frac{4}{13}$	-1 11/26
$\frac{5}{7} \times -4\frac{1}{5}$	-3	$\frac{3}{10} \times -2\frac{2}{9}$	-2/3
$-2\frac{5}{6} \times -8$	22 2/3	$-3\frac{3}{4} \times -10$	37 1/2
$-9 \times 1\frac{5}{6}$	-16 1/2	$-21 \times 2\frac{2}{9}$	-46 2/3
$5\frac{1}{4} \times -3\frac{5}{9}$	-18 2/3	$1\frac{3}{5} \times -2\frac{1}{12}$	-3 1/3
$-3\frac{1}{2} \times -2\frac{4}{7}$	9	$-2\frac{1}{7} \times 3\frac{4}{15}$	-7

DAY 71 Practice

A. Convert the mixed numbers to improper fractions.

$4\frac{1}{5}$ 21/5 $6\frac{5}{8}$ 53/8 $-4\frac{2}{9}$ -38/9 $-3\frac{6}{7}$ -27/7

B. Find each product. Simplify your answers.

$\frac{3}{8} \times -\frac{2}{9}$	-1/12	$\frac{8}{21} \times -\frac{9}{16}$	-3/14
$-\frac{2}{5} \times -9$	3 3/5	$-18 \times \frac{7}{24}$	-5 1/4
$-5\frac{1}{3} \times \frac{3}{4}$	-4	$2\frac{3}{4} \times -\frac{9}{22}$	-1 1/8
$\frac{8}{9} \times -3\frac{3}{5}$	-3 1/5	$-\frac{4}{9} \times -6\frac{3}{8}$	2 5/6
$2\frac{1}{6} \times -8$	-17 1/3	$-14 \times 1\frac{2}{8}$	-17 1/2
$-9 \times -1\frac{5}{6}$	16 1/2	$-6\frac{3}{6} \times -10$	65
$-1\frac{2}{7} \times 1\frac{5}{9}$	-2	$1\frac{2}{3} \times -1\frac{7}{15}$	-2 4/9
$1\frac{5}{6} \times -2\frac{1}{4}$	-4 1/8	$-3\frac{3}{8} \times -1\frac{5}{27}$	4

Lesson 71 – Multiplying Fractions

To multiply fractions, they multiply numerators by numerators and denominators by denominators. To make it easier, they should look for ways to reduce the fractions. They can reduce from either fraction. $\frac{1}{2}$ x $\frac{4}{5}$ = 1 x 4 over 2 x 5. Before multiplying, they could cross off the 4 and 2, dividing them both by 2, and make them 2 and 1. That leaves them with 1 x 2 over 1 x 5 or just two fifths.

To multiply mixed numbers they may want to turn the mixed number into an improper fraction. They could also use the distributive property if they want, though.

3 ¾ x 10 = $^{15}/_4$ x 10 = $^{150}/_4$ = 37 $^2/_4$ = 37 ½

3 ¾ x 10 = (3 + ¾) x 10 = 3 x 10 + ¾ x 10 = 30 + $^{30}/_4$ = 30 + 7 + $^2/_4$ = 37 ½

Review 71 – Add Negative Numbers

This is the same as the Lesson 71 review but with an extra number. They can just combine two numbers at a time.

Answers   8   -8   12

Lesson 72

DAY 72 Multiplying Fractions

A. Circle all expressions that give the same product as $^3/_5 \times 7$. Explain how you know.

$3 \div (5 \times 7)$ $\boxed{3 \div 5 \times 7}$ $(3 \times 7) \div 5$ $7 \times 3 \div 5$ $5 \div (3 \times 7)$

Note that a fraction is a division statement where the numerator is divided by the denominator.

B. Find each product. Simplify your answers.

$-\frac{4}{9} \times \frac{3}{4}$	-1/3	$-\frac{5}{18} \times \frac{3}{10}$	-1/12
$-\frac{5}{9} \times -6$	3 1/3	$16 \times -\frac{7}{24}$	-4 2/3
$\frac{7}{8} \times -4\frac{2}{7}$	-3 3/4	$\frac{3}{8} \times -6\frac{2}{9}$	-2 1/3
$-2\frac{3}{4} \times \frac{8}{9}$	-2 4/9	$-4\frac{1}{8} \times -\frac{4}{15}$	1 1/10
$-2\frac{3}{8} \times -4$	9 1/2	$-1\frac{5}{6} \times 20$	-36 2/3
$9 \times -1\frac{2}{3}$	-15	$2\frac{3}{4} \times -18$	-49 1/2
$-5\frac{1}{3} \times 2\frac{5}{8}$	-14	$-3\frac{5}{7} \times -1\frac{5}{16}$	4 7/8
$4\frac{1}{5} \times -2\frac{2}{9}$	-9 1/3	$-1\frac{7}{8} \times -2\frac{7}{10}$	5 1/16

DAY 72 Practice

Find each product. Simplify your answers.

$-\frac{2}{3} \times \frac{1}{4}$	-1/6	$\frac{9}{16} \times -\frac{4}{15}$	-3/20
$-8 \times -\frac{5}{6}$	6 2/3	$-\frac{5}{18} \times -21$	5 5/6
$\frac{5}{6} \times -2\frac{2}{5}$	-2	$5\frac{5}{6} \times -\frac{8}{25}$	-1 13/15
$-4\frac{1}{6} \times \frac{4}{5}$	-3 1/3	$\frac{5}{24} \times -7\frac{1}{9}$	-1 13/27
$7 \times -2\frac{5}{7}$	-19	$-1\frac{5}{8} \times -12$	19 1/2
$-3\frac{2}{9} \times -6$	19 1/3	$21 \times -4\frac{5}{9}$	-95 2/3
$2\frac{1}{4} \times -1\frac{3}{5}$	-3 3/5	$2\frac{3}{5} \times -2\frac{4}{13}$	-6
$-3\frac{1}{3} \times 1\frac{1}{5}$	-4	$-4\frac{2}{5} \times -1\frac{4}{11}$	6
$5\frac{1}{4} \times -2\frac{4}{7}$	-13 1/2	$-1\frac{7}{9} \times -1\frac{7}{20}$	2 2/5

Lesson 72 – Multiplying fractions

The top of the page is for figuring out, not for working out. They are supposed to think through that three fifths times seven is three times seven divided by five.

This is the same type of work as Lesson 71. They should think about reducing. One example from the page is $16 \times -^7/_{24} = 2\,(-^7/_3) = -^{14}/_3 = -4\,^2/_3$ I reduced 16 and 24 by dividing both by eight.

They need to always be remembering the sign.

Review 72 – Word problems

These word problems deal with postive and negative, so they need to make sure to use the appropriate sign. The last one uses absolute value, or if they follow the clue word "difference" they can subtract, which would give them the same answer.

Answers   -7 °C, -525 feet, 25 °C

Lesson 73

DAY 73 Dividing Fractions

A. Dividing fractions is just like multiplying fractions, except that you "flip" the divisor first. Make sure you convert any mixed and whole numbers to improper fractions before dividing! Review Day 7 if needed.

B. The sign rules are the same as the ones used for dividing integers. Review Day 63 if needed.

C. Find each quotient. Simplify your answers.

$\frac{5}{6} \div \frac{3}{4}$	-1 1/9	$-\frac{11}{12} \div \frac{22}{45}$	-1 7/8
$-8 \div -\frac{6}{7}$	9 1/3	$16 \div -\frac{4}{21}$	-84
$-\frac{3}{5} \div 9$	-1/15	$-\frac{9}{18} \div -18$	1/36
$2\frac{4}{5} \div -7$	-2/5	$3\frac{1}{5} \div -45$	-16/225
$-6 \div -1\frac{2}{7}$	4 2/3	$20 \div -3\frac{3}{4}$	-5 1/3
$1\frac{2}{7} \div -1\frac{4}{5}$	-5/7	$2\frac{2}{3} \div -1\frac{5}{11}$	-1 5/6
$-2\frac{2}{3} \div -1\frac{3}{5}$	1 2/3	$-2\frac{1}{5} \div 2\frac{5}{14}$	-14/15
$6\frac{1}{4} \div -3\frac{1}{8}$	-2	$-8\frac{3}{4} \div -2\frac{3}{16}$	4

DAY 73 Practice

Find each quotient. Simplify your answers.

$\frac{2}{3} \div -\frac{1}{4}$	-2 2/3	$\frac{9}{14} \div -\frac{16}{21}$	-27/32
$\frac{4}{5} \div -8$	-1/10	$14 \div -2\frac{5}{8}$	-5 1/3
$-3 \div 2\frac{2}{5}$	-1 1/4	$-2\frac{1}{7} \div -15$	1/7
$-2\frac{1}{4} \div -6$	3/8	$35 \div -6\frac{1}{8}$	-5 5/7
$9 \div -1\frac{1}{5}$	-7 1/2	$-6\frac{2}{3} \div -28$	5/21
$-4\frac{1}{6} \div 2\frac{2}{9}$	-1 7/8	$-2\frac{4}{9} \div 2\frac{2}{21}$	-1 1/6
$1\frac{1}{9} \div -4\frac{2}{7}$	-7/27	$1\frac{2}{7} \div -3\frac{3}{14}$	-2/5
$1\frac{1}{8} \div -1\frac{1}{4}$	-9/10	$-2\frac{5}{6} \div -2\frac{4}{15}$	1 1/4
$-4\frac{4}{5} \div -2\frac{2}{9}$	2 4/25	$-3\frac{2}{3} \div 4\frac{5}{18}$	-6/7

Lesson 73 – Dividing Fractions

Dividing fractions is just like multiplying. The extra step is to change each division problem into a multiplication problem by changing the operation sign and using the reciprocal of the second number, the reciprocal of the number being divided by. Here's an example.

½ ÷ 4 = ½ x ¼

Review 73 – Positive and Negative

This is a review. When you multiply two numbers with the same sign, the answer is positive. They can again think of the two negative signs coming together to make a plus sign. When you multiply (or divide) two numbers with opposite signs, the answer is negative.

Answers   Negative   Negative / Positive   Positive

Lesson 74

DAY 74 Rounding and Dividing Decimals

A. **Rounding** is finding the closest number. Rounded numbers are easier to use but less accurate than the originals. Rounding is a common method used for estimation. Here are the steps.

	Nearest whole number	Nearest tenth	To round a number to a given place value:
(1)	3.813	3.813	1. Underline the digit in the rounding place.
(2)	3.813	3.813	2. Look at the digit to the right of the underlined digit.
(3)	+1		3. If it is 5 or more, add 1 to the underlined digit. If it is 4 or less, leave the underlined digit as is.
(4)	4.000	3.8	4. Replace all the digits after the underlined digit with zeros. Drop the trailing zeros after the decimal point.

B. Round each number to the nearest place value indicated.

	Whole ten	Whole number	Tenth	Hundredth
15.092	20	15	15.1	15.09
364.957	360	365	365	364.96
7,819.605	7,820	7,820	7,819.6	7,819.61

C. In real life, we often round decimals to the nearest whole number to estimate a quantity or value. Round each number to the nearest whole number to estimate the quotient. Then find the actual quotient of HALF the division statements. Review Day 9 if needed.

Expression	Estimate	Actual
2.56 ÷ 3.2	1	0.8
-2.43 ÷ 0.9	-2	-2.7
-96.1 ÷ 6.2	-16	-15.5
99.18 ÷ -8.7	-11	-11.4
79.56 ÷ 10.2	8	7.8
-63.99 ÷ -3.95	16	16.2
-55.809 ÷ 7.02	-8	-7.95
15.808 ÷ -8.32	-2	-1.9

DAY 74 Practice

A. Round each number to the nearest place value indicated.

	Whole ten	Whole number	Tenth	Hundredth
5.209	10	5	5.2	5.21
11.074	10	11	11.1	11.07
28.592	30	29	28.6	28.59
105.006	110	105	105	105.01
4,296.287	4,300	4,296	4,296.3	4,296.29

B. Round each number to the nearest whole number to estimate the quotient. Then find the actual quotient.

	Estimate	Actual
44.65 ÷ -4.7	-9	-9.5
3.582 ÷ -1.8	-2	-1.99
-39.52 ÷ -5.2	8	7.6
-59.67 ÷ -3.9	15	15.3
-76.95 ÷ 11.4	-7	-6.75
41.87 ÷ -2.65	-14	-15.8
-45.147 ÷ 8.94	-5	-5.05
71.574 ÷ -7.55	-9	-9.48

C. Solve each problem.

Samuel bought a pack of 25 recordable CDs. He paid $20 and received $8.75 as change. What was the price of one CD? **$0.45**

Each CD can store data up to 700 MB. Samuel has 5.4 GB data to store. How many CDs will he use? (1 GB = 1000 MB) **8 CDs**

Lesson 74 – Rounding and Dividing Decimals

They will be rounding numbers and then dividing them. To round, they need to pay attention to what place value they are looking for, and then they need to look to the digit to the right of it. That's the only one that determines how it will round.

It asks for whole tens, which is just rounding to the nearest ten. Rounding to the nearest whole number means rounding to the nearest one.

They are going to estimate the answers at the bottom and then do SOME of them full out to compare the answers.

Review 74 – Multiplying Negative Numbers

This is just multiplying but applying the sign rules they reviewed in Lesson 73.

Answers   -54   -49   48

Lesson 75

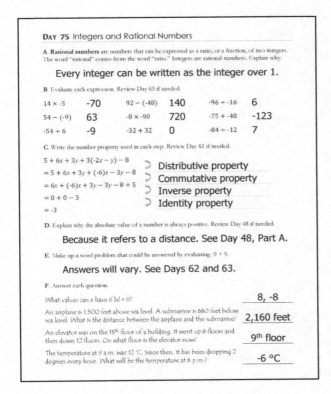

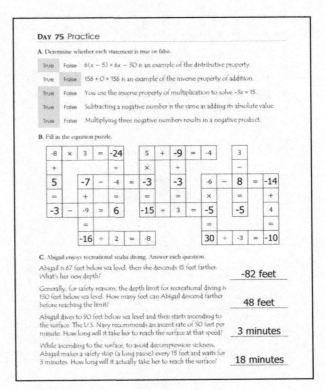

Lesson 75 – Integers and Rational Numbers

Rational numbers are something they will hear about time and time again if they continue math into algebra and beyond. There are irrational ones as well. It just comes from the word ratio. It just means a number that can be written as a ratio, which we know is just a fraction. 3 is a rational number because it can be written as 3/1.

There is also a review of number properties on the page. Distributive property is listed. It's what was use to get from the first line to the second line. What did they do on the second line to get to the third line? They need to think of things like commutative and identity property.

Review 75 – Dividing Negatives

This is the same as multiplying, since dividing is just multiplying by the reciprocal.
$8 \div 2 = 8/2 = 8(\frac{1}{2}) = 8 \times \frac{1}{2}$

Answers   -7   -5   4

Lesson 76

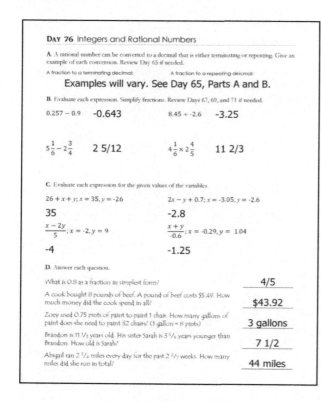

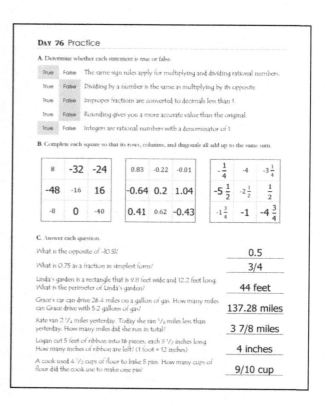

Lesson 76 – Integers and Rational Numbers

They are going to be using rational numbers today. They will be doing all the arithmetic they've been practicing with whole numbers, fractions, and decimals. They need to keep signs in mind.

They will evaluate expressions and they will figure out word problems.

Review 76 – Writing Fractions

They will write the fraction by writing the number of parts shaded in on top, as the numerator, and the total number of parts on the bottom, the denominator.

Answers   1/2   3/5   5/9

Lesson 77

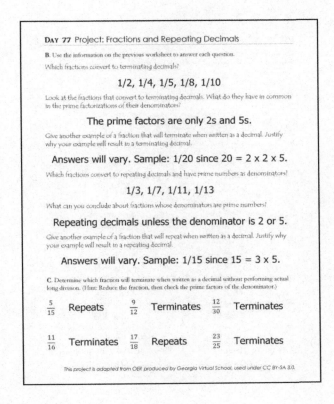

Lesson 77 – Project: Fractions and Repeating Decimals

The directions might be hard to get through, but there is an example on the page. They will find the prime factorization of the denominator. Prime factorization is multiplying only prime numbers together. The prime numbers are the ones that you can't divide by anything (other than one and themselves).

They will be identifying the answers as terminating decimals or repeating decimals.

No Review

Lesson 78

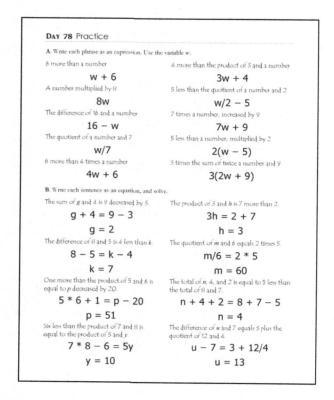

DAY 78 Translating Words to Expressions

A. When translating real-world problems into algebraic expressions, it helps to know key words and phrases that are used to describe mathematical operations. Here are some common ones.

Operation	Key words and phrases
Addition	sum, add, plus, total, and, more than, increased by
Subtraction	difference, subtract, minus, less, take away, less than, decreased by
Multiplication	product, multiply, times, double, twice, triple, multiplied by
Division	quotient, divide, over, divided into, divided by

B. Here are some examples. Cover the word phrases and read each expression in as many different ways as you can using the key words and phrases above.

$x + 4$ — the sum of a number and 4 / add 4 to a number / a number plus 4 / 4 more than a number / a number increased by 4

$2 \cdot x$ or $2x$ — the product of 2 and a number / multiply 2 by a number / 2 times a number / twice a number / 2 multiplied by a number

$x - 7$ — the difference of a number and 7 / a number less 7 / 7 less than a number / a number decreased by 7

$x \div 8$ or $\frac{x}{8}$ — the quotient of a number and 8 / a number over 8 / 8 divided into a number / a number divided by 8

C. Write each phrase as an expression. Use the variable k.

Fifteen less a number
$15 - k$

The difference of 4 times a number and 9
$4k - 9$

The product of a number and 7
$7k$

2 minus the product of a number and 3
$2 - 3k$

The sum of 5 and twice a number
$5 + 2k$

8 plus the quotient of a number and 3
$8 + k/3$

4 times a number, decreased by 6
$4k - 6$

9 less than the quotient of a number and 5
$k/5 - 9$

7 times a number, increased by 5
$7k + 5$

the sum of a number and 3, multiplied by 5
$5(k + 3)$

DAY 78 Practice

A. Write each phrase as an expression. Use the variable w.

6 more than a number
$w + 6$

4 more than the product of 3 and a number
$3w + 4$

A number multiplied by 8
$8w$

5 less than the quotient of a number and 2
$w/2 - 5$

The difference of 16 and a number
$16 - w$

7 times a number, increased by 9
$7w + 9$

The quotient of a number and 7
$w/7$

5 less than a number, multiplied by 2
$2(w - 5)$

6 more than 4 times a number
$4w + 6$

3 times the sum of twice a number and 9
$3(2w + 9)$

B. Write each sentence as an equation, and solve.

The sum of g and 4 is 9 decreased by 3.
$g + 4 = 9 - 3$
$g = 2$

The product of 3 and h is 7 more than 2.
$3h = 2 + 7$
$h = 3$

The difference of 8 and 5 is 4 less than k.
$8 - 5 = k - 4$
$k = 7$

The quotient of m and 6 equals 2 times 5.
$m/6 = 2 * 5$
$m = 60$

One more than the product of 5 and 6 is equal to p decreased by 20.
$5 * 6 + 1 = p - 20$
$p = 51$

The total of n, 4, and 2 is equal to 5 less than the total of 8 and 7.
$n + 4 + 2 = 8 + 7 - 5$
$n = 4$

Six less than the product of 7 and 8 is equal to the product of 5 and y.
$7 * 8 - 6 = 5y$
$y = 10$

The difference of u and 7 equals 3 plus the quotient of 12 and 4.
$u - 7 = 3 + 12/4$
$u = 13$

Lesson 78 Lesson – Translating Words to Expressions

Part A is for reading. Part B is for practicing. They are supposed to not look at the list of example phrases. They should cover them up and then try stating the expression in as many different ways as possible.

They will have to translate the opposite direction, taking the words and writing the mathematical expression.

Review 78 – Numerator and Denominator

The numerator is the top number and the denominator is the bottom number. The denominator is how many parts total. The numerator shows the amount we're talking about.

Answers $N = 1, D = 2$ $N = 3, D = 5$ $N = 5, D = 9$

Lesson 79

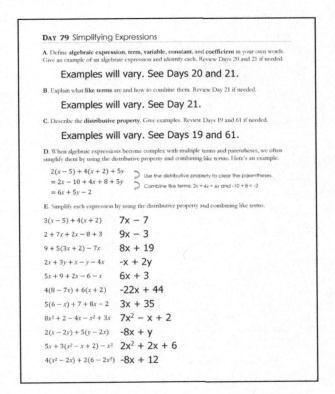

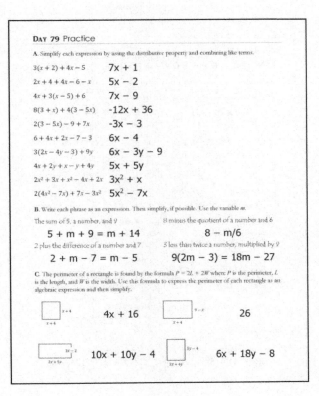

Lesson 79 – Simplifying Expressions

They are working with variables today. Their page lists some previous days if they need to go back. The term is something like 2x. The 2 is the coefficient and the X is the variable. A number by itself is constant. It's constant because that term's value is never going to change. The value of 2x is going to change as X changes. It's variable; it varies.

They are going to be using the distributive property and combining like terms. 2x and 3x are like terms. You can add them and get 5x. $2x^2$ and 3x are NOT like terms. You can't add apples and pencils. They aren't the same thing.

The distributive property means that you multiply by each term in the parentheses.
$4(x + 2) = 4x + 8$ That's 4 times X and 4 times 2.

Review 79 – Writing Fractions

They will be describing situations with fractions. They will read the description and write the corresponding fraction. The total number goes on the bottom. The amount of that being asked about goes on the top.

Answers   3/8   2/5   9/10

Lesson 80

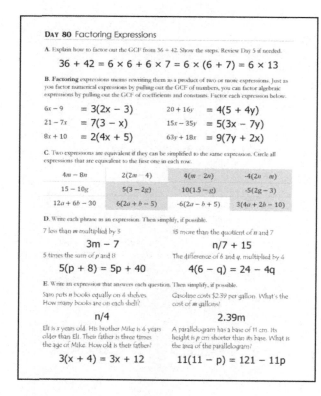

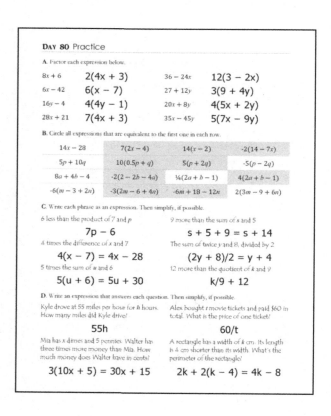

Lesson 80 – Factoring Expressions

Today they are doing the opposite of the distributive property. This is *extremely* beneficial in algebra. They will be doing it all the time. In order to do it, they need to see what can be divided out of each term. If it was something like 4x + 8y and they saw they were both even and divided out 2, they would end up with 2(2x + 4y). You could then see they were still both even and divide out another 2. 4(x + 2y) They could always distribute that and check to see if they are correct.

Using the Greatest Common Factor would keep you from having to pull out another amount like I did above, but I wanted to show that it was okay to not figure out the GCF. If you guess wrong at first, you can take out more later.

They will be writing expressions as well.

Review 80 – Writing Fractions

They just need to translate the words into numbers.

Answers   2/3   5/6   3/10

Lesson 81

DAY 81 One-Step Equations with Integers

A. Explain how to solve each equation. Show your steps. Review Days 24 and 26 if needed.

$4 + x = 9$ $k - 6 = 7$ $9 \times n = 72$ $s + 5 = 8$

x = 5   k = 13   n = 8   s = 40

B. The same rule applies to solving equations with negative numbers: perform inverse operations to isolate the variable. Compare the examples below to your steps above.

$-4 + x = 10$ $k - (-6) = 7$ $-9 \times n = 72$ $s + -5 = -8$

Add 4 on both sides.   Add -6 on both sides.   Divide both sides by -9.   Multiply both sides by -5.

$x = 14$ $k = 1$ $n = -8$ $x = 40$

C. Solve each equation.

$x + 9 = -4$ $x - 7 = -6$ $4x = -36$

x = -13   x = 1   x = -9

$29 = x - 32$ $x + 48 = 16$ $-28 + x = -25$

x = 61   x = -32   x = 3

$\frac{x}{6} = -19$ $-72 = -18x$ $-11 = \frac{x}{-7}$

x = -114   x = 4   x = 77

D. Write an equation and solve to answer each question. Use the variable x.

Sierra charges $12 per hour for babysitting. Last week she made $48. How many hours did she babysit?

12x = 48

4 hours

Jack's worksheet has 6 rows of 5 problems each. He has solved 16 problems so far. How many problems are left?

6 * 5 = 16 + x

14 problems

DAY 81 Practice

A. Solve each equation.

$x + 6 = -7$ $-8 + x = 3$ $x - 4 = -9$

x = -13   x = 11   x = -5

$48 + x = -29$ $24 = x - 59$ $x - 32 = -15$

x = -77   x = 83   x = 17

$\frac{x}{-5} = -18$ $7x = -105$ $-75 = -3x$

x = 90   x = -15   x = 25

$13x = 117$ $-11 = \frac{x}{9}$ $\frac{x}{-12} = 7$

x = 9   x = -99   x = -84

B. Write each sentence as an equation, and solve.

The quotient of m and -3 equals 8.

m/-3 = 8

m = -24

The sum of k and -7 is 5 decreased by 20.

k + -7 = 5 − 20

k = -8

C. Write an equation and solve to answer each question. Use the variable x.

A submarine was at -135 feet. Then it ascended to -50 feet. How far did the submarine ascend?

-135 + x = -50

85 feet

The perimeter of a quadrilateral is 28 cm. Three of the sides are 6 cm, 8 cm, and 5cm. What is the length of the fourth side?

6 + 8 + 5 + x = 28

9 centimeters

Lesson 81 – One-Step Equations with Integers

They are going to be solving equations today. To solve an equation, they use inverse operations to get the variable isolated. That means they will add the opposite or multiply by the reciprocal to get the variable all by itself on one side of the equation. The last step should read something like this: x = 5.

This time they will have negative numbers in the mix. They need to do the opposite so to get rid of -6 + y, they will have to add 6. They will have to divide by -9 (or multiply by negative one ninth) to figure out -9n = 72.

-9n means -9 times n

Review 81 – Recognizing the Value of Fractions

If they aren't sure about any of these, they could draw a picture like those at the top of their page. Six sevenths is almost one since almost all the parts are there. One twelfth is a very small number. It would have eleven more lines to go on the number line to get to one. Five fourths is greater than one. It's one and another one fourth. Eight fourths is two because 8/4 = 2.

Answers   B   C   A   D

Lesson 82

DAY 82 One-Step Equations with Integers

A. You solved 13x = 104 and found that x = 9. Is the solution correct? Explain how you know.

Incorrect. Substitute 9 for x. 13 * 9 is 117, not 104.

B. Solve each equation.

$x + 9 = -5$	$x - 6 = -2$	$x - (-3) = 5$
x = -14	**x = 4**	**x = 2**

$x - 16 = 8$	$-35 = 7x$	$16 = x + -15$
x = 24	**x = -5**	**x = 31**

$-6x = -42$	$-23 + x = -23$	$-5x = 125$
x = 7	**x = 0**	**x = -25**

$-17 = x - (-34)$	$11x = -110$	$x - 25 = -19$
x = -51	**x = -10**	**x = 6**

$\frac{x}{3} = -17$	$-22 = x + -48$	$14x = 98$
x = -51	**x = 26**	**x = 7**

$19 = \frac{x}{-5}$	$x - 27 = -46$	$\frac{x}{-15} = -8$
x = -95	**x = -19**	**x = 120**

$20x = -180$	$\frac{x}{17} = -70$	$14 = \frac{x}{30}$
x = -9	**x = -1190**	**x = 420**

DAY 82 Practice

A. Solve each equation.

$x - 2 = -6$	$x + -8 = 16$	$28 = -7x$
x = -4	**x = 24**	**x = -4**

$12x = -108$	$x - (-18) = 10$	$x + 35 = 18$
x = -9	**x = -8**	**x = -17**

$\frac{x}{14} = -8$	$-17 = -42 + x$	$\frac{x}{7} = 23$
x = -112	**x = 25**	**x = 161**

$-19x = -380$	$50 = \frac{x}{-16}$	$35 = x - (-11)$
x = 20	**x = -800**	**x = 24**

B. Write each sentence as an equation, and solve.

The sum of 8 and -4 equals 5 less than p.

8 + (-4) = p - 5

p = 9

The quotient of n and 5 is 42 divided by -7.

n/5 = 42/-7

n = -30

C. Write an equation and solve to answer each question. Use the variable x.

A rectangle with a width of 4 in has an area of 32 in². What is the length of the rectangle?

4x = 32

8 inches

Claire has 18 crayons. Sam has 25 crayons. Together, 9 of the crayons are broken. How many unbroken crayons do both have?

18 + 25 = 9 + x

34 crayons

Lesson 82 – One-Step Equations with Integers

This is just more practice with what they did in Lesson 81.

$\frac{x}{15}$ This is the same as one fifteenth times X or X divided by 15. To solve, you would multiply both sides by 15.

Review 82 – Simplifying Fractions

They need to use the one number given, either the numerator or denominator, to figure how what they multiplied or divided by to get there. Then they need to do the same to the other number. This is just simplifying fractions, with one step done along the way.

$\frac{1}{3}$ $\frac{5}{?}$ 1 x 5 = 5 so,

          3 x 5 = ? = 15

Answers   4, 10   9, 8   15, 4

Lesson 83

DAY 83 One-Step Equations with Decimals

A. How do operations with decimals compare to operations with integers? Explain how you handle the decimal points in each operation. Give examples. Review Days 9 and 67 if needed.

Examples will vary. See Days 9 and 67.

B. You solve equations with decimals the same way that you solve equations with integers. Find the value of x in each equation by performing the same inverse operation on both sides of the equation. Show your steps and compare them with Part A on Day 81.

$0.4 + x = 0.9$	$k - 0.6 = 0.7$	$0.9 \times n = 7.2$	$s \div 0.5 = 0.8$
$x = 0.5$	$k = 1.3$	$n = 8$	$s = 0.4$

C. Solve each equation.

$x + 11.05 = 26$	$x - 5.83 = 7.1$	$5.36 = -4.2 + x$
$x = 14.95$	$x = 12.93$	$x = 9.56$

$-12.6 = x - 7.3$	$0.92 = 2.3x$	$-1.6x = 51.2$
$x = -5.3$	$x = 0.4$	$x = -32$

$\frac{x}{0.2} = 2.4$	$\frac{x}{8} = -4.48$	$-2.6 = \frac{x}{-5.3}$
$x = 0.48$	$x = -35.84$	$x = 13.78$

D. Write an equation and solve to answer each question. Use the variable x.

One bucket holds 2.5 liters of water. Mike needs 8 liters of water for his garden. How many buckets does he need?

$2.5x = 8$

3.2 buckets

The temperature in the morning was -4.5 °C, but it went up to 3.7 °C in the evening. How much did it go up during the day?

$-4.5 + x = 3.7$

8.2 °C

DAY 83 Practice

A. Solve each equation.

$3.5 + x = 6.24$	$x - 1.83 = 0.99$	$16 = x + -0.02$
$x = 2.74$	$x = 2.82$	$x = 16.02$

$8.2 = x - (-4.6)$	$-0.48 + x = 9.5$	$4.27 + x = -8.6$
$x = 3.6$	$x = 9.98$	$x = -12.87$

$-12.5 = x - 0.78$	$20 = -0.04x$	$2.7x = -1.08$
$x = -11.72$	$x = -500$	$x = -0.4$

$\frac{x}{0.6} = 0.5$	$9.75x = 195$	$12 = \frac{x}{-7.3}$
$x = 0.3$	$x = 20$	$x = -87.6$

$0.8x = 0.64$	$\frac{x}{2.7} = -1.6$	$\frac{x}{-4.9} = -0.8$
$x = 0.8$	$x = -4.32$	$x = 3.92$

B. Write an equation and solve to answer each question. Use the variable x.

Eric scored 92% on his math test. He got 23 problems correct. How many problems were on the test?

$0.92x = 23$

25 problems

Max bought a shirt for $24.99. He had $15.80 left. How much money did Max have at first?

$x - 24.99 = 15.80$

40.79 dollars

Lesson 83 – One-Step Equations with Decimals

This is again the same thing. The difference is that there are decimals. They will still just add, subtract, multiply, or divide to find the value of the variable.

Whenever the numbers get harder, a good trick is to use smaller, simpler numbers to figure out how to solve a problem or to answer a question and then once you know how to approach it, substitute in the original numbers.

Review 83 – Simplifying Fractions

They will just be dividing the top and bottom by common factors until it can't be reduced any more. If both numerator and denominator are even, then they can at least divide each by two.

Answers   8/11   3/5   5/9

Lesson 84

DAY 84 One-Step Equations with Fractions

A. Solving equations with fractions is just like solving equations with integers and decimals: you use the properties of equality and inverse operations to isolate the variable. Just remember that dividing by a fraction is the same as multiplying by its reciprocal. For example, to solve the first equation below, you would use the subtraction property of equality and subtract $2/5$ from both sides. To solve the third equation, you would use the multiplication property of equality and multiply both sides by the reciprocal of $2/9$. Solve each equation below. Simplify your answers.

$x + \frac{2}{5} = \frac{4}{5}$

x = 2/5

$x - \frac{2}{7} = \frac{6}{7}$

x = 1 1/7

$\frac{2}{9}x = \frac{4}{9}$

x = 2

$\frac{3}{8}x = \frac{6}{7}$

x = 2 2/7

$x + \frac{2}{9} = \frac{5}{6}$

x = 11/18

$x - \frac{3}{4} = \frac{1}{5}$

x = 19/20

$x - \frac{2}{5} = -\frac{3}{4}$

x = -7/20

$\frac{2}{5}x = -6$

x = -15

$\frac{2}{3} + x = -\frac{5}{6}$

x = -1 1/2

$x + -9\frac{5}{6} = -4\frac{2}{3}$

x = 5 1/6

$x - \left(-6\frac{1}{4}\right) = 3\frac{1}{3}$

x = -2 11/12

$-2\frac{2}{7}x = -3\frac{1}{9}$

x = 1 13/36

B. Write an equation and solve to answer each question. Use the variable x.

Carmen cut a ribbon into 8 equal pieces, which made each piece ¾ inch long. How long was the ribbon?

x/8 = 3/4

6 inches

Emily had 8 ⅚ cups of flour. She used some to bake cookies, and now 2 ⅓ cups are left. How many cups of flour did she use?

x + 2 1/3 = 8 5/6

6 1/2 cups

DAY 84 Practice

A. Solve each equation.

0.5 + x = -1.74

x = -2.24

x - 0.3 = -2.1

x = -1.8

-3.7x = 2.22

x = -0.6

$x + \frac{2}{3} = \frac{5}{9}$

x = -1/9

$x - \frac{5}{6} = \frac{2}{5}$

x = 1 7/30

$\frac{2}{7}x = \frac{5}{7}$

x = 2 1/2

$x - \frac{4}{7} = -\frac{1}{4}$

x = 9/28

$\frac{2}{3}x = -\frac{3}{8}$

x = -9/16

$\frac{1}{2} + x = \frac{6}{7}$

x = 1 5/14

$x - \left(-3\frac{1}{2}\right) = -8\frac{1}{6}$

x = -11 2/3

$-6\frac{4}{5} + x = -3\frac{1}{2}$

x = 3 3/10

$-2\frac{5}{8}x = 2\frac{4}{5}$

x = -1 1/15

$-1\frac{1}{3}x = -8$

x = 6

$x - \left(-2\frac{5}{8}\right) = 8\frac{3}{8}$

x = 5 3/4

$2\frac{3}{4} + x = -4\frac{2}{3}$

x = -7 5/12

B. Write an equation and solve to answer each question. Use the variable x.

Mark ordered 6 pizzas for his birthday party. After the party, 1 ¾ pizzas were left. How many pizzas were eaten?

x + 1 3/4 = 6

4 1/4 pizzas

Sam and Eli bought the same book. Sam had $27 and spent 4/9 of his money. Eli spent ⅗ of his money. How much money did Eli have?

(3/5)x = 27 * 4/9

20 dollars

Lesson 84 – One-Step Equations with Fractions

They are working with one-step equations again, but this time with fractions. To add and subtract they will need to find a common denominator. In order to divide by a fraction, they will need to multiply by its reciprocal.

To divide by a mixed number, they should find the improper fraction and multiply by its reciprocal (flip it upside down).

Review 84 – Comparing Fractions

This is again about recognizing the value of a fraction. If the denominators are the same, the fraction with the largest numerator will be the larger number. If the numerators are the same, the fraction with the smallest denominator will be the larger number. They can use pictures to see why that's true.

Answers   False   True   True

Lesson 85

DAY 85 Two-Step Equations with Integers

A. Equations that take two steps to isolate the variable are called **two-steps equations**. Two-step equations look more complicated than one-step equations, but the principle for solving them is the same: you perform the same inverse operations on both sides of the equation until you get the variable alone on one side of the equation. Here are the steps.

$2x + 3 = 9$
$\quad -3 \quad -3$
$\quad 2x = 6$
$\quad \div 2 \quad \div 2$
$\quad x = 3$
Check:
$2 \cdot 3 + 3 = 9$

$x/2 - 3 = -1$
$\quad +3 \quad +3$
$\quad x/2 = 2$
$\quad \times 2 \quad \times 2$
$\quad x = 4$
Check:
$4/2 - 3 = -1$

To solve a two-step equation:
1. Add or subtract the same number on each side of the equation to isolate the variable term.
2. Multiply or divide each side of the equation by the same number to isolate the variable.
3. Check your solution by substituting it for the variable in the original equation.

B. Solve each equation. Check your solution.

$4x + 7 = 35$
$x = 7$

$3x - 8 = 28$
$x = 12$

$-31 = 5 + 4x$
$x = -9$

$6 - 5x = 31$
$x = -5$

$-52 = 6x - 4$
$x = -8$

$\frac{x}{2} + 9 = 17$
$x = 16$

$\frac{x}{7} - 23 = -20$
$x = 21$

$-8 - \frac{x}{5} = -11$
$x = 15$

$-7x - 15 = -92$
$x = 11$

DAY 85 Practice

Solve each equation. Check your solution.

$5x + 4 = 24$
$x = 4$

$3x - 5 = 43$
$x = 16$

$-20 = -2x - 6$
$x = 7$

$5 + 3x = -19$
$x = -8$

$58 = 7x - 26$
$x = 12$

$-38 = 7 - 3x$
$x = 15$

$4x - 45 = 79$
$x = 31$

$-13 - 8x = 59$
$x = -9$

$28 - 6x = 52$
$x = -4$

$67 = -4x - 17$
$x = -21$

$\frac{x}{9} + 11 = 14$
$x = 27$

$\frac{x}{6} + 9 = -12$
$x = -126$

$-\frac{x}{3} - 7 = -12$
$x = 15$

$15x + -44 = 61$
$x = 7$

$10 = 6 - \frac{x}{2}$
$x = -8$

Lesson 85 – Two-Step Equations with Integers

They are going to be doing the same thing, however, two steps are involved. The first step will be getting rid of the number not connected to the variable. This will involve adding or subtracting. The second step will be multiplying or dividing.

The first one on the page is $4x + 7 = 35$. The first step is to subtract seven from both sides. The second step is to divide four from both sides. The goal is the same, to get the variable, the X, all by itself.

Review 85 – Comparing Fractions

This is the same activity as Lesson 84.

Answers   True   True   True

Lesson 86

DAY 86 Two-Step Equations with Decimals and Fractions

A. **Equivalent equations** are equations that have identical solutions. Performing the same operation on both sides of an equation results in an equivalent equation. For example, if you multiply both sides of the equation $x + 3 = 4$ by 2, you get an equivalent equation $2x + 6 = 8$. Notice that the solution will be the same no matter which equation you solve.

B. When solving equations with decimals, multiply both sides by a power of 10 to clear decimals. Integers are a lot easier to work with than decimals. For example, you can rewrite the first problem below as $30x + 25 = 145$ by multiplying both sides by 100. Solve each equation below.

$0.3x + 0.25 = 1.45$ $-1.2x + 3.5 = -6.1$ $6x + -4.3 = 4.7$

x = 4   x = 8   x = 1.5

$6.5 - 4.2x = 23.3$ $-2x - 8.6 = -2.2$ $0.7x + 5 = 5.14$

x = -4   x = -3.2   x = 0.2

C. When solving equations with fractions, multiply both sides by the least common denominator to clear fractions. For example, you can rewrite the first problem below as $4x + 12 = 9$ by multiplying both sides by 12. Solve each equation below.

$\frac{1}{3}x + 1 = \frac{3}{4}$ $\frac{3}{5}x - \frac{1}{2} = \frac{1}{4}$ $3 - \frac{2}{5}x = -\frac{5}{6}$

x = -3/4   x = 1 1/4   x = 9 7/12

$\frac{5}{6} - \frac{3}{4}x = 1\frac{1}{3}$ $-1\frac{1}{2}x - \frac{6}{7} = 5\frac{1}{7}$ $1\frac{1}{3}x - 3\frac{1}{2} = -15\frac{1}{2}$

x = -2/3   x = -4   x = -9

DAY 86 Practice

Solve each equation.

$0.5x - 4.2 = -a5.2$ $-3x + 7.05 = -7.95$ $-8x + 9.5 = 63.1$

x = -2   x = 5   x = -6.7

$2.4 - 2.1x = 1.14$ $-1.74x - 6 = -14.7$ $5.7x + -2.2 = -0.49$

x = 0.6   x = 5   x = 0.3

$-\frac{5}{6} + \frac{3}{8}x = \frac{7}{12}$ $\frac{3}{5}x + \frac{3}{7} = -2$ $\frac{1}{5} - \left(\frac{7}{9}x\right) = \frac{2}{9}$

x = 3 7/9   x = -4 1/21   x = 1/35

$\frac{4}{5}x - \frac{3}{4} = -\frac{11}{20}$ $\frac{4}{7}x + \frac{5}{6} = 6$ $\frac{3}{8}x - \frac{1}{4} = 1\frac{1}{2}$

x = 1/4   x = 9 1/24   x = -4 2/3

$1\frac{1}{2}x + -2\frac{1}{3} = 1\frac{5}{12}$ $\frac{3}{4} - 1\frac{3}{5}x = -2\frac{4}{5}$ $1\frac{1}{10}x - 2\frac{1}{5} = 4\frac{1}{2}$

x = 2 1/2   x = 2 7/32   x = 6 1/11

Lesson 86 – Two-Step Equations with Decimals and Fractions

They will be doing the same thing but there will be decimals and fractions. They will add or subtract and then multiply or divide. They need to pay attention to the signs, and when using the fractions, they need to find common denominators and multiply by the reciprocal to divide.

There is another way to approach these questions. If they multiply the decimals by 10 or 100, they could get rid of the decimals. They may or may not find that helpful.

-1.2x + 3.5 = -6.1 (x10) -12x + 35 = -61

They can do a similar trick with fractions. Multiplying everything by the denominators or by the Least Common Denominator to get rid of the fractions.

1 ¼ + ½ x = 4 (x 4) 5 + 2x = 16

Review 86 – Ordering Fractions

They should be able to think this through to get the answers, but if they are stuck, they can use equivalent fractions, multiplying numerator and denominator by the same number, to compare fractions. 1/3 = 3/9 so 1/3 > 2/9.

Answers   2/5, 1/2, 5/6   1/2, 5/8, 3/4   2/9, 1/4, 1/3

Lesson 87

DAY 87 Multi-Step Equations

A. Simplify each expression by using the distributive property and combining like terms. Review Days 21 and 79 if needed.

$5x - 3 - 2x$ $4(x + 5) - 3$ $6x + 3(7 - 4x)$

$3x - 3$ $4x + 17$ $-6x + 21$

B. The first step in solving an equation is to make the equation as simple as possible. One way to simplify an equation is to make the expressions on each side of the equation as simple as possible. Simplify and solve each equation below.

$4x - 8 - x = -29$ $5(x + 2) - 3 = 47$ $3x + 4(2 - 3x) = 35$

$x = -7$ $x = 8$ $x = -3$

$7(3 + 7x) = -77$ $8 - 3(6x - 4) = -142$ $4 + 2(5x - 7) = 40$

$x = -2$ $x = 9$ $x = 5$

$5x + 2x - 9 = 19$ $-2(5x + 3) + 2 = 26$ $7(6 - 3x) = -84$

$x = 4$ $x = -3$ $x = 6$

$-3(4x - 5) = -93$ $-3x - 5(3x - 2) = 10$ $-3(2 + 8x) + 7x = 28$

$x = 9$ $x = 0$ $x = -2$

DAY 87 Practice

Simplify and solve each equation.

$-7(x - 6) = 7$ $5x + 3(2 - 7x) = -42$ $9(-4 - 2x) + 8 = 80$

$x = 5$ $x = 3$ $x = -6$

$x + 8 - 4x = -16$ $8 + 2(-3x - 5) = 16$ $-3(1 - 2x) = 39$

$x = 8$ $x = -3$ $x = 7$

$5(3x + 1) - 4x = -28$ $4(1 - 4x) + x = 79$ $6(2x + 4) - 5x = -95$

$x = -3$ $x = -5$ $x = -17$

$-9(3 + x) - 5 = -14$ $3 + 7(2x - 8) = -81$ $6x + 8 - 9(x + 2) = -43$

$x = -2$ $x = -2$ $x = 11$

$8 - 2(5 - 2x) + x = 43$ $-7(-3 + 5x) + 9 = -40$ $2(4 + x) - 5(x + 2) = 70$

$x = 9$ $x = 2$ $x = -24$

Lesson 87 – Multi-Step Equations

We're adding more steps. These basically involve the distributive property. Their first step this time will be to simplify the equation. They will distribute if needed and then combine like terms. Once all like terms are combined, they will look like the two-step equations they were just doing.

Here's the second one from part B. $5(x + 2) - 3 = 47$

$$5x + 10 - 3 = 47 \quad \text{(distribute – to get to this point)}$$
$$5x + 7 = 47 \quad \text{(combine like terms)}$$
$$5x = 40 \quad \text{(subtract 7 from both sides)}$$
$$x = 8 \quad \text{(divide each side by 5)}$$

Review 87 – Reciprocal

The reciprocal is the number upside down. The numerator becomes the denominator and the denominator becomes the numerator. Every whole number has an invisible one for its denominator. We just don't write the one because it's unnecessary.

Answers   9/7   1/8   4

Lesson 88

DAY 88 Equations with Variables on Both Sides

A. When solving equations with variables on both sides, first use inverse operations to collect all variables on one side and all constants on the other. Then solve as usual. Here are the steps.

$$2x - 3 = 9 - 4x$$
$$\underline{+ 4x \qquad\qquad + 4x}$$
$$6x - 3 = 9$$
$$\underline{+ 3 \qquad + 3}$$
$$6x = 12$$
$$\underline{\div 6 \qquad \div 6}$$
$$x = 2$$

Check:
$$2 \cdot 2 - 3 = 9 - 4 \cdot 2$$

To solve an equation with variables on both sides:
1. Add or subtract the same variable term(s) on each side of the equation to get all variable terms on one side.
2. Add or subtract the same number(s) on each side of the equation to get all constants on the other side.
3. Multiply or divide each side of the equation by the same number(s) to isolate the variable.
4. Check your solution by substituting it for the variable in the original equation.

B. Solve each equation. Check your solution.

$4x + 8 = 2x$	$42 - 3x = 4x$	$-5x = -60 + 7x$
x = -4	x = 6	x = 5

$7x + 4 = 2x - 6$	$3x - 9 = -5x + 7$	$4x + 5 = 10x - 13$
x = -2	x = 2	x = 3

$6x + 9 = -2x - 15$	$-3x + 2x = 15 + 4x$	$4x + x - 5 = 8x + 1$
x = -3	x = -3	x = -2

DAY 88 Practice

Solve each equation. Check your solution.

$8x + 5 = 3x$	$-4x = 40 + x$	$6x = 9x - 2x$
x = -1	x = -8	x = 0

$9x - 12 = -x + 8$	$6x + 8 = 3x - 7$	$21 - 2x = -5x$
x = 2	x = -5	x = -7

$4x - 4 = -16 + 8x$	$2x = 3x - 5x + 8$	$3x - 9x = 16 - 7x$
x = 3	x = 2	x = 16

$5x - 12 = 15 - 4x$	$5x - 5 = 13 - x$	$3x + x - 5 = 8x + 7$
x = 3	x = 3	x = -3

$-2x + 4 = 1 - 5x + 6$	$5 - 3x = 4x - 7 - 9$	$2 + x - 4 = 2x + 6 - 3x$
x = 1	x = 3	x = 4

Lesson 88 – Equations with Variables on Both Sides

The first step in solving these equations is to simplify them by moving all the variables to one side. Traditionally, this would be the left side of the equation, but combining them on the right sometimes will make more sense. Here's the second one on the page.

$$42 - 3x = 4x \qquad\qquad 42 - 3x = 4x$$
$$42 = 7x \qquad\qquad\qquad 42 - 7x = 0$$
$$6 = x \qquad\qquad\qquad\quad -7x = -42$$
$$\qquad\qquad\qquad\qquad\qquad x = 6$$

If they get to the end and it's a negative X, they need to multiply both sides by -1 to get rid of it. The final answer must be a positive X.

Review 88 – Improper Fractions

Multiply the denominator by the whole number and add the numerator. That's your new numerator. The denominator stays the same. They can draw a picture to see why this is true. 1 4/7 is 7/7 and 4/7. If it were 2 4/7, it would be 7/7 and 7/7 and 4/7. That's where you get the denominator times however many wholes there are plus the current numerator.

Answers   31/6   17/5   18/7

Lesson 89

DAY 89 Equations with Variables on Both Sides

A. Here are the steps for solving $3(5x + 9) = 7 + 4x - 9x$. Rewrite the equation after each step.

$15x + 27 = 7 - 5x$ First, make each side as simple as possible.

$20x + 27 = 7$ Second, collect and combine all variable terms on one side.

$20x = -20$ Third, collect and combine all constants on the other side.

$x = -1$ Fourth, get the variable x alone on one side.

B. Solve each equation. Check your solution.

$8x = -30 + 2x$ $4(x - 3) = 2x$ $20 - x = 4x$

$x = -5$ $x = 6$ $x = 4$

$3x + 5 = 5x - 13$ $7x - 9 = -2x - 18$ $7x + 4 = 2x - 6$

$x = 9$ $x = -1$ $x = -2$

$3x + 6 = 7x - 10$ $-3x + 2x = 2(7 + 3x)$ $5 - 2(x + 1) = x - 9$

$x = 4$ $x = -2$ $x = 4$

$-4x + 7 = 2 - 6x + 5$ $4 - 3x = 4(x - 2) - 9$ $7 + x - 3 = x - 5 - 3x$

$x = 0$ $x = 3$ $x = -3$

DAY 89 Practice

Solve each equation. Check your solution.

$2x - 5 = 3x$ $6x = 4(5 - x)$ $24 - x = -5x$

$x = -5$ $x = 2$ $x = -6$

$x + 7 = 3x - 11$ $4x - 22 = -x + 8$ $-5x - 6x = 35 - 4x$

$x = 9$ $x = 6$ $x = -5$

$-5x = 2x - 9x + 8$ $2(x - 2) = 20 + 8x$ $3x - x = 15 + 7x$

$x = 4$ $x = -4$ $x = -3$

$7x - 5 = 13 - 2x$ $5x - 12 = -15 + 4x$ $2(x + 5) + 6 = 7x - 9$

$x = 2$ $x = -3$ $x = 5$

$4 - 2x = 4x - 8 - 9x$ $-9x + 5 = 2 - 5x - 9$ $5 + x - 8 = 2(2x + 3) - 2x$

$x = -4$ $x = 3$ $x = -9$

Lesson 89 – Equations with Variables on Both Sides

They will be continuing this. This time there is more to do to simplify the equation. They will start by simplifying each side. Then they will combine all the variable terms on one side, typically the left, and combine all the constants, the numbers without variables on the right. Finally, they will do what's necessary to isolate the variable.

Review – Mixed Numbers

This is the opposite of Lesson 88. They will divide the denominator into the numerator to see how many wholes fit in there. That's the whole number. The remainder is the new numerator. The denominator stays the same.

Answers   7 3/5   5 5/7   2 7/9

Lesson 90

DAY 90 Review: Equations of All Types

A. Explain **equivalent equations** in your own words. Give examples. Review Day 86 if needed.

Examples will vary. See Day 86, Part A.

B. Describe how to clear decimals and fractions to make an equation easier to work with. Give examples. Review Day 86 if needed.

Examples will vary. See Day 86, Parts B and C.

C. Solve each equation. Simplify fractions.

$x + 15 = -17$	$3.65 = x - 4.3$	$1.26 = -0.7x$
x = -32	x = 7.95	x = -1.8

$\frac{x}{5} = -14$	$\frac{4}{5}x = -\frac{2}{5}$	$x - \frac{3}{4} = \frac{4}{5}$
x = -70	x = -1/2	x = 1 11/20

$14 + 7x = 35$	$-27 = 5 + 4x$	$4x + 2.3 = 5.7$
x = 3	x = -8	x = 0.85

$\frac{x}{3} + 5 = -10$	$\frac{4}{5}x - \frac{2}{3} = -\frac{2}{5}$	$1\frac{1}{6}x + 2\frac{2}{3} = 4\frac{1}{2}$
x = -45	x = 1/3	x = 1 4/7

$8x + 4 = 3x - 6$	$-6x + 4x = 5(7 + x)$	$4 - 3(x + 7) = x - 9$
x = -2	x = -5	x = -2

DAY 90 Practice

Solve each equation. Simplify fractions.

$x + 23 = 14$	$-0.8x = 1.92$	$1.06 = 4.2 + x$
x = -9	x = -2.4	x = -3.14

$-12 = \frac{x}{-7}$	$x + \frac{2}{3} = \frac{5}{9}$	$\frac{2}{9}x = \frac{4}{5}$
x = 84	x = -1/9	x = 3 3/5

$3x - 12 = 27$	$16 - 5x = 31$	$1.7x + 8 = 10.04$
x = 13	x = -3	x = 1.2

$\frac{x}{7} - 24 = -25$	$\frac{1}{5}x - \frac{3}{8} = -\frac{1}{4}$	$-1\frac{1}{2}x + \frac{3}{4} = 2\frac{1}{2}$
x = -7	x = 5/8	x = -1 1/6

$6(x - 1) = -x - 20$	$8x + 2x - 9 = -19$	$9 - 5x = 3(x - 2) - 9$
x = -2	x = -1	x = 3

$\frac{1}{2}x - 2x = -1\frac{1}{2}$	$\frac{2}{3}x + 4x = -\frac{1}{3} - 2$	$2\frac{1}{5} + \frac{4}{5}x = \frac{2}{5}x + \frac{3}{5}$
x = 1	x = -1/2	x = -4

Lesson 90 – Review: Equations of All Types

This is a review of all the types of equations they've been working with. They can look back at other pages if they need any reminders.

No Review

Lesson 91

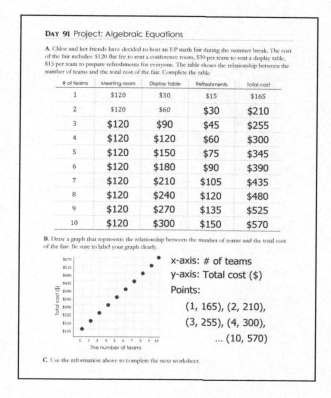

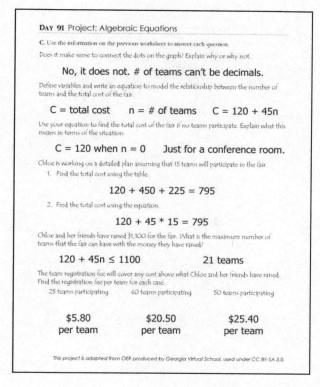

Lesson 91– Project: Algebraic Equations

They are going to be completing a chart and then drawing a graph that shows total cost verses number of teams, the two end columns on the chart. They will plot points on the graph first. They will look at those points and decide if it makes sense to connect the dots.

They need to turn the page. There is a second page for today. They will need to write an equation that you can enter the number of teams into and it will tell you the total cost.

number of teams x ? + ? = total cost

No Review

Lesson 92

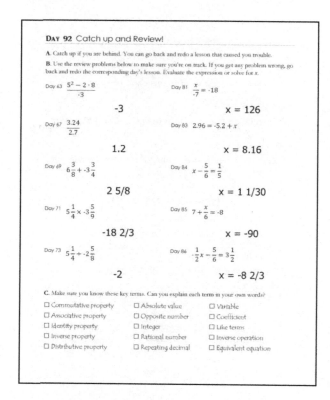

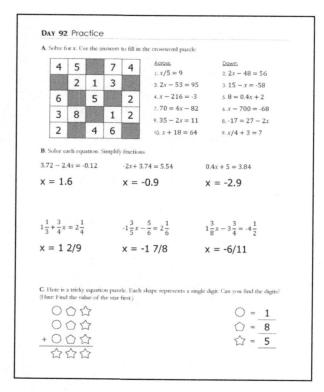

Lesson 92 Catch Up and Review

Have your child check themselves using the lesson page and go back to work on problem areas. See if your child can explain the terms on the page. If they are doing well, have them use the practice page today to stay sharp.

No Review

Lesson 93

DAY 93 Addition and Subtraction Inequalities

A. You can solve inequalities involving addition and subtraction in the same way that you solve addition and subtraction equations. Below are some examples showing the steps. Which inequality is solved correctly? Select all that apply. Review Days 29 and 30 if needed.

$15 + x < 32$	$x + 20 \geq 58$	$x - 27 \geq 14$
$-15 \quad -15$	$-20 \quad -20$	$+27 \quad +27$
$x < 17$	$x \leq 38$	$x \geq 41$

B. Solve each inequality.

$x + 19 > 34$
$x > 15$

$x - 26 \leq 18$
$x \leq 44$

$-47 \geq 15 + x$
$x \leq -62$

$x - 0.46 \leq 2.8$
$x \leq 3.26$

$x + 1.9 > -4.28$
$x > -6.18$

$-4.5 + x \leq 18$
$x \leq 22.5$

$-\frac{3}{4} > x - \frac{1}{2}$
$x < -1/4$

$\frac{1}{6} \leq \frac{3}{8} + x$
$x \geq -5/24$

$x - \frac{2}{3} > -\frac{4}{9}$
$x > 2/9$

$x + 1\frac{2}{5} \geq 2\frac{1}{2}$
$x \geq 1\ 1/10$

$x - \left(-2\frac{3}{4}\right) < 1\frac{1}{3}$
$x < -1\ 5/12$

$x + -4\frac{1}{7} \leq -2\frac{2}{3}$
$x \leq 1\ 10/21$

C. Write an inequality and solve to answer each question. Then interpret your solution.

Dan has 32 coins. Together, Dan and Laura have fewer than 50 coins. How many coins does Laura have?

$32 + x < 50$
Fewer than 18 coins

Walker ran 11 miles this week. His goal was at least 20 miles. How many more miles does he need to run?

$11 + x \geq 20$
At least 9 miles

DAY 93 Practice

A. Solve each inequality.

$32 + x > 41$
$x > 9$

$x - 16 \geq -20$
$x \geq -4$

$-27 + x < -19$
$x < 8$

$x + 3.02 \leq 4.52$
$x \leq 1.5$

$-2.8 + x < -0.5$
$x < 2.3$

$-14.07 < x - 8.27$
$x > -5.8$

$x - \frac{2}{5} < \frac{1}{4}$
$x < 3/20$

$-\frac{7}{8} + x \geq \frac{1}{4}$
$x \geq 1\ 1/8$

$\frac{3}{4} + x \geq \frac{5}{6}$
$x \geq 1/12$

$5\frac{1}{2} \leq x + 2\frac{3}{4}$
$x \geq 2\ 3/4$

$-3\frac{2}{3} + x \leq -2\frac{1}{2}$
$x \leq 1\ 1/6$

$x - \left(-4\frac{1}{5}\right) < 2\frac{1}{3}$
$x < -1\ 13/15$

B. Write an inequality and solve to answer each question. Then interpret your solution.

Lisa needs at least $70 for a camping trip. She has saved $47 so far. How much more money does Lisa need to save?

$47 + x \geq 70$
At least 23 dollars

An elevator can hold up to 3,000 pounds and it currently weighs 1,190 pounds. How much more can the elevator hold?

$1,190 + x \leq 3,000$
Up to 1,810 pounds

Eli went to a mall with $45 and bought a shirt for $18. How much more can he spend at the mall?

$18 + x \leq 45$
At most 27 dollars

Ron scored 87 and 88 on the first two math quizzes. What does Ron need to score on the 3rd quiz to get an average of at least 90?

$87 + 88 + x \geq 90 * 3$
At least 95

Lesson 93 – Addition and Subtraction Inequalities

They will add or subtract the opposite to get the X, the variable, by itself. This is just like solving equations. The greater than/less than sign needs to stay the same way. There will be a time when the sign will flip, when they multiply or divide by a negative number. They are just adding and subtracting here.

You can have them explain why the middle one in Part A is incorrect. The sign should not flip. That's only when multiplying or dividing. You can also have them explain what the answers mean. The answer is any number less than 17 for the first one and any number equal or greater than 41 for the last answer.

To solve the ones with fractions, they will need to find a common denominator.

Review 93 – Comparing Fractions

They are comparing fractions. They do not have to find equivalent fractions. They just need to think it through what the whole numbers mean and what the fractions mean.

Answers   True   False   False

Lesson 94

DAY 94 Multiplication and Division Inequalities

A. When solving inequalities with multiplication and division, solve exactly like multiplication and division equations except for one thing: you must flip the inequality sign when multiplying or dividing by a negative number. Below are some examples showing the steps. Which inequality is solved correctly? Select all that apply. Review Days 29 and 30 if needed.

$6x \le 54$	$8x \ge 96$	$x/-3 > 18$
$-6 \quad -6$	$\div 8 \quad \div 8$	$\times -3 \quad \times -3$
$x \le 48$	$x \ge 12$	$x < -54$

C. Solve each inequality.

$5x < 45$	$-14x \ge 56$	$x \div 8 < -14$
$x < 9$	$x \le -4$	$x < -112$

$-6x > 48$	$12x > -9$	$x \div -0.3 < -9$
$x < -8$	$x > -0.75$	$x > 2.7$

$1.3x \ge -0.91$	$-2.25 \ge 0.9x$	$-1.6x < -14.08$
$x \ge -0.7$	$x \le -2.5$	$x > 8.8$

$\frac{x}{4} < -17$	$\frac{x}{-3} \ge \frac{7}{5}$	$-6 < -1\frac{1}{5}x$
$x < -68$	$x \le -4 \, 1/5$	$x < 5$

D. Write an inequality and solve to answer each question. Then interpret your solution.

Dale used a $25 gift card to buy some cookies. Cookies cost $2 each. How many cookies can Dale buy with the gift card?

$2x \le 25$

At most 12 cookies

A cuboid has a width of 5 cm and a length of 8 cm. Its volume is greater than 120 cm³. What are the possible heights of the cuboid?

$(5 * 8)x > 120$

Greater than 3 cm

DAY 94 Practice

A. Solve each inequality.

$-9x > 81$	$7x < 49$	$13x \ge -91$
$x < -9$	$x < 7$	$x \ge -7$

$-0.74 \ge 0.4x$	$4.2x \ge -2.1$	$-8.9x < -23.14$
$x \le -1.85$	$x \ge -0.5$	$x > 2.6$

$\frac{5}{7}x > -10$	$\frac{x}{-9} < -21$	$\frac{6}{7} \le -\frac{2}{3}x$
$x > -14$	$x > 189$	$x \le -1 \, 2/7$

$1\frac{2}{9}x \le -33$	$-2\frac{1}{7}x > -\frac{5}{21}$	$1\frac{2}{3}x > 2\frac{2}{9}$
$x \le -27$	$x < 1/9$	$x > 1 \, 1/3$

B. Write an inequality and solve to answer each question. Then interpret your solution.

Pam earns $12 per hour working at a store. How many hours does Pam have to work to earn at least $180?

$12x \ge 180$

At least 15 hours

The width of a rectangle is 6 inches. Its area is no more than 54 square inches. What are the possible lengths of the rectangle?

$6x \le 54$

No more than 9 inches

Isabella bought a hat. She paid with a $20 bill and received change of more than $2. How much does the hat cost?

$20 - x > 2$

Less than 18 dollars

Max solved 14 algebra problems, fewer than half the problems Paul solved. How many problems did Paul solve?

$14 < (1/2)x$

More than 28 problems

Lesson 94 – Multiplication and Division Inequalities

They will be multiplying and dividing to solve inequalities. They will be doing the opposite to get the X, the variable, all by itself, just like in solving equations. There are examples on the page.

The greater than/less than sign stays facing the same way UNLESS they multiply or divide by a negative number. You can see below how that works out.

$-x > 1$ The opposite of X is greater than 1: -2, -3, -4,….

Multiply/Divide both sides by negative one. Which produces the same answer?

$x > -1$ X is greater than negative one: 0, 1, 2, 3, 4,…

$x < -1$ X is less than negative one: -2, -3, -4,…

In Part A, the wrong answer subtracts six instead of dividing.

Review 94 – Comparing Fractions

This time they will need to do some figuring, changing the improper fractions into mixed numbers and finding equivalent fractions in order to really compare.

Answers   True   False   True

Lesson 95

DAY 95 One-Step Inequalities

A. Just like there are properties of equality, there are also **properties of inequality**. In fact, you've been using the properties below to solve inequalities. Review each property and examples.

Property of inequality	In symbols	Examples
Addition property	If $a < b$, then $a + c < b + c$	If $x - 3 < 5$, then $x - 3 + 3 < 5 + 3$
Subtraction property	If $a < b$, then $a - c < b - c$	If $x + 4 < 2$, then $x + 4 - 4 < 2 - 4$
Multiplication property	If $a < b$ and $c > 0$, then $ac < bc$ If $a < b$ and $c < 0$, then $ac > bc$	If $x/5 < 2$, then $x/5 \cdot 5 < 2 \cdot 5$ If $x/-4 < 3$, then $x/-4 \cdot -4 > 3 \cdot -4$
Division property	If $a < b$ and $c > 0$, then $a/c < b/c$ If $a < b$ and $c < 0$, then $a/c > b/c$	If $6x < 12$, then $6x \div 6 < 12 \div 6$ If $-7x < 21$, then $-7x \div -7 > 21 \div -7$

B. Solve each inequality.

$x + 45 > 21$	$5x > -40$	$5.4 > -0.09x$
x > -24	x > -8	x > -60

$-2.7x \geq -24.3$	$x - 18 \leq 23$	$-1.9 + x > -2.5$
x ≤ 9	x ≤ 41	x > -0.6

$\frac{1}{4} \leq -\frac{1}{3} + x$	$-\frac{x}{3} \leq -27$	$\frac{2}{5}x > \frac{3}{4}$
x ≥ 7/12	x ≥ 81	x < -1 7/8

$\frac{x}{19} \leq -9$	$\frac{3}{4} + x \geq -\frac{1}{6}$	$-5x < \frac{5}{8}$
x ≤ -171	x ≥ -11/12	x > 1/8

$-\frac{x}{4} > 2\frac{1}{8}$	$27 \geq 4\frac{1}{2}x$	$x + 2\frac{3}{5} \geq 2\frac{1}{2}$
x < -8 1/2	x ≤ 6	x ≥ -1/10

DAY 95 Practice

Solve each inequality. Simplify fractions.

$-17 + x < 26$	$x - 43 \leq -29$	$8x \geq -72$
x < 43	x ≤ 14	x ≥ -9

$-6.4x < 1.92$	$3.7 + x \leq -5.4$	$40 \leq x - (-15)$
x > -0.3	x ≤ -9.1	x ≥ 25

$x - 0.79 \leq 5.8$	$0.4x \geq -0.9$	$7.02 + x > 2.99$
x ≤ 6.59	x ≥ -2.25	x > -4.03

$5 > \frac{x}{16}$	$x - \frac{1}{6} < \frac{3}{8}$	$-\frac{4}{7}x \leq \frac{8}{9}$
x < 80	x < -5/24	x ≥ -1 5/9

$\frac{3}{5} + x \geq \frac{7}{15}$	$\frac{x}{-8} \geq -24$	$\frac{x}{-4} \geq \frac{2}{5}$
x ≥ -2/15	x ≤ 192	x ≤ -1 3/5

$-6x \leq \frac{4}{7}$	$5 \leq \frac{2}{9} + x$	$x - 9 < -4\frac{1}{3}$
x ≥ -2/21	x ≥ 4 7/9	x < 4 2/3

$\frac{x}{10} \geq 1\frac{3}{4}$	$-1\frac{2}{5}x < 4\frac{3}{8}$	$x - \left(-6\frac{1}{4}\right) < 1\frac{1}{2}$
x ≥ 17 1/2	x > -3 1/8	x < -4 3/4

Lesson 95 – One-Step Inequalities

They will be doing the same thing as Lessons 93 and 94. This time they aren't all the same. Some will be adding and subtracting and some will be multiplying and dividing. They need to keep the inequality facing the same directions except for the one case of multiplying (or dividing) by a negative number.

Review 95 – Adding Fractions

They will be adding fractions with common denominators. The denominators will stay the same. They just add the numerators and then reduce the fractions. If the numerator and denominator are both even, then they can divide both by two to reduce. If they both end in either a 0 or a 5, then they can both be divided by 5.

Answers   1   1/2   2/3

Lesson 96

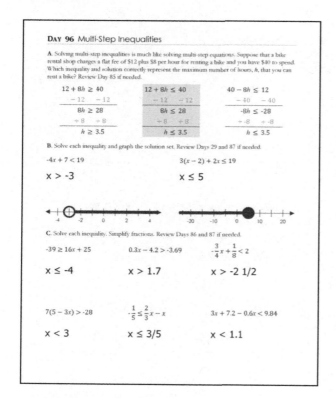

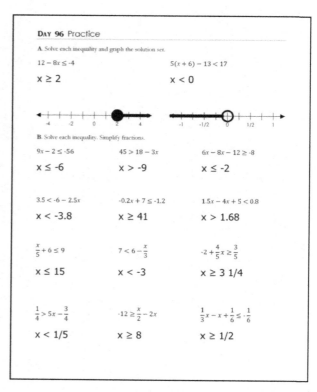

Lesson 96 – Multi-Step Inequalities

They will be combining what they've been practicing. There are lesson numbers on there if they need to go back and remind themselves of how to do it. Here are the steps:

1. simplify the equation
   - distribute if necessary such as $2(x - 1) = 2x - 2$
   - combine like terms such as $3 + x - 2 + 2x = 1 + 3x$
   - remember that $x = 1x$ **Hint: 1x = (3/3)x**
   - This all still applies when the coefficient is a fraction, that number by X.
2. get the variable alone
   - first add the opposite if needed
   - then multiply by the opposite, switch the sign if you multiplied by a negative

When they graph the inequalities, they need to remember to use an open circle for greater than or less than and a closed circle if it's also equal.

Review 96 – Subtracting Fractions

They will be subtracting fractions with common denominators. The denominators will stay the same. They just add the numerators and then reduce the fractions. If the numerator and denominator are both even, then they can divide both by two to reduce. They both end in either a 0 or a 5, then they can both be divided by 5.

Answers   2/7   1/4   4/5

Lesson 97

DAY 97 Inequalities with Variables on Both Sides

A. Remember how we solved equations with variables on both sides? Here are the steps for solving $2(5 - 3x) \le 2x - 6$. Rewrite the inequality after each step. Review Day 88 if needed.

$10 - 6x \le 2x - 6$	First, make each side as simple as possible.
$10 - 8x \le -6$	Second, collect and combine all variable terms on one side.
$-8x \le -16$	Third, collect and combine all constants on the other side.
$x \ge 2$	Fourth, get the variable x alone on one side.

B. Solve each inequality. Simplify fractions.

$x - 6 < 7x - 8$	$-8x + 5 \ge -6x + 3$	$2x - 4 > -3x - 7$
x > 1/3	x ≤ 1	x > -3/5

$-3(x + 1) \ge 9x + 5$	$6x - 5 < x + 8 - 2x$	$6 - 4x < 2(4x + 1)$
x ≤ -2/3	x < 1 6/7	x > 1/3

$\frac{3}{5}x - \frac{2}{5}x < \frac{1}{10}$	$\frac{2}{9}x \ge \frac{1}{3}x + 4$	$2 - \frac{1}{7}x < 3 - \frac{2}{7}x$
x < 1/2	x ≤ -36	x < 7

$-\frac{1}{2}x > \frac{1}{3}x - 5$	$\frac{1}{2}x \le 1\frac{1}{4} + 2x$	$\frac{1}{6}x - \frac{2}{3}x > 2 + \frac{1}{2}x$
x < 6	x ≥ -5/6	x < -2

DAY 97 Practice

Solve each inequality. Simplify fractions.

$3x - 4 < 5x + 1$	$6x - 9 \le -4 - x$	$-6x + 4 < 3x - 5$
x > -2 1/2	x ≤ 5/7	x > 1

$10x - 9 > 3 - 6x$	$6(x - 1) \ge -2 - 3x$	$7 - 2x > 3x + 9$
x > 3/4	x ≥ 4/9	x < -2/5

$-5x + 7 > 3x - 9$	$3x - 9 < 9x - 8$	$2x + 1 \ge 10x + 3$
x < 2	x > -1/6	x ≤ -1/4

$\frac{3}{4} - x > \frac{1}{2}x$	$\frac{1}{3}x - \frac{2}{3}x > -2$	$8 + \frac{3}{4}x \le \frac{2}{5}x - 6$
x < 1/2	x < 6	x ≤ -40

$1\frac{1}{2}x + x > 1\frac{5}{6}$	$\frac{1}{6}x \ge \frac{3}{8}x + \frac{5}{6}$	$\frac{1}{9}x + \frac{2}{3} < \frac{4}{9} - \frac{2}{3}x$
x > 11/15	x ≤ -4	x < -2/7

Lesson 97 – Inequalities with Variables on Both Sides

This is just like Lesson 96 except that the X is on both sides of the inequality. Here's an example.

$$
\begin{array}{rcl}
2x - 4 & > & -4x + 8 \\
+4x + 4 & & +4x + 4 \\
\hline
6x & > & 12 \\
/6 & & /6 \\
\hline
x & > & 2
\end{array}
$$

Simplify each side first. Then start moving variables and constants. Typically we'd move variables onto the left.

Review 97 – Adding Mixed Numbers

They can separate out these just like separating place values to add.

$123 + 456 = 100 + 400 + 20 + 50 + 3 + 6$
$1\frac{1}{2} + 2\frac{3}{4} = 1 + 2 + \frac{1}{2} + \frac{3}{4}$

They need to make sure their answers are in the simplest form. Reduce!

Answers   5 3/5   6 1/3   6

Lesson 98

DAY 98 Unit Rates with Complex Fractions

A. Define ratio, rate, and unit rate in your own words. Give examples. Review Day 11 if needed.

Examples will vary. See Day 11.

B. When one or both quantities being compared are fractions, the rate becomes a **complex fraction** (a fraction where the numerator, denominator, or both are fractions). To find a unit rate, you must simplify the complex fraction by dividing its numerator by its denominator. For example, suppose you walked 2 miles in 2/3 hour. What is the unit rate in miles per hour?

$$\frac{2\ miles}{\frac{2}{3}\ hour} = \frac{2}{1} \div \frac{2}{3} = \frac{2}{1} \times \frac{3}{2} = 3\ miles/hour$$

To simplify a complex fraction, rewrite it as a division expression and use the rules for division of fractions.

C. Simplify each complex fraction.

$\frac{\frac{2}{4}}{\frac{2}{5}}$ 2 1/2 $\frac{\frac{6}{7}}{8}$ 3/28

$\frac{\frac{2}{3}}{\frac{5}{6}}$ 4/5 $\frac{\frac{3}{4}}{\frac{9}{16}}$ 1 1/3

D. Determine whether each pair is equivalent or not. Answer yes or no.

$28 for 5 tickets and $39.20 for 7 tickets — **Yes**

102 words in 3 minutes and 232 words in 7 ¼ minutes — **No**

128 miles on 4 gallons and 80 miles on 2 ½ gallons — **Yes**

E. Solve each problem.

Brian divided 5/8 gallons of milk evenly into 5 bottles. How much milk did he put in each bottle? — **1/8 gallon**

Store P sells 5 pounds of beef for $14.40. Store Q sells 4 pounds of beef for $19.60. Which store has the better price? — **Store P**

Ella and Josh baked large pizzas of the same size. Ella used 9 cups of cheese on every four pizzas. Josh used 7 1/4 cups of cheese on every three and a half pizzas. Who used more cheese on one pizza? — **Ella**

DAY 98 Practice

A. Simplify each complex fraction.

$\frac{4}{\frac{6}{7}}$ 4 2/3 $\frac{7}{\frac{7}{15}}$ 15

$\frac{\frac{3}{4}}{9}$ 1/12 $\frac{\frac{9}{10}}{12}$ 3/40

$\frac{\frac{4}{5}}{\frac{2}{3}}$ 1 1/5 $\frac{\frac{3}{8}}{\frac{7}{12}}$ 9/14

B. Determine whether each pair is equivalent or not. Answer yes or no.

54 students in 3 groups and 153 students in 9 groups — **No**

$8.40 for 7 cupcakes and $14.40 for 12 cupcakes — **Yes**

$18 for 200 copies and $40.50 for 450 copies — **Yes**

330 miles in 6 hours and 169 miles in 3 ¼ hours — **No**

C. Solve each problem.

Adam rode his bike 18 miles in 45 minutes. What was his average speed in miles per hour (mph)? — **24 mph**

Kyle jogged 4 miles in three quarters of an hour. Jayden jogged two and a half miles in 30 minutes. Who jogged at a faster rate? — **Kyle**

Marsha used three and a half cups of flour to bake 2 dozen cupcakes. How many cups of flour would she use for a dozen cupcakes? — **1 3/4 cups**

It took James seven and a half minutes to drain his 30-gallon fish tank. How many gallons of water went down the drain each minute? — **4 gallons**

Josh's car can go 169 miles on 6 ½ gallons of gas. Amanda's car can go 252 miles on 9 gallons of gas. Whose car gets better gas mileage (miles per gallon of gas)? — **Amanda's**

Lesson 98 – Unit Rates with Complex Fractions

This isn't as complex as it sounds. $^4/_2 = 4 \div 2$ Saying something is a complex fraction just means you are dividing a fraction by a fraction.

They know how to divide by a fraction, they just multiply by the reciprocal.

When trying to figure out the rate, they can use simple numbers to help them figure it out. For example one set of numbers is 232 words in seven and a quarter minutes. Well, what would 200 words in 2 minutes be as a rate, 100 words a minute. Then they can see they take the number of words and divide by the number of minutes, even if it's a fraction.

Review 98 – Subtracting Mixed Numbers

This is just like adding mixed numbers because subtracting is just adding a negative number. They don't have to "borrow" to do these, so it's simple to just subtract since they have common denominators. They need to reduce their answers though.

Answers   3/4   1 2/3   2 3/5

Lesson 99

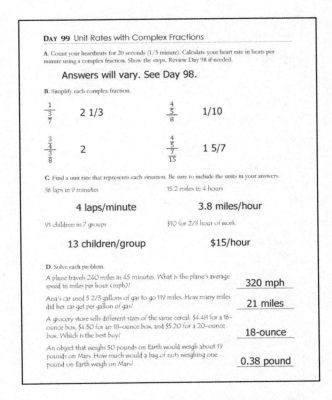

DAY 99 Unit Rates with Complex Fractions

A. Count your heartbeats for 20 seconds (1/3 minute). Calculate your heart rate in beats per minute using a complex fraction. Show the steps. Review Day 98 if needed.

Answers will vary. See Day 98.

B. Simplify each complex fraction.

$\frac{\frac{1}{3}}{7}$ **2 1/3** $\frac{\frac{4}{5}}{8}$ **1/10**

$\frac{\frac{3}{4}}{\frac{3}{8}}$ **2** $\frac{\frac{4}{5}}{\frac{7}{15}}$ **1 5/7**

C. Find a unit rate that represents each situation. Be sure to include the units in your answers.

36 laps in 9 minutes   15.2 miles in 4 hours

4 laps/minute   **3.8 miles/hour**

91 children in 7 groups $10 for 2/3 hour of work

13 children/group   **$15/hour**

D. Solve each problem.

A plane travels 240 miles in 45 minutes. What is the plane's average speed in miles per hour (mph)?   **320 mph**

Ana's car used 5 2/3 gallons of gas to go 119 miles. How many miles did her car get per gallon of gas?   **21 miles**

A grocery store sells different sizes of the same cereal: $4.48 for a 16-ounce box, $4.50 for an 18-ounce box, and $5.20 for a 20-ounce box. Which is the best buy?   **18-ounce**

An object that weighs 50 pounds on Earth would weigh about 19 pounds on Mars. How much would a bag of nuts weighing one pound on Earth weigh on Mars?   **0.38 pound**

DAY 99 Practice

A. Simplify each complex fraction.

$\frac{4}{\frac{2}{7}}$ **14** $\frac{8}{\frac{6}{11}}$ **14 2/3**

$\frac{\frac{4}{9}}{6}$ **2/27** $\frac{\frac{5}{12}}{15}$ **1/36**

$\frac{\frac{2}{5}}{\frac{4}{9}}$ **9/10** $\frac{\frac{5}{12}}{\frac{7}{18}}$ **1 1/14**

B. Find a unit rate that represents each situation. Be sure to include the units in your answers.

312 pages in 6 days $57.60 for 8 tickets

52 pages/day   **$7.20/ticket**

486 points in 18 games   150 miles in 2 1/2 hours

27 points/game   **60 miles/hour**

C. Solve each problem.

A freight train travels 1,320 miles in 24 hours. What is the train's average speed in miles per hour (mph)?   **55 mph**

Jayden is trying to decide whether or not he should buy a 12-ounce can of ground coffee on sale for $8.40 or a 2-pound can of coffee for $19.20. Which is the better buy? (1 pound = 16 ounces)   **2-pound**

Emily's recipe uses two and a quarter cups of sugar to make 2 dozen cookies. Mike's recipe uses 3 cups of sugar to make two and a half dozen cookies. Which recipe uses more sugar for a dozen cookies?   **Mike's**

It took Owen 20 minutes to type 4 pages that had an average of 250 words per page. It took Cathy 32 minutes to type 6 pages that had an average of 240 words per page. Who typed faster?   **Owen**

Lesson 99 – Unit Rates with Complex Fractions

They are supposed to measure their heartrate by counting heartbeats over twenty seconds and then divide that by one third to get their heartrate, beats per minute.

They will be doing the same thing different ways down the page. If they become stuck on a word problem, remind them to start with simple numbers.

Review 99 – Fraction Word Problems

If the word problems are confusing, encourage them to use whole numbers in the question to figure out how to approach it and then substitute in the fractions.

Answers   3/4 of an hour, 2/3 of the box, 2/5 of the box

Lesson 100

DAY 100 Percent of Change

A. Explain how to find 20% of 55 in two different ways: using multiplication and using a proportion. Show your steps. Review Day 16 if needed.

$$20\% \text{ of } 55 = 11 \qquad \text{See Day 16, Parts B and C.}$$

B. When a quantity changes from one amount to another, we often express the change as a percentage of the original amount. It is called the **percent change** or **percent of change**. If a quantity increases, the percent of change is called a **percent increase**. If a quantity decreases, the percent of change is called a **percent decrease**. Here are some examples and related formulas.

The percent decrease from 20 to 15:
$$\frac{|20 - 15|}{20} = \frac{5}{20} = 0.25 = 25\%$$

The new amount when 40 is increased by 20%:
$$40 + 20\% \text{ of } 40 = 40 + 0.2 \times 40 = 48$$

The new amount when 40 is decreased by 20%:
$$40 - 20\% \text{ of } 40 = 40 - 0.2 \times 40 = 32$$

Percent of change formulas:
- $\frac{\text{Amount of change}}{\text{Original amount}} = \frac{\% \text{ change}}{100}$
- Amount of change = | New amount − Original amount | = Percent of original amount
- New amount = Original amount ± Amount of change

C. Find the percent of each change. Indicate an increase with a plus sign (+), and a decrease with a minus sign (-), followed by the percentage change.

From 50 to 90	From 200 to 120	From 40 to 140
+80%	−40%	+250%

D. Find each new amount.

Increase 30 by 40%	Increase 80 by 155%	Decrease 140 by 15%
42	204	119

E. Solve each problem.

An electrician cut 9 feet from a 75-foot electric cable. What is the percent decrease in length? — 12%

The population of Lisa's city increased from 52,000 to 65,000 over a period of 5 years. What is the percent increase in population? — 25%

Last year Ali was 5 feet tall and Ryan was 4 feet and 8 inches tall. This year Ali grew by 4% and Ryan by 10%. Who's taller? (1 foot = 12 inches) — Ali

DAY 100 Practice

A. Find the percent of each change. Indicate an increase with a plus sign (+), and a decrease with a minus sign (-), followed by the percentage change.

From 40 to 60	From 70 to 210	From 450 to 315
+50%	+200%	−30%

From 112 to 84	From 58 to 145	From 2,020 to 101
−25%	+150%	−95%

B. Find each new amount.

Increase 310 by 30%	Increase 15 by 120%	Decrease 280 by 15%
403	33	238

Decrease 1,200 by 73%	Decrease 712 by 25%	Increase 1,620 by 40%
324	534	2,268

C. Solve each problem.

Ann's book club grew from 16 to 22 members. What is the percent increase in members? — 37.5%

A laptop originally cost $820, but it is now on sale for $697. What is the percent decrease in price? — 15%

Ariana saved $60. Her sister Sophia saved 24% more than Ariana. How much money did they save all together? — $134.40

The regular price of the shirt is $20. Store M has it on sale at $16. Store N offers an 18% discount. Which store offers a better deal? — Store M

Last year Andrew bought 120 shares of a company at $16 per share. Since then the stock price of the company has risen by 5%. What are his shares worth now? — $2,016

Noah drew a rectangle with width 15 inches and height 20 inches. Then he made the rectangle bigger by extending its width and height by 3 inches each. What's the percent increase in area? — 38%

Lesson 100 – Percentage of Change

This is called something different but these concepts are all related. Ratios, proportions, scale factors, even variations. They are one number over another. This time we're going to divide to find a decimal and convert that to a percent.

We're finding percent increase or decrease, this is just like saying the side of the triangle went from 4 to 2 = (4 − 2) / 4. It changed by 50%. 2/4 = 0.5 = 50 %

When they are finding the new amount, they need to find the amount increased or decreased and then add that on to the original amount.

They just need to remember that a percent is the hundredth.   0.3 = 30%   1.25 = 125%

Review 100 – Common Denominators

They are to find the least common denominator, not just any. Multiplying the denominators together won't work. My trick is to think through the multiples of the larger number.
3 and 4, 4 is larger: 4, 8, 12. I know three goes into 12 and can stop there.

Answers   4/12, 9/12   9/24, 20/24   15/48, 18/48

Lesson 101

A. Explain how to find the new amount when 80 is decreased by 15%. Show your steps. Review Days 16 and 100 if needed.

$$80 - 15\% \text{ of } 80 = 80 - 0.15 \times 80 = 80 - 12 = 68$$

B. Complete the table.

From	To	% change
50	8	−84%
25	60	+140%
75	15	−80%
84	126	+50%
12.5	30	+140%
24	19.2	−20%
710	852	+20%
0.9	6.3	+600%
440	330	−25%
120	128.4	+7%

C. Solve each problem.

Ryan's rent was $650 per month. Starting this month, it went up by 4%. What will be his rent payment now? — **$676**

Andrew was 140 cm tall three years ago. Today he is 161 cm tall. What is the percent increase in his height? — **15%**

The home owner dropped the selling price of his home from $150,000 to $135,000. What is the percent decrease in price? — **10%**

Natalie bought a shirt for $16 and a book for $12. She had a coupon for 20% off clothing. How much did she pay in total? — **$24.80**

Levi scored 92% on his first math test. He got 2 more problems correct on the second test than on the first one. Both tests had 25 problems. What is his average score? — **24 or 96%**

A. Complete the table.

From	To	% change
20	12	−40%
78	117	+50%
64	80	+25%
150	45	−70%
1100	11	−99%
50	37.5	−25%
16.8	42	+150%
8.4	2.1	−75%
36	55.8	+55%
5.5	24.2	+340%

B. Solve each problem. Round your answers to the nearest tenth or cent, if necessary.

In September, Sandy saved $55. In October, she saved 12% less. How much did she save in October? — **$48.40**

The price of a computer monitor is marked down from $420 to $357. What is the percent decrease in price? — **15%**

A plumber cut 10 inches from a 5-foot PVC pipe. What is the percent decrease in length? (1 foot = 12 inches) — **16.7%**

The temperature at noon was 80 °F. By midnight, it had dropped to 54 °F. What was the percent decrease in temperature? — **32.5%**

Zoey had a rectangular board 12 inches long and 15 inches wide. For her craft project, she cut it by 2 inches along its length and width. What is the percent decrease in the area of the board? — **27.8%**

In 2019, Arizona increased the state minimum wage from $10.50 to $11. Florida increased its minimum wage from $8.25 to $8.46 and South Dakota from $8.85 to $9.10. Which state had the largest percent increase in minimum wage? — **Arizona**

Lesson 101 – Percent of Change

When they divide to find the percent change, they should check to make sure the answer makes sense. If the percent is 100%, that means double. If percent is 50%, that means half.

When they are doing word problems, they should also make sure their answer makes sense, that they are answering the final question being asked.

Review 101 – Adding Fractions

They will need to find common denominators before adding. They should first see if the smaller number divides evenly into the larger number. If not, they should double the larger number and check that before moving on. They will always need to check to see if the answer can be simplified.

Answers   8/9   9/10   2/3

Lesson 102

Lesson 102 – Commission, Tip, Sales Tax, and Discount

There are several definitions or things they should have a general idea of their meaning. They are all figured by multiplying by a percent.

There are a few word problems on the page. If they are figuring a discount, they need to find the discount and then subtract that off the total cost. They need to see it through like that if necessary in order to find the final answer.

Review 102 – Subtracting Fractions

Subtract fractions by first finding common denominators. Then reduce the answer if possible.

Answers   7/15   1/14   1/60

Lesson 103

DAY 103 Commission, Tip, Sales Tax, and Discount

A. Explain how to calculate the total bill with a 15% tip on top of $36. Review Day 102 if needed.

Total bill = 36 + 36 * 0.15 = 36 + 5.40 = 41.40

B. Complete each table.

Sales amount	Commission rate	Commission
$810	9%	$72.90
$4,150	8.5%	$352.75
$17,900	6%	$1,074
$41,200	7.25%	$2,987

Purchase price	Sales tax rate	Sales tax	Total cost
$90	5.5%	$4.95	$94.95
$46.5	6%	$2.79	$49.29
$720	10%	$72	$792
$1,300	11%	$143	$1,443

C. Solve each problem.

Lillian bought a computer game at 15% off the regular price of $46. How much did she pay for the game? — $39.10

The dinner bill was $38.20, and Camila left a 20% tip. How much did Camila pay for the dinner? — $45.84

A jacket priced at $76 has a sales tax of $3.80. What is the sales tax rate? Express your answer as a percent. — 5%

A jewelry store pays 18% commission on all sales. How much commission does an employee earn on the sale of a $700 necklace? — $126

A $70 jacket is marked down by 10%. Justin has a 20% coupon off the sale price. How much can he get the jacket for? — $50.40

Sarah found that two stores price the same shirt differently. Store P sells it at $19.99. Store Q lists it for $24.99 but has it on sale at 25% off. Which store offers the lower price? — Store Q

DAY 103 Practice

A. Complete each table.

Sales amount	Commission rate	Commission
$6,500	4.25%	$276.25
$32,250	8%	$2,580
$51,000	9.5%	$4,845

Bill amount	Tip rate	Tip	Total bill
$60	15%	$9	$69
$45	16%	$7.20	$52.20
$92.50	20%	$18.50	$111

Regular price	Discount rate	Discount	Sale price
$40	15%	$6	$34
$70	25%	$17.50	$52.5
$80.90	30%	$24.27	$56.63

B. Solve each problem.

Henry spent $180 at a department store. If the sales tax is 7%, what was his final bill? — $192.60

A real estate agent made a $13,200 commission on the sale of a $220,000 house. What was her commission rate in percent? — 6%

The regular price of a skateboard is $120, but it is now on sale at a 28% discount. What is the sale price? — $86.40

A group of five friends went out for dinner. The bill was $110 plus a 15% tip. If they split the bill evenly, how much will each pay? — $25.30

Aiden bought a pair of sneakers for 25% off the regular price of $62. The sales tax was 8%. How much did he pay in total? — $50.22

A furniture store is offing a one day sale of 20% off. James bought a desk originally priced at $460. The sales tax in his city is 6%. What was the final price of the desk, including tax? — $390.08

Lesson 103 – Commission, Tip, Sales Tax, and Discount

They should have a general idea of the meaning of several definitions or terms. These are the same activities as Lesson 102. They can turn back to Lesson 102 to look for examples and definitions if needed.

Make sure their word problems are answered with labeled answers.

Review 103 – Word Problems

They are going to be doing word problems with fractions. They can use simpler numbers to figure out what to do in order to answer the question, and then put the fractions back in.

Answers   1/2 of the carton, 1/10 of the room, 1/4 cup of flour

Lesson 104

DAY 104 Simple Interest

A. Interest is another everyday use of percent. **Interest** is a fee paid for the use of someone else's money. Banks pay customers interests on their deposits, and lenders pay banks interests on their loans. **Principal** is the initial amount deposited or borrowed. **Rate of interest** or **interest rate** is the percent earned or charged. **Simple interest** is a fixed percent of the principal. The formula for simple interest is $I = Prt$ where I is the interest, P is the principal, r is the annual interest rate in decimal form, and t is the time in years. Let's see an example. Suppose you deposit $400 into an account that earns 5% annual simple interest. What will be the final balance of the account after 18 months? Try to work out on your own before checking the solution on the right. Note that all time units must be in years.

First, find the interest:
$P = 400$
$r = 0.05$ per year
$t = 1.5$ years
$I = Prt = 30$

Then, add to the principal:
$400 + 30 = 430$

B. Complete each table.

Principal	Annual simple interest rate	Period (years)	Interest	Total amount
$120	6%	4	$28.80	$148.80
$280	5%	2.5	$35	$315
$165	7%	1	$11.55	$176.55
$1,210	4%	5	$242	$1452
$3,200	3.5%	7	$784	$3984
$830	9%	3	$224.10	$1054.10
$300	6%	6	$108	$408
$1,365	8.2%	2	$223.86	$1588.86

C. Solve each problem.

Alexa put $5,000 in her savings account at a simple interest rate of 3% per year. How much interest will Alexa earn in five years? — **$750**

Greg deposited $500 in his savings account for 24 months. His current balance is $524. What was the annual simple interest rate? — **4%**

Charlotte deposits $8,000 in her savings account that earns 6% simple interest per year. About how long will it take for her account balance to reach $10,000? — **About 4.2 years**

DAY 104 Practice

A. Complete each table.

Principal	Annual simple interest rate	Period (years)	Interest	Total amount
$520	2%	5	$52	$572
$1,410	1%	3	$42.30	$1452.30
$830	3%	1	$24.90	$854.90
$400	6%	2.5	$60	$460
$612	2.25%	4	$55.08	$667.08
$524	2%	2	$20.96	$544.96
$1,690	4.5%	5	$380.25	$2070.25
$3,000	7%	3	$630	$3630
$2,620	2%	1	$52.40	$2672.40
$700	5.5%	4	$154	$854

B. Solve each problem.

Joshua borrowed $8,000 from a bank at an annual simple interest rate of 9%. How much interest will he pay each year? — **$720**

Amy purchased a Certificate of Deposit for $2,000. It pays an annual interest rate of 6%. How much interest will she earn in 3 years? — **$360**

Ella borrowed $2,500 from her parents and paid them back $2,650 in 6 months. What was the annual simple interest rate? — **12%**

Mike invested $1,200 at a simple interest rate of 6% per year. Now his balance is $1,560. For how long did he invest his money? — **5 years**

Sam borrowed $18,000 at an annual simple interest rate of 8.5% to buy a new car. He paid the entire loan off at the end of the fourth year. What was the total amount that he paid for the car? — **$24,120**

Ron borrowed $6,000 at an annual simple interest rate of 7% for 8 years. Mason borrowed the same amount at an annual simple interest rate of 6% for 10 years. Who paid more interest in total? — **Mason**

Lesson 104 – Simple Interest

Interest rates is just another form of what we've been practicing. It's how numbers relate to each other in a predictible way. There are definitions at the top of the page. It would be good to have your child tell you about each one. If they can explain them, they understand them.

They need to multiply the numbers given to find the interest amount they earned. Here's a good lesson for saving.

If they get any word problems wrong, make sure they get the concepts behind them.

Review 104 – Adding Mixed Numbers

Add the mixed numbers. They will need to find a common denominator. They can use improper fractions, but they can also just break apart the place values and add the ones and then add the fractions and then put them back together.

Answers   3 11/12   7 24/35   4 17/30

Lesson 105

DAY 105 Simple Interest

A. Explain how to use the simple interest formula $I = Prt$ to calculate the interest on $650 at 8% annual simple interest for 3 years. Review Day 104 if needed.

$$I = Prt = \$650 \times 0.08 \times 3 = \$156$$

B. Complete each table.

Principal	Annual simple interest rate	Period (years)	Interest	Total amount
$500	2%	2	$20	$520
$483	1%	5	$24.15	$507.15
$1,500	5.25%	1	$78.75	$1578.75
$236	3%	3	$21.24	$257.24
$700	2%	3.5	$49	$749
$2,115	6%	4	$507.60	$2622.60
$449	4%	6	$107.76	$556.76
$500	8%	1.5	$60	$560
$3,000	1%	3	$90	$3090
$1,860	7%	5	$651	$2511

C. Solve each problem.

A bank is offering 5.5% simple interest on a savings account. If Violet deposits $800, how much interest will she earn in 4 years? $176

Ryan borrowed $800 from a bank and paid back $840 after one year. At what simple interest rate did Ryan borrow the money? 5%

Camila deposited $10,000 in her savings account, which pays 2% simple interest for the first two years and 4% simple interest from the third year on. How much interest will Camila earn in five years? $1,600

Ella invested $1,200 at an annual simple interest rate of 8% for five years. Carter invested $1,500 at an annual simple interest rate of 5% for six years. Who earned more interest? Ella

---

DAY 105 Practice

A. Complete each table.

Principal	Annual simple interest rate	Period (years)	Interest	Total amount
$824	1%	2	$16.48	$840.48
$1,316	4%	5	$263.20	$1579.20
$500	1.25%	3	$18.75	$518.75
$710	3%	2	$42.60	$752.60
$650	2%	1	$13	$663
$4,215	1%	4	$168.60	$4383.60
$900	4%	2	$72	$972
$1,677	6%	3	$301.86	$1978.86
$2,900	2.8%	1	$81.20	$2981.20
$440	7%	3	$92.40	$532.40

B. Solve each problem.

Ethan borrowed $2,000 from a bank at an annual simple interest rate of 8%. How much interest will he pay each year? $160

Adam deposited $3,000 in his savings account for 1 year. His current balance is $3,180. What was the annual simple interest rate? 6%

Isaac invested $4,000 at a simple interest rate of 4% per year. He earned $480 in interest. For how long did he invest his money? 3 years

Jack put $1,500 in his savings account at a simple interest rate of 6% per year. How much interest will he earn in 18 months? $135

Hunter borrowed $12,000 from a bank at an annual simple interest rate of 7.5%. He paid the entire loan off at the end of the fifth year. What was the total amount that he paid the bank? $16,500

Kyle invested $1,800 at a simple interest rate of 5% per year. Jack invested the same amount at a simple interest rate of 6.5% per year. How much more interest will Jack earn than Kyle after four years? $108

Lesson 105 – Simple Interest

This has the same types of activities as Lesson 104.

Review 105 – Subtracting Mixed Numbers

This is the same as Lesson 104 but with subtracting. The same thing applies.

Answers   2 1/8   3 1/2   3/14

Lesson 106

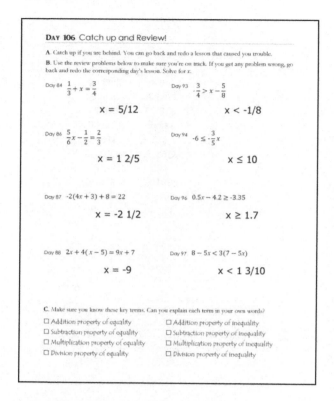

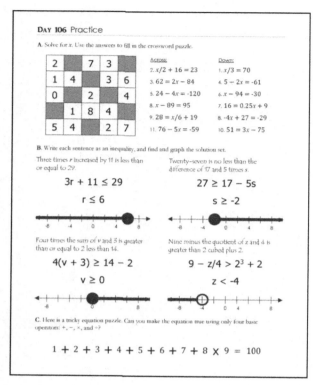

Lesson 106 Catch Up and Review

Have your child check themselves using the lesson page and go back to work on problem areas. See if your child can explain the terms on the page. If they are doing well, have them use the practice page today to stay sharp.

No Review

Lesson 107

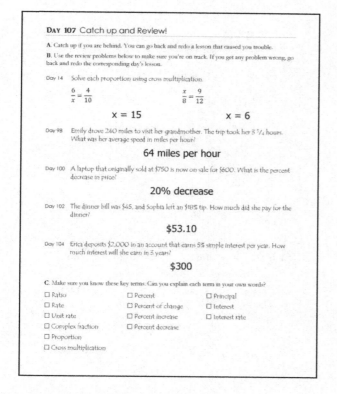

DAY 107 Catch up and Review!

A. Catch up if you are behind. You can go back and redo a lesson that caused you trouble.

B. Use the review problems below to make sure you're on track. If you get any problem wrong, go back and redo the corresponding day's lesson.

Day 14 Solve each proportion using cross multiplication.

$\frac{6}{x} = \frac{4}{10}$ $\frac{x}{8} = \frac{9}{12}$

x = 15   x = 6

Day 98 Emily drove 240 miles to visit her grandmother. The trip took her 3 3/4 hours. What was her average speed in miles per hour?

64 miles per hour

Day 100 A laptop that originally sold at $750 is now on sale for $600. What is the percent decrease in price?

20% decrease

Day 102 The dinner bill was $45, and Sophia left an 18% tip. How much did she pay for the dinner?

$53.10

Day 104 Erica deposits $2,000 in an account that earns 5% simple interest per year. How much interest will she earn in 3 years?

$300

C. Make sure you know these key terms. Can you explain each term in your own words?

☐ Ratio   ☐ Percent   ☐ Principal
☐ Rate   ☐ Percent of change   ☐ Interest
☐ Unit rate   ☐ Percent increase   ☐ Interest rate
☐ Complex fraction   ☐ Percent decrease
☐ Proportion
☐ Cross multiplication

DAY 107 Practice

A. Solve each proportion using cross multiplication. Simplify fractions.

$\frac{x}{8} = \frac{4}{6}$ x = 5 1/3 $\frac{x}{20} = \frac{18}{30}$ x = 12

$\frac{3}{4} = \frac{9}{x}$ x = 12 $\frac{10}{x} = \frac{25}{12}$ x = 4 4/5

$\frac{2}{9} = \frac{x}{12}$ x = 2 2/3 $\frac{28}{35} = \frac{11}{x}$ x = 13 3/4

$\frac{6}{x} = \frac{15}{8}$ x = 3 1/5 $\frac{x}{12} = \frac{40}{15}$ x = 32

B. Find a unit rate that represents each situation.

1,980 words on 9 pages $34.95 for 5 pounds of beef

220 words/page   ### $6.99/pound

$90 for 4 1/2 hours of work   77 miles on 2 3/4 gallons of gas

$20/hour   ### 28 miles/gallon

C. Find the mystery numbers.

Start with the constant of variation in 2y = 10x. Subtract the denominator of a unit rate. Increase the result by 25%. What number do you have?   5

Start with the fraction form of 48:32. Convert to a decimal. Round to the nearest whole number. Multiply by the number of meters in one kilometer. Take 1% of the result. What number do you have?   20

Start with the ratio of the number of quarters to pennies in three dollars. Simplify the ratio and take 140% of the second number. Add the amount of discount when a $360 TV is sold at 15% off. What number do you have?   89

Lesson 107 Catch Up and Review

Have your child check themselves using the lesson page and go back to work on problem areas. See if your child can explain the terms on the page. If they are doing well, have them use the practice page today to stay sharp.

No Review

Lesson 108

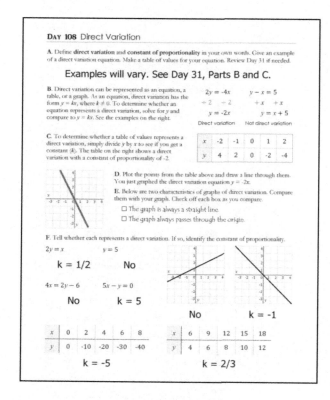

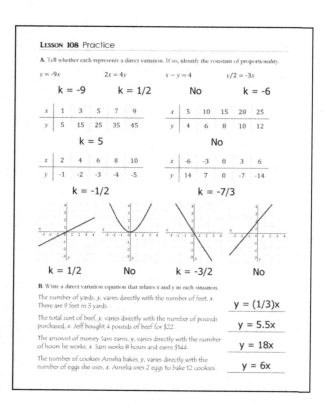

Lesson 108 – Direct Variation

Direct variation makes a graph of a straight line that goes through the center, the point (0,0). It looks like variable = constant times variable. Otherwise, it isn't direct variation. It may not look like that at first, but it might after the equation is simplified.

The first thing they should do it get it into the form y = …

Review 108 – Adding Mixed Numbers

The difference today is that the fractions will add to greater than 1. This is like carrying. Here's an example. $2\frac{3}{4} + 1\frac{1}{2} = 3 + 1\frac{1}{4} = 4\frac{1}{4}$

Answers   9 1/12   6 1/3   5 7/24

Lesson 109

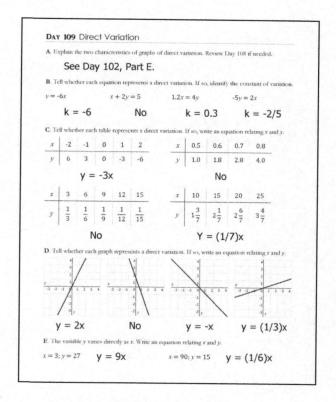

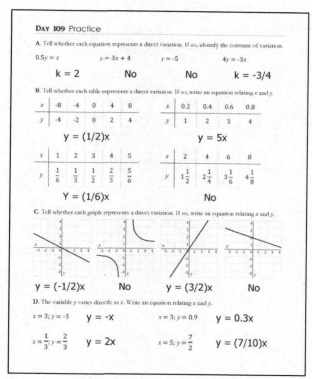

Lesson 109 – Direct Variation

For part B, they need to rewrite the equation so that it starts with y =…. Then it will show them if it is direct variation.

For part C, they will divide. Does Y divided by X equal the same thing in each instance? If it does, then it is an example of direct variation.

For part D, if the graph is a straight line and goes through the center at point (0,0), then it is direct variation.

For part E, they should divide Y by X to see what the constant is they need to use to multiply.

Review 109 – Subtracting Mixed Numbers

They are subtracting mixed numbers with common denominators, however, they will have to "borrow." Here are two ways to do it.

$3 \frac{1}{4} - 1 \frac{3}{4} = 3 - 1 = 2$ and $\frac{1}{4} - \frac{3}{4} = -\frac{2}{4} = -\frac{1}{2}$ $2 - \frac{1}{2} = 1 \frac{1}{2}$

$= \frac{13}{4} - \frac{7}{4} = \frac{6}{4} = 1\frac{2}{4} = 1 \frac{1}{2}$

Answers   4 2/3   2 2/3   3/5

Lesson 110

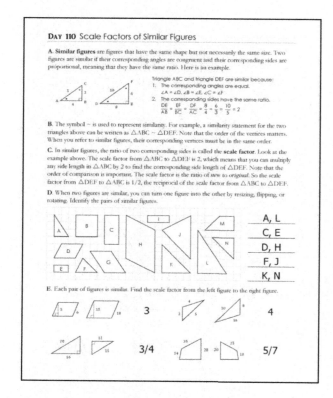

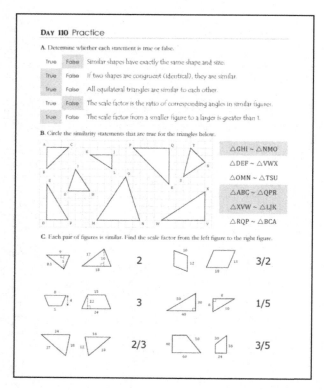

Lesson 110 – Scale Factors of Similar Figures

A scale factor is another kind of rate, a proportion, a ratio. These are all related concepts.

A similar figure is one that is the same shape, just a different size. If you could perfectly shrink or grow the one, it would be identical to the other.

All of the letters and symbols are just ways of identifying things. ∠A is angle A. DE is the side of the shape that goes from point D to point E.

If triangle ABC is similar to triangle DEF, let's say DEF is twice as big, then we could double the length of side AB to get the length of DE. And you'd double the length of BC to get the length of EF. The order of the letters matter otherwise your triangle won't come up looking right! We'd say that the scale factor of ABC to DEF is 2 since each DEF measurement is double that of ABC. The official ratio would be 2 to 1, 2/1.

Review 110 – Subtracting Mixed Numbers

They will be subtracting mixed numbers today. This time they don't get to start with common denominators, so there is an extra step.

Answers   1 5/6   11/14   1 17/20

Lesson 111

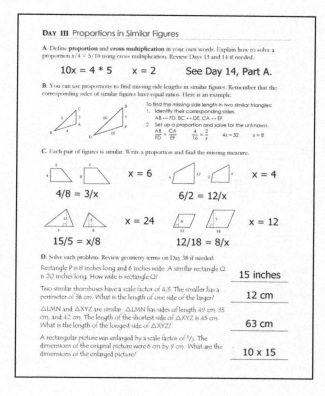

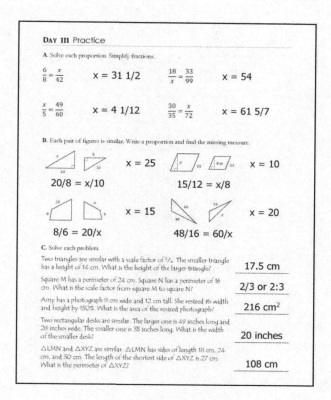

Lesson 111 – Proportions in Similar Figures

They will be setting up proportions and solving by cross multiplication. Multiply the opposite denominators and numerators together and then solve.

$$\frac{9}{x} \text{ as } \frac{3}{4} \quad 9 * 4 = 3x \quad 36 \div 3 = x \quad 12 = x$$

$$\frac{y}{20} \text{ as } \frac{3}{4} \quad 4y = 3 \times 20 \quad y = 60 \div 4 \quad y = 15$$

Review 111 – Word Problems

They will be answering questions that require them to use mixed numbers.

Answers   6 1/4 miles, 3 1/2 feet, 15 3/10 pounds

Lesson 112

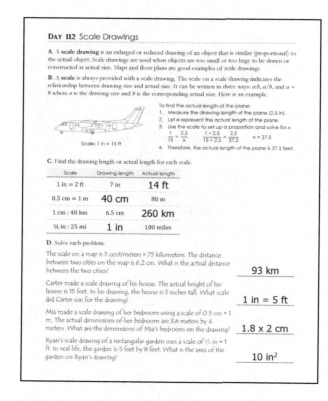

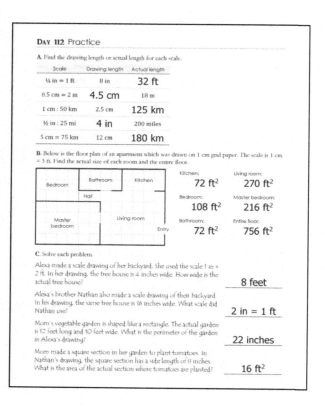

Lesson 112 – Scale Drawings

This is the same concept they've done a lot on recently: scale, proportion, rates, and such.

They can look at the Similar Figures pages for a reminder. The important thing to compare the same things.

    Drawing length to Actual length = Drawing width to Acual width
        BUT NOT
    Drawing length to Actual length = Actual width to Drawing width

$$\frac{D}{A} = \frac{D}{A}$$

Here's the first word problem.

$5/75 = 6.2/?$ Cross multiply $5? = 6.2 \times 75$ $5? = 465$ $? = 93$ kilometers

Review 112 – Multiplying Fractions and Whole Numbers

To multiply fractions and whole numbers, consider the whole numbers as a fraction over one. Multiply the numerators together and multiply the denominators together. They will need to simplify their answers, which means making sure there isn't an improper fraction.

Answers   1 1/2   2 4/5   5 1/3

Lesson 113 (ruler)

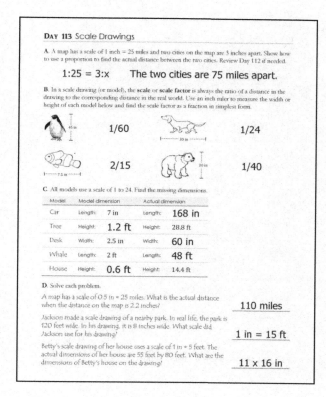

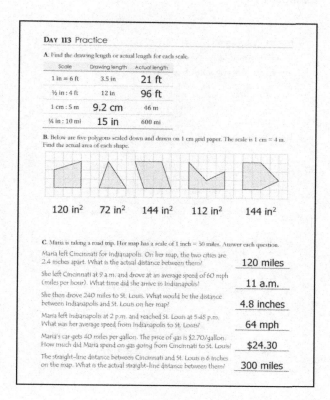

Lesson 113 – Scale Drawings

They will be doing the same type of exercises as in Lesson 112. They will set up proportions using the scale given. In part B they are finding the scale, the ratio, the fraction of the one measurement over the other.

The first image is ¾ of an inch. ¾ is to 45 inches as 1 is to ? in. Using cross multiplying, you'd end up with ¾ x ? = 45 x 1 which is 45 x 4/3.

Review 113 – Multiplying Fractions

Multiply numerators and denominators. Reduce the fractions and simplify the answers.

Answers   2/5   1/3   3/5

Lesson 114

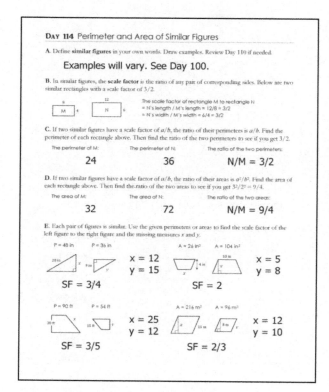

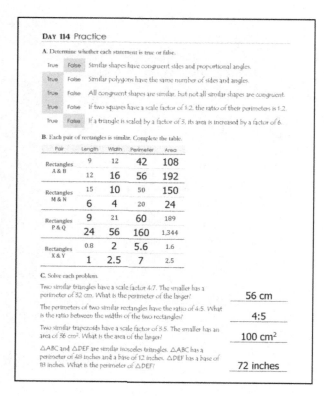

Lesson 114 – Perimeter and Area of Similar Figures

When they are reading explanations such as "have a scale factor of a/b, the ratio of their perimeters is a/b" and their eyes glaze over and they proclaim that they have no idea what it's talking about, have them substitute in numbers. If the one has sides ½ of the other, then its perimeter is going to be ½. Just talking it through with an example can make it clear and make "a/b" understandable.

The rest is the same idea of comparing the known sides to the unknown to find what's missing. Cross multiplying is a useful tool that will be used for years throughout algebra and geometry, so encourage them to use it.

Review 114 – Multiplying with Mixed Numbers

This is *different* than adding mixed numbers. While you can separate the place values, you have to make sure to multiply all the parts. You can't just multiply the whole numbers together.

1 ½ x 5 is NOT 1 x 5 + ½. It's 1 x 5 and ½ x 5.

Answers   9 1/2   9 5/7   26 2/3

Lesson 115

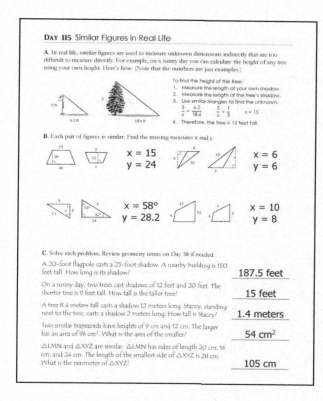

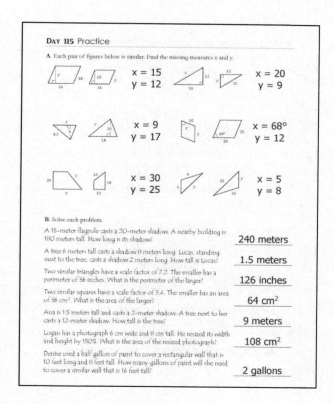

Lesson 115 – Similar Figures in Real Life

Bonus points for trying to figure out the height of a tree!

It may be helpful to your child to redraw the similar figures so that they are pointing in the same direction. I know in my mind it's really hard for me to visualize how they rotate and match up. They need to make sure they are comparing the same sides on each figure, not just both tops and both bottoms, but the sides that line up as similar figures. The first shape, for instance, is a trapezoid. The top of the one corresponds to the bottom of the other.

Drawing pictures might also help for the word problems!

Review 115 – Word Problems

The word "of" is a cue to multiply. They will be multiplying whole numbers and fractions. Make sure they are answering the questions, not just solving a math problem. Their answers should be labeled.

Answers   Lisa, 2/15 of the pets, 5 problems

Lesson 116

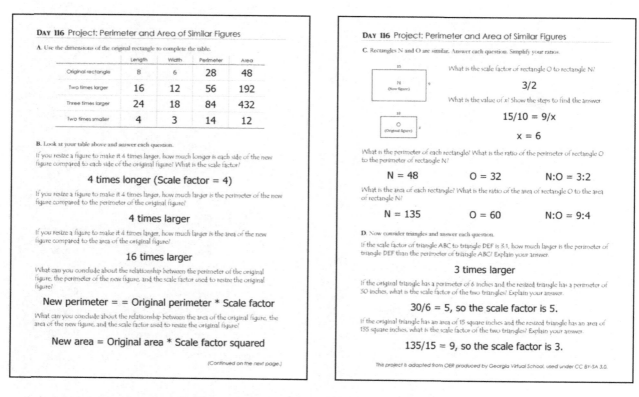

DAY 116 Project: Perimeter and Area of Similar Figures

A. Use the dimensions of the original rectangle to complete the table.

	Length	Width	Perimeter	Area
Original rectangle	8	6	28	48
Two times larger	16	12	56	192
Three times larger	24	18	84	432
Two times smaller	4	3	14	12

B. Look at your table above and answer each question.

If you resize a figure to make it 4 times larger, how much longer is each side of the new figure compared to each side of the original figure? What is the scale factor?

4 times longer (Scale factor = 4)

If you resize a figure to make it 4 times larger, how much larger is the perimeter of the new figure compared to the perimeter of the original figure?

4 times larger

If you resize a figure to make it 4 times larger, how much larger is the area of the new figure compared to the area of the original figure?

16 times larger

What can you conclude about the relationship between the perimeter of the original figure, the perimeter of the new figure, and the scale factor used to resize the original figure?

New perimeter = = Original perimeter * Scale factor

What can you conclude about the relationship between the area of the original figure, the area of the new figure, and the scale factor used to resize the original figure?

New area = Original area * Scale factor squared

(Continued on the next page.)

DAY 116 Project: Perimeter and Area of Similar Figures

C. Rectangles N and O are similar. Answer each question. Simplify your ratios.

What is the scale factor of rectangle O to rectangle N?

3/2

What is the value of x? Show the steps to find the answer

15/10 = 9/x

x = 6

What is the perimeter of each rectangle? What is the ratio of the perimeter of rectangle O to the perimeter of rectangle N?

N = 48   **O = 32**   **N:O = 3:2**

What is the area of each rectangle? What is the ratio of the area of rectangle O to the area of rectangle N?

N = 135   **O = 60**   **N:O = 9:4**

D. Now consider triangles and answer each question.

If the scale factor of triangle ABC to triangle DEF is 3:1, how much larger is the perimeter of triangle DEF than the perimeter of triangle ABC? Explain your answer.

3 times larger

If the original triangle has a perimeter of 6 inches and the resized triangle has a perimeter of 30 inches, what is the scale factor of the two triangles? Explain your answer.

30/6 = 5, so the scale factor is 5.

If the original triangle has an area of 15 square inches and the resized triangle has an area of 135 square inches, what is the scale factor of the two triangles? Explain your answer.

135/15 = 9, so the scale factor is 3.

This project is adapted from OER produced by Georgia Virtual School, used under CC BY-SA 3.0.

Lesson 116 – Project: Perimeter and Area of Similar Figures

They will calculate the perimter and area and then use scale to finish the chart and answer the questions.

There is a second page! Make sure they turn the page and continue.

No Review

Lesson 117

DAY 117 Review: Proportional Relationships

A. Describe the relationships between scale factor, perimeter, and area in similar figures. Give examples. Review Day 114 if needed.

Examples will vary. See Day 114, Parts C and D.

B. Use proportions to solve each problem. Review Days 100, 112, and 115 if needed.

Erica drove 125 miles in two and a half hours. What was Erica's speed in miles per hour?	50 mph
Kim is 4.5 feet tall and casts a shadow 6 feet long. A nearby flagpole casts a shadow 24 feet long. How tall is the flagpole?	18 feet
Twelve inches equals 30.48 centimeters. How many centimeters are there in 20 inches?	50.8 cm
One U.S. dollar is the same as 0.85 euros. How many U.S. dollars will you get in exchange for 17 euros?	$20
The property tax in Emily's city is $30 per $1,000 of property value. How much property tax would the owner of a $150,000 house pay?	$4,500
Henry can run 6 miles per hour. If he runs 1 ½ hours each day, how many days will it take him to run 100 miles?	12 days
A 12-foot flagpole casts an 18-foot shadow. A nearby building is 30 feet tall. How long is its shadow?	45 feet
A book club has 35 members, and the ratio of boys to girls is 3:4. How many boys are in the book club?	15 boys
The scale on a map is 5 cm = 75 km. Two cities on the map are 6.2 cm apart. What is the actual distance between the two cities?	93 km
Cammy bought a hat at $16.80. The price was 40% off its regular price. What was the original price?	$28
At a free throw contest, Aiden and Jacob tried 25 shots each. Aiden made 21 and Jacob made 88%. Who made more shots?	Jacob
Sound travels through air at 1,100 feet per second. How many miles does it travel in one hour? (1 mile = 5,280 feet)	750 miles
On average, seawater has a salinity of about 3.5% or 35 g/L. That is, every liter of seawater has approximately 35 grams of salt dissolved in it. How many grams of salt are in 2.8 liters of seawater?	98 grams

---

DAY 117 Practice

A. Determine whether each statement is true or false.

True	False	A unit rate is a rate whose second number equals 1.
True	False	Two ratios form a proportion if their cross products are equal.
True	False	Similar shapes have congruent angles and proportional sides.
True	**False**	Two parallelograms are similar if their angles are proportional.
True	False	The perimeter of a square is doubled if its side length is doubled.

B. Use proportions to solve each problem.

A tree 10 feet tall casts a 6-foot shadow. A statue next to the tree is 8 feet tall. How long is the statue's shadow?	4.8 feet
A book club has 16 members, and 62.5% of them are boys. How many girls are in the club?	6 girls
A map has a scale of 0.5 in = 30 miles. What is the actual distance when the distance on the map is 2.6 inches?	156 miles
Each week Ryan saves 25% of his weekly allowance. For 6 weeks, he has saved $39. What's his weekly allowance?	$26
An object which weighs 100 pounds on Earth would weigh about 38 pounds on Mars. If an object weighs 250 pounds on Earth, how much would it weigh on Mars?	95 pounds

C. Here are some tricky proportion problems. See if you can solve them!

A zoo has 100 mammals. The ratio of mammals to reptiles is 5:4. How many reptiles does the zoo have?	80 reptiles
If the zoo brings in 10 more reptiles, the ratio of reptiles to birds will become 3:4. How many birds are in the zoo?	120 birds
If the zoo brings in 20 more mammals, how many more birds does it need to keep the ratio of mammals to birds the same?	24 birds
On average 1,200 people visit the zoo each day. The ratio of adults to children is 7 to 5. How many children visit the zoo each day?	500 children
The average ratio of first-time visitors to repeat visitors is 1:3. How many first-time visitors does the zoo have each day?	300 visitors

Lesson 117 – Review: Proportional Relationships

This is practice with everything they've been doing with scale. Give them paper to draw and work. Drawings help!

No Review

Lesson 118

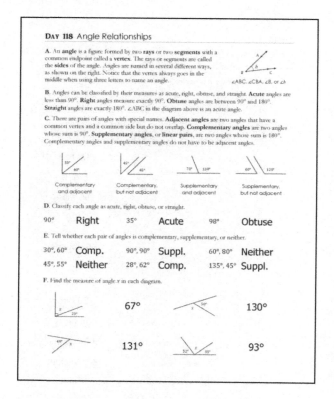

DAY 118 Angle Relationships

A. An **angle** is a figure formed by two **rays** or two **segments** with a common endpoint called a **vertex**. The rays or segments are called the **sides** of the angle. Angles are named in several different ways, as shown on the right. Notice that the vertex always goes in the middle when using three letters to name an angle.

∠ABC, ∠CBA, ∠B, or ∠b

B. Angles can be classified by their measures as acute, right, obtuse, and straight. **Acute** angles are less than 90°. **Right** angles measure exactly 90°. **Obtuse** angles are between 90° and 180°. **Straight** angles are exactly 180°. ∠ABC in the diagram above is an acute angle.

C. There are pairs of angles with special names. **Adjacent angles** are two angles that have a common vertex and a common side but do not overlap. **Complementary angles** are two angles whose sum is 90°. **Supplementary angles**, or **linear pairs**, are two angles whose sum is 180°. Complementary angles and supplementary angles do not have to be adjacent angles.

Complementary and adjacent | Complementary, but not adjacent | Supplementary and adjacent | Supplementary, but not adjacent

D. Classify each angle as acute, right, obtuse, or straight.

90° **Right**   35° **Acute**   98° **Obtuse**

E. Tell whether each pair of angles is complementary, supplementary, or neither.

30°, 60° **Comp.**   90°, 90° **Suppl.**   60°, 80° **Neither**

45°, 55° **Neither**   28°, 62° **Comp.**   135°, 45° **Suppl.**

F. Find the measure of angle x in each diagram.

67°   **130°**

131°   **93°**

DAY 118 Practice

A. Classify each angle as acute, right, obtuse, or straight.

96° **Obtuse**   55° **Acute**   28° **Acute**

14° **Acute**   105° **Obtuse**   180° **Straight**

B. Find the measure of the complementary angle for each angle.

45° **45°**   30° **60°**   42° **48°**

20° **70°**   84° **6°**   59° **31°**

C. Find the measure of the supplementary angle for each angle.

25° **155°**   100° **80°**   60° **120°**

90° **90°**   57° **123°**   135° **45°**

D. Look at the diagram and identify all statements that are true.

☐ ∠AOC and ∠COD are adjacent angles.
☑ ∠AOB and ∠AOD are right and supplementary angles.
☑ ∠BOC and ∠COD are adjacent and supplementary angles.
☐ ∠AOC and ∠BOC are adjacent and complementary angles.

E. Find the measure of angle x in each diagram.

60°   **35°**

44°   **73°**

74°   **31°**

Lesson 118 – Angle Relationships

There is again a bunch of vocabulary. Use the vocabulary. It will turn it into your language instead of a foreign language.

A right angle is 90 degrees and is marked with a little square.

An acute angle is less than 90° and an obtuse angle is more.

Angles that "complement" each other add up to 90 degrees (a perpendicular line).

Angles that "supplement" each other add up to 180 degrees (a straight line).

Angles that are adjacent, touch each other. Where the one stops, the other starts.

To find the measures at the bottom of the page, they can think of them like equations.

For instance: x + 23 = 90

Review 118 – Dividing Fractions by Whole Numbers

½ ÷ 4 = ½ x ¼ To divide, they multiply by the reciprocal.

Answers   1/20   1/14   1/18

Lesson 119

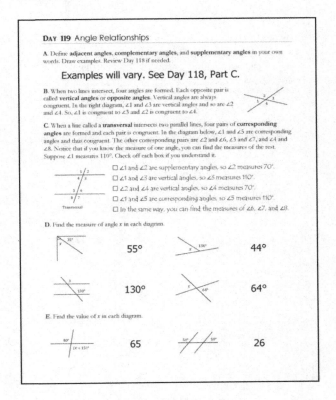

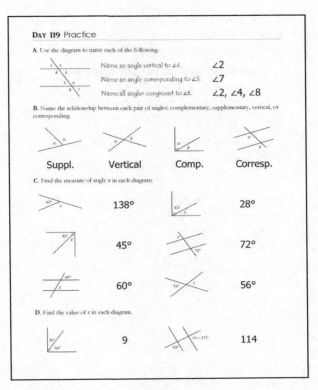

Lesson 119 – Angle Relationships

More vocabulary! Opposite and vertical angles are the same thing. Congruent means the same. In the picture, the angles at 2 and 4 are the same; they are congruent. Same with 1 and 3.

A transversal is just a line drawn through other lines.

Corresponding angles are like the same angles in similar figures. They are going to be the same. They are congruent. You can look in the book to see how the picture made with angles 1, 2, 3, 4 is the same as 5, 6, 7, 8.

Review 119 – Dividing Whole Numbers by Fractions

They will multiply by the reciprocal. This makes it easier!

$4 \div \frac{1}{2} = 4 \times 2$

Answers   21   45   16

Lesson 120

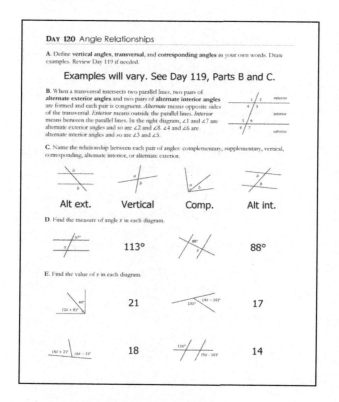

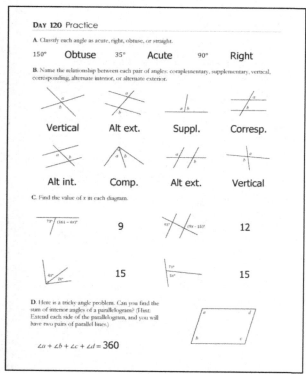

Lesson 120 – Angle Relationships

There is more defining going on. I would recommend having them color in between the parallel lines in Part B to show the difference between interior and exterior. They would be coloring over numbers 3-6.

Review 120 – Dividing Fractions

To divide the fractions, they need to multiply by the reciprocals.

Answers   1 1/9   2 2/3   1 1/7

Lesson 121 (ruler, protractor)

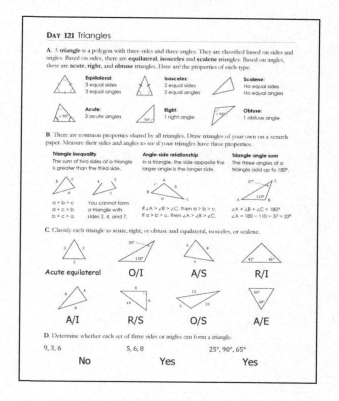

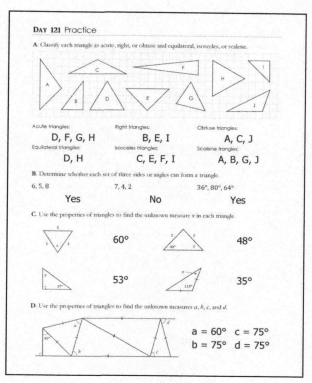

Lesson 121 Lesson – Triangles

The top of the page defines the different types of triangles. The little dashes mean those sides are equal. The identical angle markings mean those angles are equal. The acute triangle, where all angles are less than 90 degrees, has three different angle markings. That's show all of the angles are different, or at least could be different.

Part B is asking them to investigate a little on their own. They should see that these triangle properties are always true. Angle-side relationship is easy to see. Place your palms together. Keep your wrists together and start opening your hands like a V. The greater the angle you open your hands, the greater the distance between the fingers on your two hands.

Review 121 – Reciprocal of Mixed Numbers

They need to convert the mixed numbers into improper fractions. They will multiply the denominator by the whole number and then add the numerator. That becomes the new denominator in the reciprocal. The current denominator becomes the numerator in the reciprocal.

Answers   2/7   5/22   6/17

Lesson 122

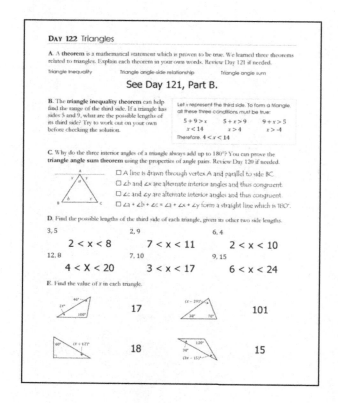

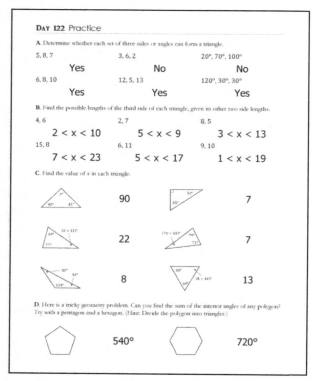

Lesson 122 – Triangles

A theorem is something that is proved true. Theory is supposed to be truth, not just an idea. A mathematical theorem has never, ever been later shown to be false, as some of our science truths have.

Part C is a proof. In geometry they will be doing these often. This proof is done for them. Have them explain it to you. The proof starts with the understanding that a line is 180 degrees. Since the angles that make up the line are the same as (congruent to) those that make up the triangle, then the triangle's angles must equal 180 degrees.

Review 122 – Dividing Mixed Numbers

They should turn the mixed numbers into improper fractions and then multiply by the reciprocal. They should definitely look for ways to reduce before they multiply.

Answers   12   5 1/4   4/9

Lesson 123

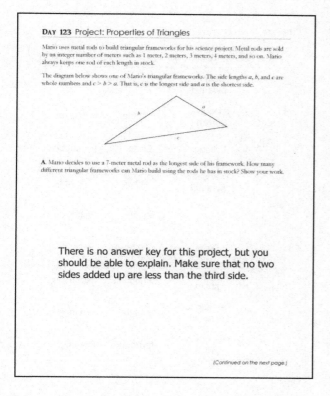

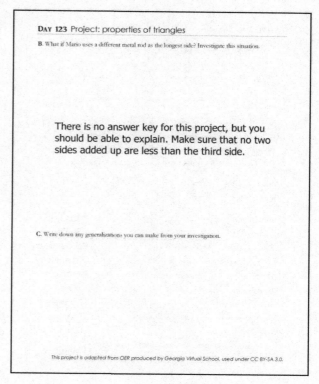

Lesson 123 – Project: Properties of Triangles

They are thinking today! They need to use the triangle property about side length to figure out how long the other sides could be. Basically, any two sides added together must equal more than the third side.

No Review 123

Lesson 124

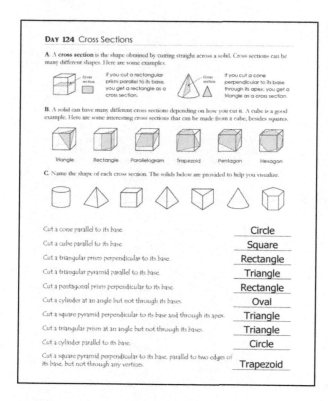

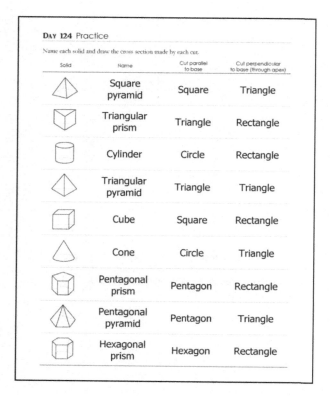

Lesson 124 – Cross Sections

This lesson involves visualizing. For me personally, I struggle visualizing in my head. Sketching out the shapes is helpful to me. They can use the pictures to draw in the cross section as best they can. They should take the time to work down the page and make sure they can picture the cross sections already drawn in the examples.

Review 124 – Word Problems

These are word problems using dividing mixed numbers. If they are confused on how to begin, they should use whole numbers to think through how to approach the question. They also need to make sure they are answering what is being asked and labeling their answers.

Answers   30 pieces, 1 5/8 gallons, 4 1/2 miles

Lesson 125

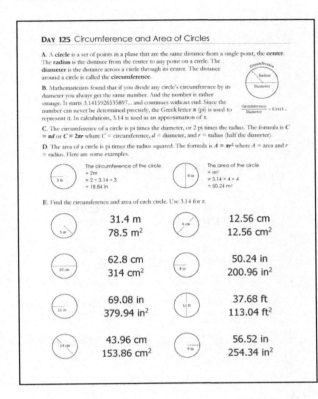

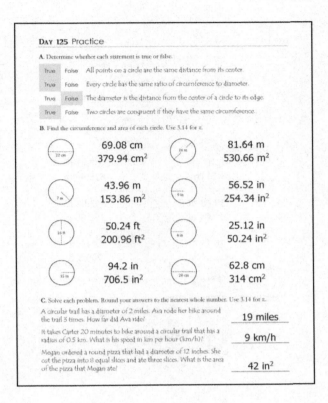

Lesson 125 – Circumference and Area of Circles

Circumference is the perimeter of a circle. The measure across the circle through the center is the diameter and half of that is the radius.

There are forumlas that they should understand and be comfortable with. Ask them to read the formulas to you in English.

Getting comfortable plugging numbers into formulas will be important.

This lesson introduces pi. Pi is a ratio. It's the ratio of the circumference to the diameter. It is the same ratio for every single circle ever. It's an infinite decimal. We use 3.14 as an approximate value of pi.

Review 125 – Word Problems

These word problems use mixed numbers and fractions and multiplication. They can use simpler numbers and draw pictures and all that to help them figure out how to approach them. The word "of" is the cue for multiplying.

Answers   5/14 of the money, 9/10 cup, 55 miles

Lesson 126

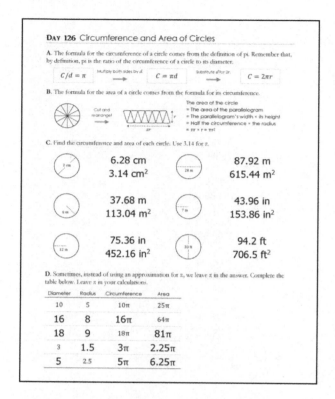

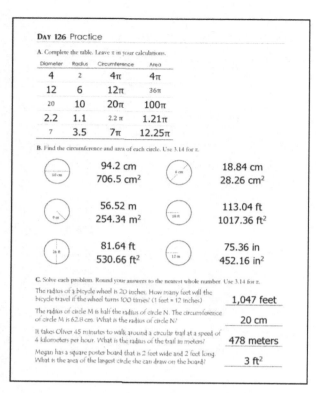

Lesson 126 – Circumference and Area of Circles

Have your child explain parts A and B to you. They are trying to see how things fit together, where these formulas come from. It's not out of thin air.

Review 126 – Decimals

They are just writing the decimals. A decimal has the number of decimal places as the place value has zeros. Hundreths has two decimal places, like 100 has two zeros.

Answers   12.15   0.005   0.592

Lesson 127

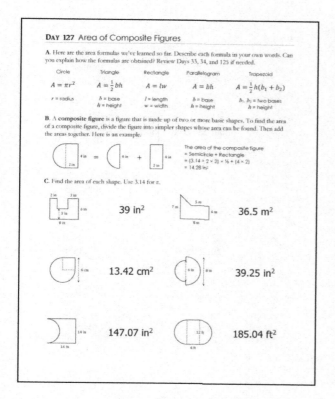

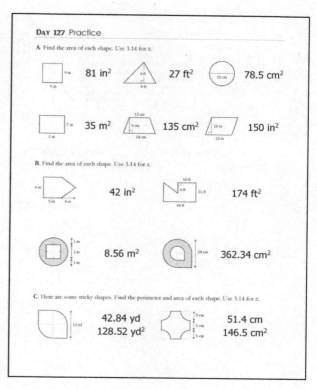

Lesson 127 – Area of Composite Figures

Part A asks them to explain. Teaching something is the best way to learn it, so please ask your child to teach you by explaining the formulas.

To figure out the composite areas, they should draw lines on the shapes to divide them into smaller shapes. Part B shows a dotted line in the composite figure, dividing it into a rectangle and a semi-circle. That's what I'm talking about, draw in lines to make shapes they know how to find the area of. Sometimes they will draw in parts of shapes that are missing, and they will need to subtract off an area.

Review 127 – Place Value

They need to name the place value such as: tens, ones, tenths, hundredths, thousandths

Answers   Tenths   Thousandths   Hundredths

Lesson 128

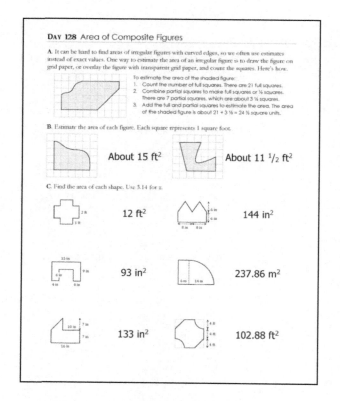

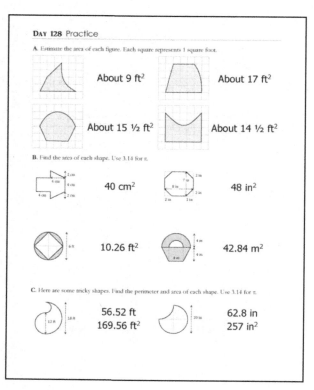

Lesson 128 – Area of Composite Figures

In Part B is explained in Part A, just using the squares there to count up the area.

In Part C, this is the same type of activity as Lesson 127. They need to look for the shapes. Have them draw on what's missing if needed. A quarter circle has the area that's ¼ of a full circle's area. The last one in the corner is a full square missing half a square in two places and two quarters of a circle.

Review 128 – Expanded Form

They need to expand the numbers by adding together each place value.

$12.34 = 10 + 2 + 0.3 + 0.04$

Answers $6 + 0.4 + 0.07 + 0.002$ $20 + 5 + 0.08 + 0.003$ $700 + 2 + 0.3 + 0.009$

Lesson 129

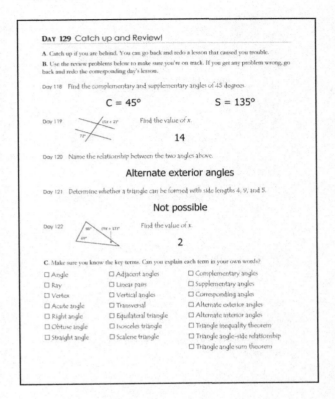

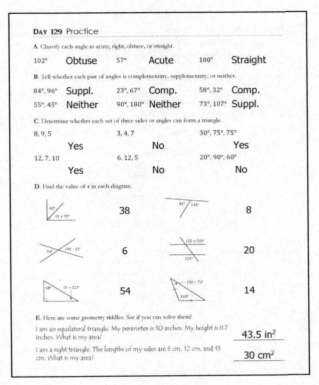

Lesson 129 Catch Up and Review

Have your child check themselves using the lesson page and go back to work on problem areas. See if your child can explain the terms on the page. If they are doing well, have them use the practice page today to stay sharp.

No Review

Lesson 130

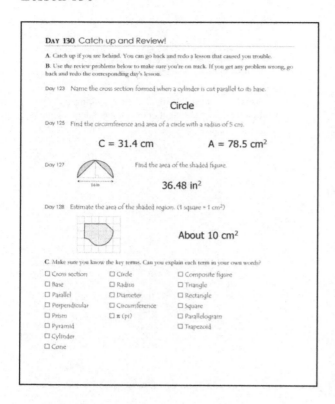

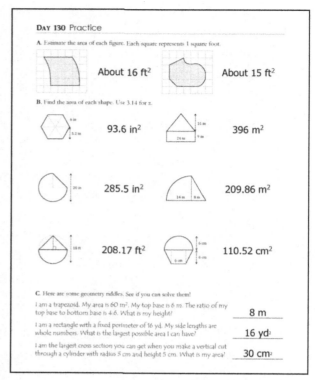

Lesson 130 Catch Up and Review

Have your child check themselves using the lesson page and go back to work on problem areas. See if your child can explain the terms on the page. If they are doing well, have them use the practice page today to stay sharp.

No Review

Lesson 131

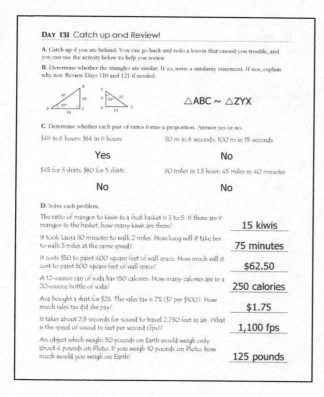

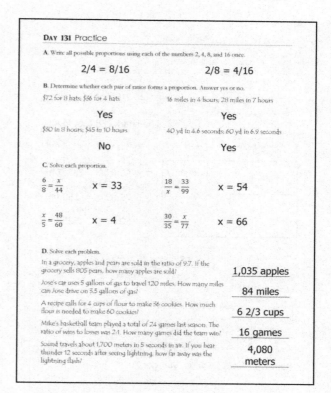

Lesson 131 Catch Up and Review

Have your child check themselves using the lesson page and go back to work on problem areas. If they are doing well, have them use the practice page today to stay sharp.

No Review

Lesson 132

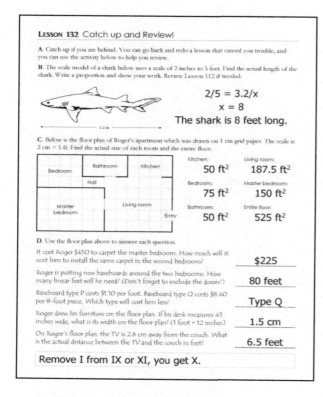

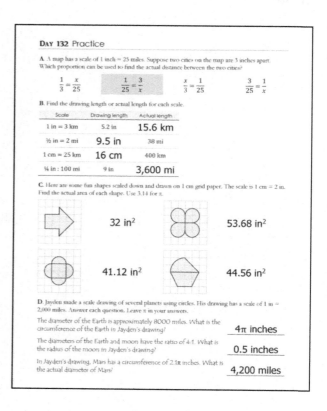

Lesson 132 Catch Up and Review

Have your child check themselves using the lesson page and go back to work on problem areas. If they are doing well, have them use the practice page today to stay sharp.

No Review

Lesson 133

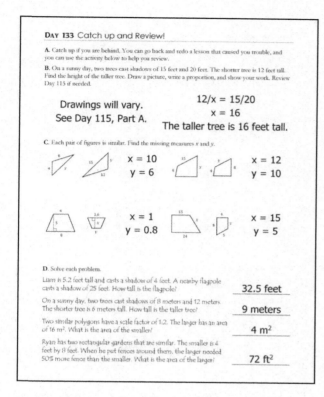

DAY 133 Catch up and Review!

A. Catch up if you are behind. You can go back and redo a lesson that caused you trouble, and you can use the activity below to help you review.

B. On a sunny day, two trees cast shadows of 15 feet and 20 feet. The shorter tree is 12 feet tall. Find the height of the taller tree. Draw a picture, write a proportion, and show your work. Review Day 115 if needed.

Drawings will vary.
See Day 115, Part A.

$12/x = 15/20$
$x = 16$
The taller tree is 16 feet tall.

C. Each pair of figures is similar. Find the missing measures x and y.

$x = 10$
$y = 6$

$x = 12$
$y = 10$

$x = 1$
$y = 0.8$

$x = 15$
$y = 5$

D. Solve each problem.

Liam is 5.2 feet tall and casts a shadow of 4 feet. A nearby flagpole casts a shadow of 25 feet. How tall is the flagpole?
32.5 feet

On a sunny day, two trees cast shadows of 8 meters and 12 meters. The shorter tree is 6 meters tall. How tall is the taller tree?
9 meters

Two similar polygons have a scale factor of 1:2. The larger has an area of 16 m². What is the area of the smaller?
4 m²

Ryan has two rectangular gardens that are similar. The smaller is 4 feet by 8 feet. When he put fences around them, the larger needed 50% more fence than the smaller. What is the area of the larger?
72 ft²

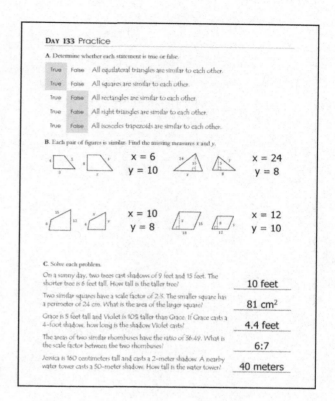

DAY 133 Practice

A. Determine whether each statement is true or false.

True / False All equilateral triangles are similar to each other.

True / False All squares are similar to each other.

True / False All rectangles are similar to each other.

True / False All right triangles are similar to each other.

True / False All isosceles trapezoids are similar to each other.

B. Each pair of figures is similar. Find the missing measures x and y.

$x = 6$
$y = 10$

$x = 24$
$y = 8$

$x = 10$
$y = 8$

$x = 12$
$y = 10$

C. Solve each problem.

On a sunny day, two trees cast shadows of 9 feet and 15 feet. The shorter tree is 6 feet tall. How tall is the taller tree?
10 feet

Two similar squares have a scale factor of 2:3. The smaller square has a perimeter of 24 cm. What is the area of the larger square?
81 cm²

Grace is 5 feet tall and Violet is 10% taller than Grace. If Grace casts a 4-foot shadow, how long is the shadow Violet casts?
4.4 feet

The areas of two similar rhombuses have the ratio of 36:49. What is the scale factor between the two rhombuses?
6:7

Jessica is 160 centimeters tall and casts a 2-meter shadow. A nearby water tower casts a 50-meter shadow. How tall is the water tower?
40 meters

Lesson 133 Catch Up and Review

Have your child check themselves using the lesson page and go back to work on problem areas. If they are doing well, have them use the practice page today to stay sharp.

No Review

Lesson 134

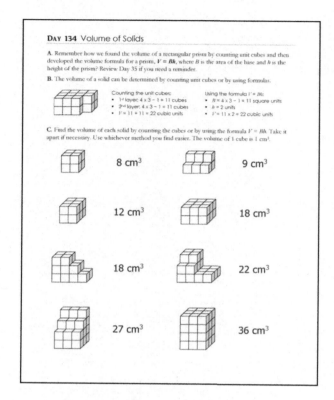

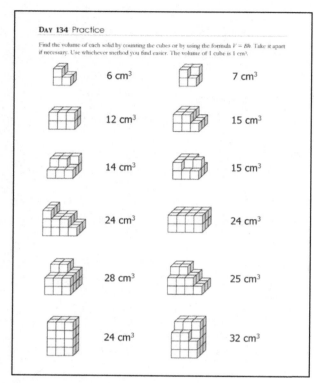

Lesson 134 – Volume of Solids

This looks like a little kid lesson today. They are counting cubes. They should first take the opportunity to use the formula. Where there is a stack, they should count the base and multiply it by the height. Then they can count cubes to see if they are doing it correctly.

Review 134 – Writing Decimals

They need to decide the place value shown, tenths or hundreths. Then they count up the parts being shown. If two of ten lines are colored in, that's 0.2, two tenths. If twenty-five hundredths is colored in, that's 0.25 or twenty-five hundredths.

Answers   0.4   0.9   0.06   0.78

Lesson 135

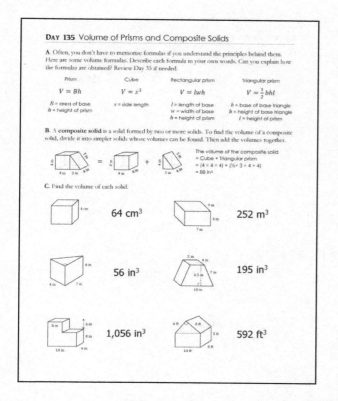

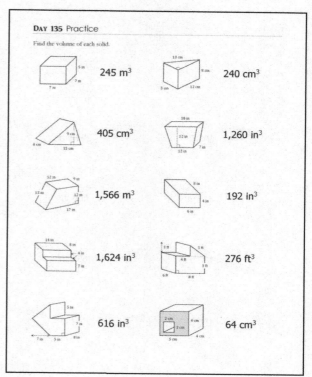

Lesson 135 – Volume of Prisms and Composite Solids

There are several formulas, but they are all based on the same thing. The volume of a cube is still the area of the base by the height, which is just length times width times height, but those measurements are all the same in a cube. A triangle is just half the square.

A trapezoid is a rectangle and two triangles.

A little square marks where there is a right angle.

Review 135 – Writing Decimals

They need to see that each line is moving up one tenth. 0 0.1 0.2 0.3...

Answers   0.1   0.3   0.6   0.9

Lesson 136

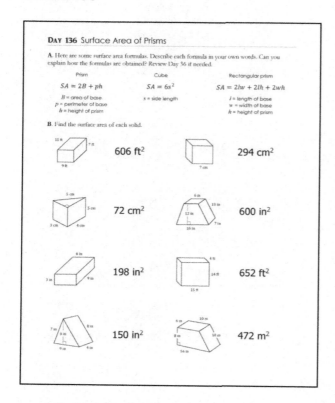

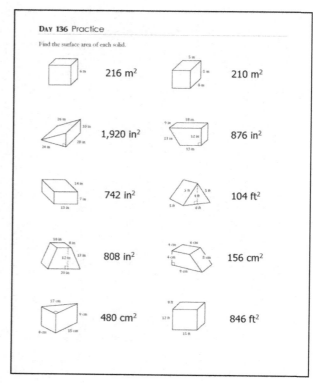

Lesson 136 – Surface Area of Prisms

Now instead of the inside, they are measuring the outside. They need to try to picture all the sides of the shapes. They could look for the shapes in the house if they need help counting the sides.

There are formulas there. Those are basically just like combining like terms. The surface area of a cube is the area of one side six times over. The area is length times width. For a square, those are the same number, so the area is just the length of the side times the length of the side. Area of a square is s^2. The surface area of a cube is $s^2 + s^2 + s^2 + s^2 + s^2 + s^2$. The formula is $SA = 6s^2$. Those are the same thing.

Review 136 – Writing Decimals

They need to count up the lines between the numbers to see that it is divided into ten parts. The first answer isn't 0.2 but 4.2.

Answers   4.2   4.7   5.3   5.6

Lesson 137

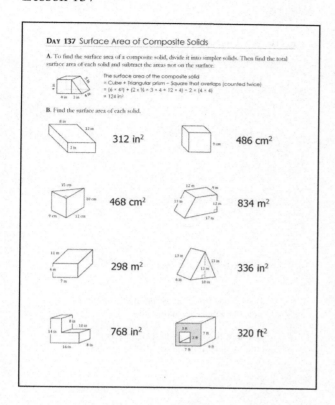

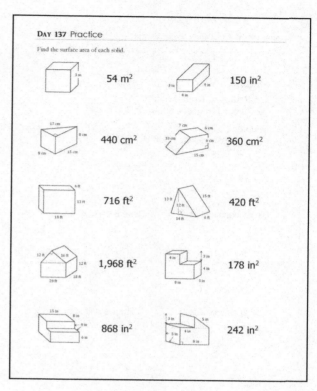

Lesson 137 – Surface Area of Composite Solids

They should divide the irregular shapes into simpler shapes such as cubes and rectangular and triangular prisms. For the final shape, they will need to subtract out a shape.

This is surface area, not volume. They are finding the area of the outside surface of each composite shape.

Review 137 – Writing Decimals

They are writing decimals again. This time it is hundredths.

Answers   0.02   0.04   0.07   0.09

Lesson 138

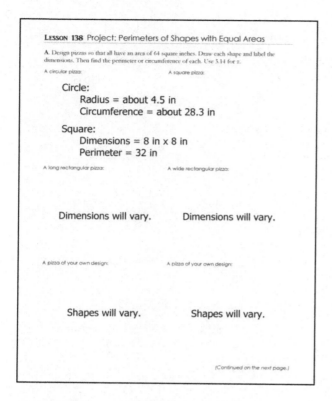

LESSON 138 Project: Perimeters of Shapes with Equal Areas

A. Design pizzas so that all have an area of 64 square inches. Draw each shape and label the dimensions. Then find the perimeter or circumference of each. Use 3.14 for π.

A circular pizza: A square pizza:

> Circle:
>   Radius = about 4.5 in
>   Circumference = about 28.3 in
>
> Square:
>   Dimensions = 8 in x 8 in
>   Perimeter = 32 in

A long rectangular pizza: A wide rectangular pizza:

Dimensions will vary.   Dimensions will vary.

A pizza of your own design: A pizza of your own design:

Shapes will vary.   Shapes will vary.

(Continued on the next page.)

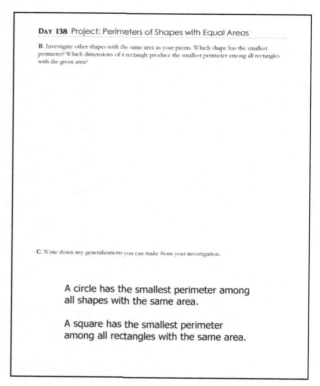

DAY 138 Project: Perimeters of Shapes with Equal Areas

B. Investigate other shapes with the same area as your pizzas. Which shape has the smallest perimeter? Which dimensions of a rectangle produce the smallest perimeter among all rectangles with the given area?

C. Write down any generalizations you can make from your investigation.

A circle has the smallest perimeter among all shapes with the same area.

A square has the smallest perimeter among all rectangles with the same area.

Lesson 138 – Project: Perimeters of Shapes with Equal Areas

There is no answer key for this. They should come up with their answers and then explain them to you. They should draw their pizza with labeled measurements and then solve for the area.

No Review

Lesson 139

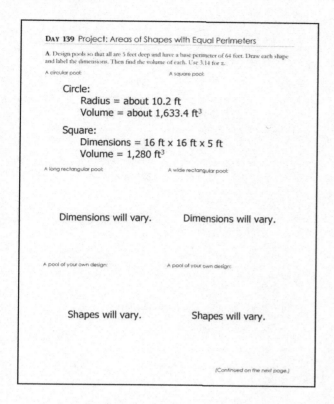

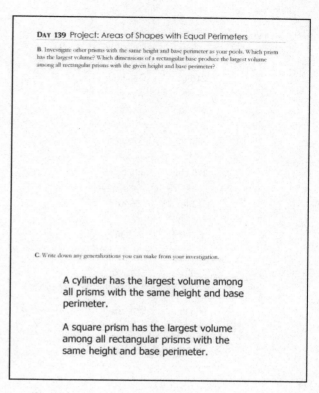

DAY 139 Project: Areas of Shapes with Equal Perimeters

A. Design pools so that all are 5 feet deep and have a base perimeter of 64 feet. Draw each shape and label the dimensions. Then find the volume of each. Use 3.14 for π.

A circular pool: A square pool:

Circle:
     Radius = about 10.2 ft
     Volume = about 1,633.4 ft³

Square:
     Dimensions = 16 ft x 16 ft x 5 ft
     Volume = 1,280 ft³

A long rectangular pool: A wide rectangular pool:

Dimensions will vary.   Dimensions will vary.

A pool of your own design: A pool of your own design:

Shapes will vary.   Shapes will vary.

(Continued on the next page.)

DAY 139 Project: Areas of Shapes with Equal Perimeters

B. Investigate other prisms with the same height and base perimeter as your pools. Which prism has the largest volume? Which dimensions of a rectangular base produce the largest volume among all rectangular prisms with the given height and base perimeter?

C. Write down any generalizations you can make from your investigation.

A cylinder has the largest volume among all prisms with the same height and base perimeter.

A square prism has the largest volume among all rectangular prisms with the same height and base perimeter.

Lesson 139 – Project: Areas of Shapes with Equal Perimeters

This is similar to the project in Lesson 138. This time they are finding volume. They should draw and label a picture for each and then write their equaion and solve.

No Review

Lesson 140

DAY 140 Volume and Surface Area of Prisms

Find the volume and surface area of each solid described. Review Days 35 and 36 if needed.

A cube with a side length of 6 inches.

$$216 \text{ in}^3 \qquad 216 \text{ in}^2$$

A square prism with a base side length of 7 inches and a height of 8 inches.

$$392 \text{ in}^3 \qquad 322 \text{ in}^2$$

A rectangular prism that is 6 inches long, 8 inches wide, and 10 inches tall.

$$480 \text{ in}^3 \qquad 376 \text{ in}^2$$

A rectangular prism with a length of 3 cm, a width of 6 cm, and a height of 15 cm.

$$270 \text{ cm}^3 \qquad 306 \text{ cm}^2$$

A prism that is 2 m tall and whose bases are right triangles with sides 3 m, 4 m, and 5 m.

$$12 \text{ m}^3 \qquad 36 \text{ m}^2$$

A prism that is 6 m tall and whose bases are right triangles with sides 5 m, 12 m, and 13 m.

$$180 \text{ m}^3 \qquad 240 \text{ m}^2$$

A prism whose height is 5 ft and whose bases are equilateral triangles with side lengths of 6 ft and a height of 5.2 ft.

$$78 \text{ ft}^3 \qquad 121.2 \text{ ft}^2$$

A prism whose height is 8 cm and whose bases are isosceles trapezoids with bases of 5 cm and 15 cm, sides of 13 cm, and a height of 12 cm.

$$960 \text{ cm}^3 \qquad 608 \text{ cm}^2$$

A prism whose height is 6 m and whose bases are isosceles trapezoids with bases of 4 m and 12 m, sides of 5 m, and a height of 3 m.

$$144 \text{ m}^3 \qquad 204 \text{ m}^2$$

DAY 140 Practice

A. Find the volume and surface area of each solid described.

A cube with a side length of 8 inches.

$$512 \text{ in}^3 \qquad 384 \text{ in}^2$$

A square prism with a base side length of 4 inches and a height of 9 inches.

$$144 \text{ in}^3 \qquad 176 \text{ in}^2$$

A rectangular prism that is 9 inches long, 4 inches wide, and 5 inches tall.

$$180 \text{ in}^3 \qquad 202 \text{ in}^2$$

A prism that is 6 m tall and whose bases are right triangles with sides 9 m, 12 m, and 15 m.

$$324 \text{ m}^3 \qquad 324 \text{ m}^2$$

A prism whose height is 10 cm and whose bases are isosceles trapezoids with bases of 6 cm and 12 cm, sides of 5 cm, and a height of 4 cm.

$$360 \text{ cm}^3 \qquad 352 \text{ cm}^2$$

B. Here are some geometry riddles. See if you can solve them!

I am a cube, a prism with six identical square faces. One of my faces has an area of 16 in². What is my surface area?

$$96 \text{ in}^2$$

I am a rectangular prism. My bases are squares with perimeter of 12 cm. My height is twice the side of my base. What is my volume?

$$54 \text{ cm}^3$$

I am a rectangular prism with a volume of 126 in³. My width is 7 inches and my height is 6 inches. What is my surface area?

$$162 \text{ in}^2$$

I am a rectangular prism with a volume of 225 cm³. My height is 9 cm. My bases are squares. What is my surface area?

$$230 \text{ cm}^2$$

I am a rectangular prism with integer side lengths. The sum of my three dimensions is 6 feet. What is my largest possible volume?

$$8 \text{ ft}^3$$

I am a cuboid. My dimensions are in inches. My height is a common factor of 84 and 98. My width is a solution to $9 - x \geq 4$. My length is 4 less than 2 cubed. What is my largest possible volume?

$$280 \text{ in}^3$$

Lesson 140 – Volume and Surface Area of Prisms

This is review of finding the volume and surface area. They are being asked to find BOTH for each shape described. They should draw little diagrams to make sure that they are thinking the right way.

Review 140 – Writing Decimals

The first answer is 2.73. The markings are showing hundredths (ten parts of a tenth).

Answers   2.73   2.77   2.82   2.88

Lesson 141

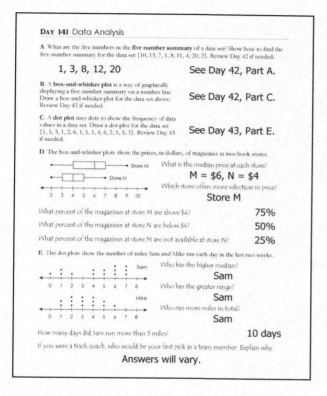

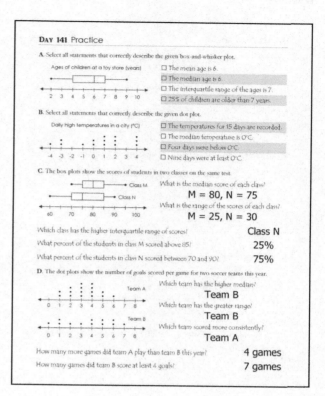

Lesson 141 – Data Analysis

They are working again with box-and-whisker plot.

Part A is asking for five numbers. The high, low, median, and the median between the median and the high and low.

Part B is to draw a picture of Part A. There is an example they can look at. The dots are the high and low. The line in the middle of the box is the median. The ends of the box are the medians of each half.

Part C is a graph of the data set in Part A. There is an example they can look at.

Review 141 – Rounding Decimals

They need to look to the digit to the right of the place value they are rounding to. To round to the nearest whole number, they just need to look at the tenths.

Answers   7, 6.8, 6.77   2, 2.2, 2.2   18, 18.4, 18.4

Lesson 142

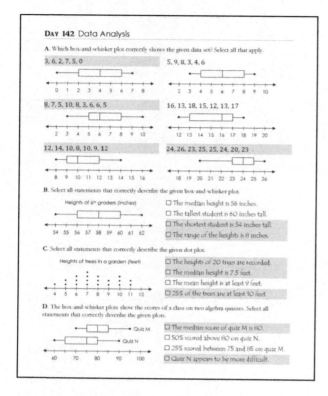

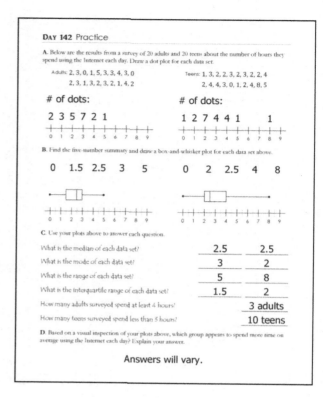

Lesson 142 – Data Anaylsis

There are more practices today for data graphs.

At the top of the page, they are to say which are correct. Here's what's wrong with the incorrect ones. The top two on the right are incorrect. The top one should have a median of five and a half. The second one should have a median of 15.

Review 142 – Recognizing Decimal Values

This is just checking their understanding of place value.

Answers   True   True   False

Lesson 143

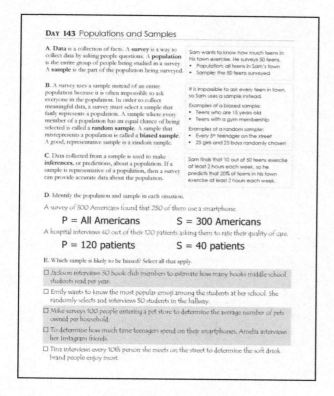
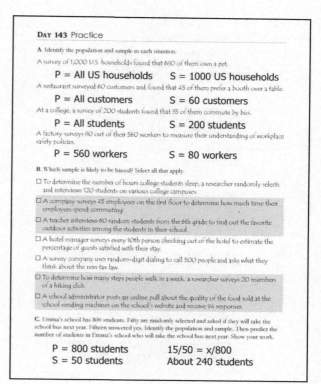

Lesson 143 – Populations and Samples

They should read through the top and look at the example for each.

Here are explanations of answers in Parts D and E. For Part D, the populations are the whole group being studied, not just the ones actually asked the survey questions. So the populations are Americans and hospital patients.

For Part E, the first one isn't asking the population they are studying. The next one is unbiased; she's randomly interviewing those she's studying. The next one about pets is biased because he's interviewing pet owners when he should be going house to house or something like that. The same problem exists with the next one. It's not a random population. She's interviewing only friends and people on Instagram. The last one is unbiased.

Review 143 – Comparing Decimals

This is again checking their understanding of decimal place value.

Answers   False   True   True

Lesson 144

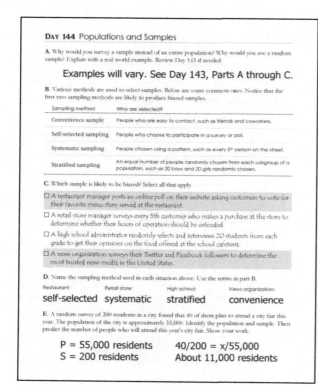

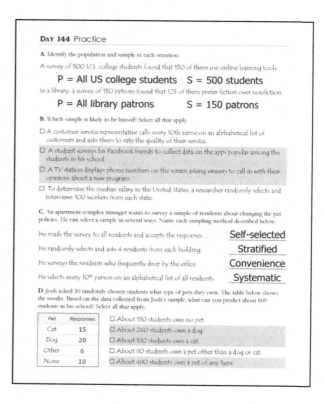

Lesson 144 – Populations and Samples

In Part C, the last one is biased because they are asking only their followers when they say their population is all Americans.

This is why all statistics should be questioned! You need to know if the numbers are biased.

In Part D, they will choose their answers from the list in Part B.

Part E is a proportion! 200 is to 55,000 as 40 is to ? That can be rewritten 1/275 = 40/? by simplyfying the first fraction. Cross multiply: ? = 275 x 40

Review 144 – Decimals

They will need to think through (or write out) what decimal is being described and compare it to the answer given.

Answers   True   False   False

Lesson 145

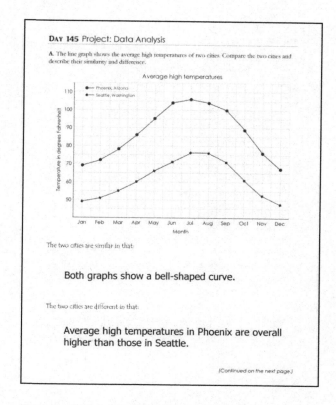

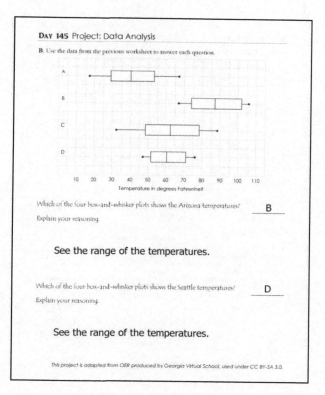

Lesson 145 – Project: Data Analysis

They are going to be reading graphs today. This should be short and easy.

No Review 145

Lesson 146

DAY 146 Probability of Simple Events

A. The **probability** of an event is a measure of the likelihood that the event will occur. An **outcome** is the result of an **experiment** or activity. An **event** is a particular outcome or set of outcomes looked for. The specific sought-after outcomes for a certain event are called **favorable outcomes**. The probability of an event is the number of favorable outcomes divided by the total number of possible outcomes. Let's see what all of this means using an example. Check off each box if you understand it.

Abe rolls a die. What's the probability that he rolls an odd number?

☐ The experiment or activity is rolling a die.
☐ The outcome is the result of rolling a die.
☐ The event is rolling an odd number.
☐ The favorable outcomes are 1, 3, and 5.
☐ The possible outcomes are 1 through 6.
☐ The probability that Abe rolls an odd number is 3 divided by 6, which is ½.

B. The probability of event E is written P(E). It can be expressed as a fraction, a decimal, or a percent. Suppose a die is rolled. Find the probability of each event as a fraction.

Event	Favorable outcomes	Probability
Rolling a number at least 6	6	P(at least 6) = 1/6
Rolling a number less than 5	1, 2, 3, 4	P(less than 5) = 2/3
Rolling a prime number	2, 3, 5	P(prime) = 1/2
Rolling a multiple of 3	3, 6	P(3's multiple) = 1/3

C. Probabilities are always between 0 and 1. The probability of an **impossible** event is 0. The probability of a **certain** event is 1. The probability 0.5 means that the event is **as likely as not** to occur. Events with a probability closer to 1 are **likely** to occur. Events with a probability closer to 0 are **unlikely** to occur. Suppose you randomly select a card from a pack of 10 cards numbered from 1 to 10. Determine whether each event is impossible, unlikely, as likely as not, likely, or certain.

Selecting a card with a number divisible by 2	As likely ~
Selecting a card with a single-digit number	Likely
Selecting a card with a negative number	Impossible
Selecting a card with a number greater than 0	Certain
Selecting a card with a number that is a multiple of 4	Unlikely

DAY 146 Practice

A. Determine whether each statement is true or false.

True	False	Probability is how likely something is to happen.
True	False	A probability of ½ could also be written as 0.5 or 50%.
True	False	The probability of an event ranges from –1 to 1.
True	False	A high probability means an event is unlikely to occur.
True	False	The probability of an event that will never occur is 1.

B. A die is rolled. Find the probability of each event as a fraction.

Event of rolling a die	Favorable outcomes	Probability
Rolling an even number	2, 4, 6	P(even) = 1/2
Rolling a number less than 7	1, 2, 3, 4, 5, 6	P(less than 7) = 1
Rolling a negative number	None	P(negative) = 0
Rolling a composite number	4, 6	P(composite) = 1/3
Rolling a factor of 30	1, 2, 3, 5, 6	P(30's factor) = 5/6

C. Determine whether each event is impossible, unlikely, as likely as not, likely, or certain.

Flipping a coin and getting heads	As likely ~
Rolling a die and getting a multiple of 8	Impossible
Rolling a die and getting a number at most 2	Unlikely
Picking a red ball from a bag containing 1 blue ball and 6 red balls	Likely
Picking a black marble from a bag containing 8 black marbles	Certain
Rolling a die and getting a number less than or equal to 4	Likely
Picking a blue marble from a bag that contains 12 white marbles and 12 blue marbles	As likely ~
Spinning a spinner with 10 equal sections marked 1 through 10 and landing on a factor of 10	Unlikely

Lesson 146 – Probability of Simple Events

The definitions can get convoluted. There is an example below the definitions that uses the terms to show what they mean.

A probability of 0 means it can't happen. A probability of 1 means it always will happen. All other probabilities fall between 0 and 1. If they get a probability over 1, they divided the wrong way.

In Part B, P(less than 5) means the probabilty that when you roll the die and the number that comes up will be less then five.

Review 146 – Ordering Decimals

To compare decimals, you use place value. They will start with the ones, then move to the tenths, etc.

Answers   2.9, 6.2, 9.3   3.9, 4.75, 4.78   0.02, 0.576, 1.576

Lesson 147

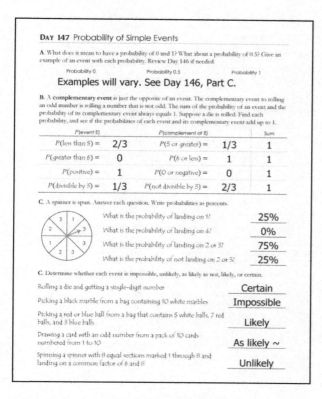

DAY 147 Probability of Simple Events

A. What does it mean to have a probability of 0 and 1? What about a probability of 0.5? Give an example of an event with each probability. Review Day 146 if needed.

Probability 0   Probability 0.5   Probability 1

Examples will vary. See Day 146, Part C.

B. A complementary event is just the opposite of an event. The complementary event to rolling an odd number is rolling a number that is not odd. The sum of the probability of an event and the probability of its complementary event always equals 1. Suppose a die is rolled. Find each probability, and see if the probabilities of each event and its complementary event add up to 1.

P(event E)		P(complement of E)		Sum
P(less than 5) =	2/3	P(5 or greater) =	1/3	1
P(greater than 6) =	0	P(6 or less) =	1	1
P(positive) =	1	P(0 or negative) =	0	1
P(divisible by 3) =	1/3	P(not divisible by 3) =	2/3	1

C. A spinner is spun. Answer each question. Write probabilities as percents.

What is the probability of landing on 1?   25%
What is the probability of landing on 4?   0%
What is the probability of landing on 2 or 3?   75%
What is the probability of not landing on 2 or 3? 25%

C. Determine whether each event is impossible, unlikely, as likely as not, likely, or certain.

Rolling a die and getting a single-digit number   Certain
Picking a black marble from a bag containing 10 white marbles   Impossible
Picking a red or blue ball from a bag that contains 5 white balls, 7 red balls, and 3 blue balls   Likely
Drawing a card with an odd number from a pack of 10 cards numbered from 1 to 10   As likely ~
Spinning a spinner with 8 equal sections marked 1 through 8 and landing on a common factor of 6 and 8   Unlikely

DAY 147 Practice

A. A bag contains 14 red marbles, 4 blue marbles, and 2 clear marbles. Answer each question. Write probabilities as decimals.

Which color of marble are you least likely to pick without looking?   Clear
What is the total number of possible outcomes?   20
What is the probability of picking a blue marble?   0.2
What is the probability of not picking a blue marble?   0.8
What is the probability of picking a red or blue marble?   0.9
What is the probability of not picking a red or blue marble?   0.1

B. A spinner is spun. Answer each question. Write probabilities as fractions.

What is the probability of landing on 2?   1/4
What is the probability of not landing on 2?   3/4
What is the probability of landing on 1 or 3?   3/8
What is the probability of not landing on 1 or 3? 5/8

C. A card is randomly selected from a pack of 100 cards numbered from 1 to 100. Determine whether each event is impossible, unlikely, as likely as not, likely, or certain.

Selecting a card with a multiple of 10   Unlikely
Selecting a card with not a multiple of 10   Likely
Selecting a card with a number divisible by 2   As likely ~
Selecting a card with a number not divisible by 2   As likely ~
Selecting a card with a number divisible by 1   Certain
Selecting a card with a number not divisible by 1   Impossible
Selecting a card with not a multiple of 9   Likely
Selecting a card with not a common multiple of 5 and 6   Likely
Selecting a card with not a perfect square number   Likely

Lesson 147 – Probability of Simple Events

In Part B, the answer to sum should always be one.

In part C, the total number of outcomes is eight. The probabilty of landing on 3 is 4 out of 8. 4/8 = ½

Review 147 – Converting Fractions to Decimals

They just need to read it out loud and write that same number as a decimal. They will be writing the numerator and give it the same number of decimal places as there are zeros.

Answers   0.7   1.62   0.315

Lesson 148

DAY 148 Experimental Probability

A. Suppose you tried 10 free throws and made 8. Based on your trials, we can predict that you have 80% chance of making the next shot. That is an **experimental probability**, the actual probability of an event determined by repeating an experiment and observing the outcomes. Experimental probability is used to make predictions. Here is how to calculate it.

$$P(E) = \frac{\text{Number of times event E occurs}}{\text{Total number of trials}} \quad \xrightarrow{\text{Apply to our example:}} \quad \frac{8 \text{ shots made}}{10 \text{ shots tried}} = 0.8 = 80\%$$

B. What if you tried 100 free throws and made 70? Then, it would be more accurate to say that you have 70% chance of making the next shot. Note that the more trials you carry out, the more accurate your prediction is likely to be.

C. Dana rolled a die 50 times and recorded the results in the table. Find each experimental probability as a percent.

Outcome	1	2	3	4	5	6
Frequency	8	10	7	6	14	5

What is the experimental probability of rolling a 4?   12%

What is the experimental probability of rolling a 2?   20%

What is the experimental probability of not rolling a 6?   90%

What is the experimental probability of rolling a number less than 3?   36%

What is the experimental probability of rolling an even number?   42%

D. Find each experimental probability as a fraction.

Jayden tossed a coin 25 times and got heads 10 times. What is the experimental probability of getting heads?   2/5

Luke shot 27 free throws and made 18 of them. What is the experimental probability that he misses the next free throw?   1/3

Logan hit a baseball on 14 out of 30 tries during practice. What is the experimental probability that he will hit the ball on his next try?   7/15

Cam's softball team has won 12 out of 22 games so far. What is the experimental probability that the team will win the next game?   6/11

A bakery sold 24 cakes, nine of which were birthday cakes. What is the experimental probability that the next cake sold is a birthday cake?   3/8

An inspector at a monitor factory checked 200 monitors and found 8 defective. What is the experimental probability that a monitor is defective?   1/25

DAY 148 Practice

A. A spinner with 4 equal sections labeled A, B, C, and D is spun 25 times. The results are in the table. Find each experimental probability as a percent.

Outcome	A	B	C	D
Frequency	4	5	8	8

What is the experimental probability of landing on section A?   16%

What is the experimental probability of landing on section B?   20%

What is the experimental probability of landing on section C or D?   64%

What is the experimental probability of not landing on section B?   80%

B. Chris rolled a die 40 times and recorded the results in the table. Find each experimental probability as a fraction.

Outcome	1	2	3	4	5	6
frequency	6	8	11	5	3	7

What is the experimental probability of rolling a 1?   3/20

What is the experimental probability of rolling a 3 or 4?   2/5

What is the experimental probability of rolling a number at least 5?   1/4

What is the experimental probability of rolling an odd number?   1/2

What is the experimental probability of not rolling an odd number?   1/2

C. Find each experimental probability as a fraction.

Stephanie made 10 out of 15 shots in basketball. What is the experimental probability that she will make the next shot?   2/3

Zoey tossed a coin 45 times and got tails 18 times. What is the experimental probability of getting heads?   3/5

Olivia pulled 28 marbles from a bag. Seven of them were red. What is the experimental probability that she will pull a red marble?   1/4

An appliance store sold 18 appliances, four of which were washers. What is the experimental probability that the next appliance sold will be a washer?   2/9

A donut shop sold 55 plain donuts and 20 glazed donuts. What is the experimental probability that the next donut sold will be plain?   7/11

Out of 26 games, Aiden's baseball team won 16 games and tied 4 games. What is the experimental probability that the team will lose the next game?   3/13

Lesson 148 – Experimental Probability

Part C, the total number of trials is 50. The frequencies are the number of times that favorable outcome came up out of those fifty times.

Here's the first word problem in Part D. He got the favorable outcome ten out of twenty-five times. 10/25 = 2/5

They need to reduce!

Review 148 – Writing Fractions and Decimals

They will interpret the pictures as fractions and decials. They will need to count up the blocks that are colored in and that is out of ten or one hundred total blocks.

Answers   F = 1/10, D = 0.1   F = 5/10, D = 0.5   F = 9/100, D = 0.09   F = 42/100, D = 0.42

Lesson 149 (coin)

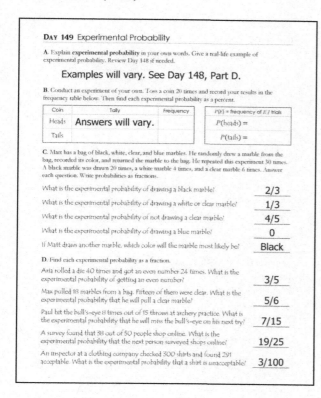

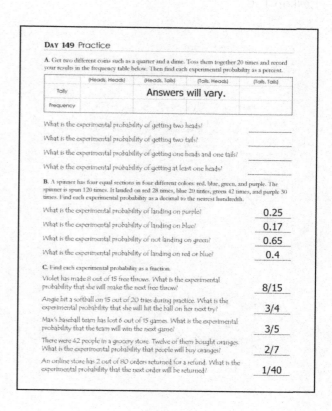

Lesson 149 – Experimental Probability

In Part B, they are doing an experiment, flipping a coin and making a tally mark for each time heads or tales comes up and then finding the probability based on their trial. The theoretical probabilty is 50%, ½, 0.5. But the experimental probability will likely be different.

In Part C, the total number is 30. We don't know how many of each color marble are in the bag. They can only go by the experimental probability.

Here's the first word problem in Part D.   24 out of 40 = 24/40 = 3/5

Review 149 – Converting Decimals to Fractions

They just need to read the decimal out loud and then write that fraction. There will be the same number of zeros in the denominator as decimal places.

Answers   3/5   9/20   5/8

Lesson 150

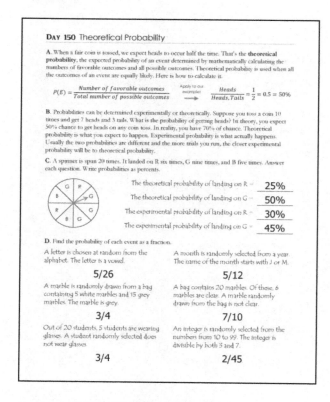

DAY 150 Theoretical Probability

A. When a fair coin is tossed, we expect heads to occur half the time. That's the **theoretical probability**, the expected probability of an event determined by mathematically calculating the numbers of favorable outcomes and all possible outcomes. Theoretical probability is used when all the outcomes of an event are equally likely. Here is how to calculate it.

$$P(E) = \frac{Number\ of\ favorable\ outcomes}{Total\ number\ of\ possible\ outcomes} \longrightarrow \frac{Heads}{Heads, Tails} = \frac{1}{2} = 0.5 = 50\%$$

B. Probabilities can be determined experimentally or theoretically. Suppose you toss a coin 10 times and get 7 heads and 3 tails. What is the probability of getting heads? In theory, you expect 50% chance to get heads on any coin toss. In reality, you have 70% of chance. Theoretical probability is what you expect to happen. Experimental probability is what actually happens. Usually the two probabilities are different and the more trials you run, the closer experimental probability will be to theoretical probability.

C. A spinner is spun 20 times. It landed on R six times, G nine times, and B five times. Answer each question. Write probabilities as percents.

The theoretical probability of landing on R — **25%**
The theoretical probability of landing on G — **50%**
The experimental probability of landing on R — **30%**
The experimental probability of landing on G — **45%**

D. Find the probability of each event as a fraction.

A letter is chosen at random from the alphabet. The letter is a vowel.
5/26

A month is randomly selected from a year. The name of the month starts with J or M.
5/12

A marble is randomly drawn from a bag containing 5 white marbles and 15 grey marbles. The marble is grey.
3/4

A bag contains 20 marbles. Of these, 6 marbles are clear. A marble randomly drawn from the bag is not clear.
7/10

Out of 20 students, 5 students are wearing glasses. A student randomly selected does not wear glasses.
3/4

An integer is randomly selected from the numbers from 10 to 99. The integer is divisible by both 3 and 7.
2/45

DAY 150 Practice

A. Determine whether each statement is true or false.

True **False** Picking a red marble from a bag containing 5 red marbles is unlikely.

True False The probabilities of an event and its complement must always total to 1.

True **False** Theoretical probability is based on the outcomes of experiments.

True **False** Experimental probability is the chance of an event occurring in theory.

True False Theoretical probability and experimental probability are often different.

B. Andy rolled a die 30 times and recorded the results in the table. Find each probability as a fraction.

Outcome	1	2	3	4	5	6
Frequency	7	3	5	6	2	7

What is the theoretical probability of rolling an even number? **1/2**
What is the theoretical probability of rolling a number less than 3? **1/3**
What is the experimental probability of rolling an even number? **8/15**
What is the experimental probability of rolling a number less than 3? **1/3**

C. Kyle randomly draws a marble from a bag containing 18 black marbles, 6 white marbles, 10 clear marbles, and 2 blue marbles. Answer each question. Write probabilities as fractions.

What is the probability of drawing a black marble? **1/2**
What is the probability of drawing a white or clear marble? **4/9**
What is the probability of drawing a green marble? **0**
What is the probability of not drawing a clear marble? **13/18**

D. Find the probability of each event as a fraction.

There are 15 boys and 10 girls in the library. A child selected at random is a boy.
3/5

A box contains 20 red balls and 20 blue balls. Ten red balls are removed from the box, and a ball is randomly selected. The ball is blue.
2/3

A card is randomly drawn from a pack of 20 cards numbered from 1 to 20. The card has a composite number, a number with more than 2 factors.
11/20

Lesson 150 – Theoretical Probability

This is what they've already been doing. It just puts a name on it. I gave an example in Lesson 149. The theoretical probability of a coin toss is ½ or 0.5. In practice, you could flip a coin ten times and have it be heads seven times. That would make the experimental probability of heads be 7/10 or 0.7.

For the first word problem, there are 26 letters in the alphabet and five vowels. 5/26 is the probability.

Review 150 – Converting Fractions to Decimals

There are two ways to do this. They can divide the denominator into the numerator. Or, they can find an equivalent fraction with ten or one hundred or one thousand in the denominator.

Answers   0.5   0.36   0.29

Lesson 151

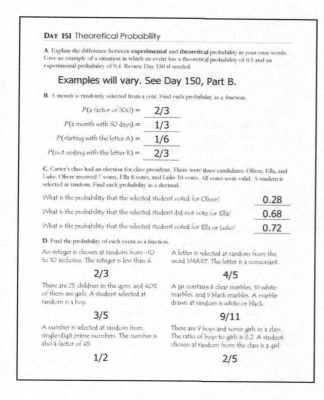
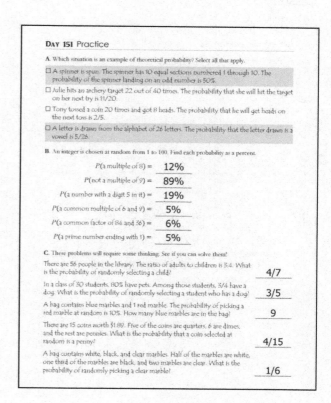

Lesson 151 – Theoretical Probability

Part A can have any answer that has two possibilities, a fifty/fifty chance.

Part B requires them to know how many months have those different things, like doesn't end in R. The first one, factor of 300, means like months 1 (January), 2 (February), 3, 4, 5, 6… The factors of 300 are 1, 2, 3, 4, 5, 6, and 12. There are five months with 30 days. There is one month that starts with A. There are 8 months that don't end in R.

Part C has 25 total votes. Remember that the probability will always be between 0 and 1. They will divide the votes for one student divided by the total votes. They are supposed to find decimals.

Part D is looking for a fraction.

Review 151 – Convert Decimals to Mixed Numbers

The whole number just stays the same. 1.5 is the same as 1 ½ . They just need to covert the decimal part into a fraction and then add that onto the whole number.

Answers   9 4/5   1 9/20   9 7/250

Lesson 152

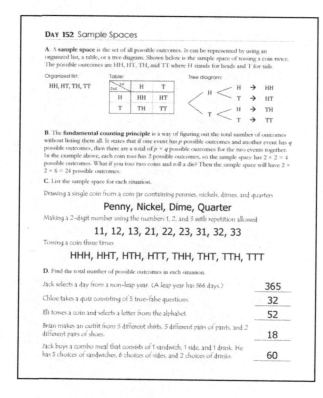

DAY 152 Sample Spaces

A. A **sample space** is the set of all possible outcomes. It can be represented by using an organized list, a table, or a tree diagram. Shown below is the sample space of tossing a coin twice. The possible outcomes are HH, HT, TH, and TT where H stands for heads and T for tails.

Organized list: Table: Tree diagram:

HH, HT, TH, TT

B. The **fundamental counting principle** is a way of figuring out the total number of outcomes without listing them all. It states that if one event has *p* possible outcomes and another event has *q* possible outcomes, then there are a total of $p \times q$ possible outcomes for the two events together. In the example above, each coin toss has 2 possible outcomes, so the sample space has $2 \times 2 = 4$ possible outcomes. What if you toss two coins and roll a die? Then the sample space will have $2 \times 2 \times 6 = 24$ possible outcomes.

C. List the sample space for each situation.

Drawing a single coin from a jar containing pennies, nickels, dimes, and quarters

Penny, Nickel, Dime, Quarter

Making a 2-digit number using the numbers 1, 2, and 3 with repetition allowed

11, 12, 13, 21, 22, 23, 31, 32, 33

Tossing a coin three times

HHH, HHT, HTH, HTT, THH, THT, TTH, TTT

D. Find the total number of possible outcomes in each situation.

Jack selects a day from a non-leap year. (A leap year has 366 days.) 365

Chloe takes a quiz consisting of 5 true-false questions. 32

Eli tosses a coin and selects a letter from the alphabet. 52

Brian makes an outfit from 3 different shirts, 3 different pairs of pants, and 2 different pairs of shoes. 18

Jack buys a combo meal that consists of 1 sandwich, 1 side, and 1 drink. He has 5 choices of sandwiches, 6 choices of sides, and 2 choices of drinks. 60

DAY 152 Practice

A. List the sample space for each situation.

Drawing a number from 2-digit square numbers

16, 25, 36, 49, 64, 81

Drawing a letter from the alphabet of 26 letters

26 alphabet letters

Tossing a coin and rolling a die

H1, H2, H3, H4, H5, H6, T1, T2, T3, T4, T5, T6

Answering 3 true-false questions

TTT, TTF, TFT, TFF, FTT, FTF, FFT, FFF

Making an outfit from 3 shirts (red, blue, and tan) and 2 pairs of pants (tan and blue)

R/T, R/B, B/T, B/B, T/T, T/B

B. Find the total number of possible outcomes in each situation.

Jacob rolls a die twice. 36

Larry tosses a coin five times. 32

Jamal rolls a die and selects one day of the week. 42

Cheryl tosses a coin and selects a month of the year. 24

Mark selects an integer from 1 to 10 and a letter from the word SAMPLE. 60

Ron has a choice of ham, tuna, or turkey and a choice of white or wheat bread to make a sandwich. 6

A café sells fruit smoothies. Chad can choose small, medium, or large. Then he can choose bananas, kiwis, or oranges. 9

Cheyenne tosses two coins and spins a spinner with eight equal sections numbered 1 through 8. 32

Alison takes a multiple choice test which consists of 4 questions. Each question has 4 choices. You may use a calculator. 256

Grace makes a 4-digit password using the numbers 1 to 9 with repetition allowed. You may use a calculator. 6,561

Lesson 152 – Sample Spaces

A sample space is all the possible outcomes of the whole experiment. If you tossed a coin once, the sample space would be heads and tails (H or T). If you flipped a coin twice, the outcomes could be heads both time (HH), tails both times (TT), or one of each (HT or TH). Those are the sample space, all the possible outcomes in all their possible combinations.

Part B says that you can figure out the total number of sample spaces by multiplying together the number of outcomes from each "event." Rolling a die has six possible outcomes. Rolling a die twice has six times six possible outcomes.

When they are doing Part C, they can use that knowledge from Part B to figure out if they've thought of all possible outcomes. The number of possible outcomes in the sample spaces are:
Part C #of outcomes in sample space: 1 x 4   3 x 3   2 x 2 x 2

For Part D: 1 x 366   2 x 2 x 2 x 2 x 2   2 x 26   3 x 3 x 2   5 x 6 x 2

Review 152 – Adding Decimals

Adding decimals is just like adding regular numbers, but they need to make sure to add together the correct place values. Just like they would add tens and tens and hundreds to hundreds, they need to make sure they are adding tenths to tenths and hundredths to hundredths. If they feel stuck, they can get rid of the decimal point and then just put it back in after they add.
Answers   1.4   11.9   11.3

Lesson 153

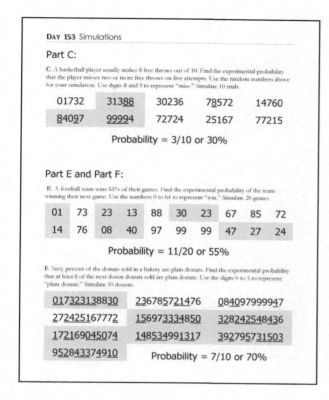

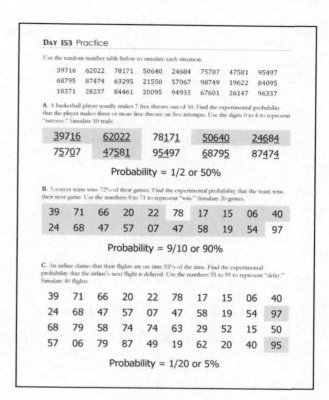

Lesson 153 – Simulations

In Part A they are just reading.

In Part B they take the digits in order, not the first three from each set of numbers. It's walking them through the process.

In Part C they take the new example and apply the steps in Part B. The ten tries are represented by the ten digits of 0 through 9. Digits 0 – 7 will represent making the shot.

Turn the page! There's more.

In Part D there is another example. They will copy that example to do Part E, where numbers 0 - 64 would be a winning game and numbers 65 – 99 would be a losing game. Then they would look at the first 20 pairs of digits looking for those numbers.

The last one, Part F, they will take groups of 10 numbers and see if at least 8 are five or less in each group of ten. Each group of ten that has that many is one out of ten trials.

Review 153 – Adding Decimals

They will need to follow the directions laid out in Lesson 152.
Answers   5.82   4.08   11.06

Lesson 154

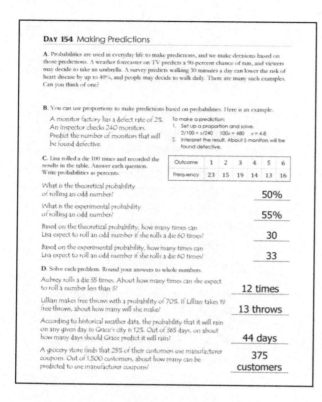

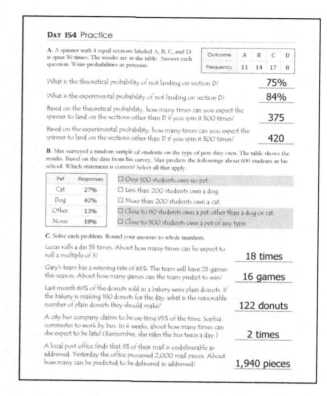

Lesson 154 – Making Predictions

To make the prediction, you multiply the total by the probability.

In Part C there are 100 trials, so one result is one percent of the total, one out of the 100. Those frequencies can be considered as percents. To find the experimental probablity of rolling an odd number would just be adding together the frequencies of the odd numbers. That's the total percent, which is the same as the probability.

Review 154 – Adding Decimals

They will need to follow the directions laid out in Lesson 152.

Answers   6.218   7.034   11.064

Lesson 155

DAY 155 Making Predictions

A. An online poll says 45% of eligible voters will participate in the coming presidential election. Ella's city has 52,000 people of voting age. Based on the poll, Ella predicts that more than 25,000 people will vote in the coming presidential election. Is her prediction accurate? Explain.

Inaccurate. 45/100 = x/52000, Less than 25000.

B. Jenna tossed two different coins 50 times and recorded the results in the table. Answer each question. Write probabilities as percents.

Outcome	HH	HT	TH	TT
Frequency	13	9	12	16

What is the theoretical probability of getting at least one heads? **75%**

What is the experimental probability of getting at least one heads? **68%**

Based on the theoretical probability, how many times can Jenna expect to get at least one heads if she tosses the two coins 250 times? **188**

Based on the experimental probability, how many times can Jenna expect to get at least one heads if she tosses the two coins 250 times? **170**

C. Solve each problem. Round your answers to whole numbers.

Oliver rolls a die 80 times. About how many times can he expect to roll a number greater than 5? **13 times**

Henry flips 2 quarters 60 times. About how many times can he expect to flip two tails? **15 times**

Landon rolls two dice 25 times. About how many times can he expect to roll the same numbers? **4 times**

Natalie's team has a winning rate of 72%. Out of 24 games, about how many games can the team expect to tie or lose? **7 games**

Zoey flips a coin 38 times and gets 15 heads. If she flips the coin 70 times, how many heads can she expect to get based on her experiment? **28 heads**

A box contains 5 red balls and 8 blue balls. Gil randomly picks a ball, records its color, and return the ball to the box. If she repeats this 40 times, how many times can she expect to pick a red ball? **15 times**

An airline claims that their flights are on time 98% of the time. The airline has 440 flights scheduled next month. About how many flights can be predicted to be delayed? **9 flights**

DAY 155 Practice

A. Four students are trying to predict how many times they would get a prime number from rolling a die 36 times. Who set up the proportion correctly? Select all that apply.

Addison	Grace	Scott	Amanda
$\frac{6}{3} = \frac{x}{36}$	$\frac{3}{6} = \frac{x}{36}$	$\frac{1}{2} = \frac{36}{x}$	$\frac{1}{2} = \frac{x}{36}$

B. A bag contains 13 red, 8 blue, 10 green, and 9 yellow marbles. Answer each question. Write probabilities as percents.

If a marble is drawn from the bag, what is the probability that it is green? **25%**

If 12 marbles are drawn from the bag, how many are expected to be green? **3**

If a marble is drawn from the bag, what is the probability that it is not blue? **80%**

If 15 marbles are drawn from the bag, how many are expected to be not blue? **12**

C. Solve each problem. Round your answers to whole numbers.

Hannah flips 2 pennies 40 times. About how many times can she expect to flip two tails? **10 times**

Landon rolls two dice 25 times. About how many times can he expect to roll two even numbers? **6 times**

Alexa flips 3 dimes 90 times. About how many times can she expect to flip three heads? **11 times**

Owen makes free throws with a probability of 75%. Out of 55 free throws, about how many will he miss? **14 throws**

The probability of rain on any given day in Jim's city is 21%. Jim can predict it will rain on about how many days during one year? **77 days**

Matt rolls a die 25 times and gets a 2 four times. If he rolls the die 30 times, how many times can he expect to get a 2? **5 times**

A survey of 100 adults finds that 57 of them plan to get a flu shot this year. Out of 11,000 adults, about how many can be predicted to get a flu shot? **6,270 adults**

An appliance company sells an extended warranty to 15% of its customers. Out of 2,500 customers, about how many are expected to purchase an extended warranty? **375 customers**

Lesson 155 – Making Predictions

In Part B these frequencies are out of 50. 13/50 = x/100 They can cross multiply to figure out the probability/frequency out of 100. But maybe they can just realize they can double each frequency because double 50 is 100.

Here are some set ups from Part C.

* Oliver: Probability is one out of six. 1/6 times 80 is the answer.
* Henry: ¼ times 60 is the answer. The sample space is 4 possibilities. Two tails is one out of the   four possibilities. One out of four is ¼ .
* Landon: Probability is 6 (1-1, 2-2, 3-3, 4-4, 5-5, 6-6) out of 6 x 6 possibilities. 1/6 times 25 is the answer.
* Natalie: The probability is 72% or .72. The prediction is .72 times 24.
* Zoey: Probability is 15/38. Prediction is 15/38 times 70.

Review 155 – Subtracting Decimals

They will need to follow the directions laid out in Lesson 152. The difference is that they are subtracting.

Answers   0.7   1.8   24.5

Lesson 156

DAY 156 Probability of Compound Events

A. A **simple event** is an event with one outcome. A **compound event** is an event composed of two or more events. Tossing heads is a simple event. Tossing two heads is a compound event.

B. Two events are **independent** if the outcome of one event does not affect the probability of the other event. Coin tosses are independent events because the outcome of one toss does not affect the outcome of the next toss. When events A and B are independent, the probability of both occurring is $P(A$ and $B) = P(A) \times P(B)$.

C. Let's see an example. Suppose you toss a coin and roll a die. What is the probability of tossing heads and rolling an odd number? Using the formula above, we first find the probability of each event, then multiply the probabilities.

Using the formula:
- $P(heads) = 1/2$
- $P(odd) = P(1, 3, or 5) = 1/2$
- $P(heads$ and $odd)$ $= P(heads) \times P(odd) = 1/2 \times 1/2 = 1/4$

D. Remember that you can always find the probability of an event using the sample space also. Use whichever method you find easier! Whether you use the probability formula or the sample space, the result will be the same.

Using the sample space:
- There are 12 possible outcomes: H1, H2, H3, H4, H5, H6, T1, T2, T3, T4, T5, T6
- There are 3 favorable outcomes: H1, H3, H5
- $P(heads$ and $odd) = 3/12 = 1/4$

E. A die is rolled twice. Find the probability of each event as a fraction.

Rolling a 4 first and a 5 second	1/36
Rolling a 3 first and an odd number second	1/12
Rolling a prime number on both rolls	1/4

F. You randomly draw a card from a stack of five cards numbered 1 to 5, put the card back in the stack, and then randomly draw another card. Find the probability of each event as a fraction.

Selecting 2 first and 4 second	1/25
Selecting an odd number first and an even number second	6/25
Selecting two numbers greater than 4	1/25

G. A bag contains 2 red balls and 4 blue balls. You randomly draw a ball from the bag two times, with replacement (putting the ball drawn back in the bag before drawing the next ball). Find the probability of each event as a fraction.

Selecting a red ball first and a blue ball second	2/9
Selecting two blue balls	4/9
Selecting at least one blue ball	8/9

DAY 156 Practice

A. A coin is tossed and a die is rolled. Find the probability of each event as a fraction.

Tossing heads and rolling a 5	1/12
Tossing tails and rolling a multiple of 3	1/6
Tossing tails and rolling a negative number	0

B. A dime and a nickel are tossed. Find the probability of each event as a fraction.

Tossing heads on the dime and tails on the nickel	1/4
Tossing one heads and one tails	1/2
Tossing at least one heads	3/4

C. A 2-digit number is formed from the digits 1 through 9 with repetition allowed. Find each probability as a fraction.

$P(number$ is $25) =$	1/81
$P(number$ is $88) =$	1/81
$P(number$ is even$) =$	4/9
$P(number$ is less than $40) =$	1/3

D. Find each probability as a fraction.

Three coins are tossed. What is the probability of landing three heads?	1/8
Three dice are rolled. What is the probability that all three numbers are greater than or equal to 5?	1/27
A quiz consists of 5 true-false questions. If you choose answers randomly, what is the probability of getting all 5 questions correct?	1/32
Jamal rolls a die and randomly selects one day of the week. What is the probability that he rolls an odd number and selects Monday or Tuesday?	1/7
A bag contains 3 red balls and 6 blue balls. Two balls are drawn at random with replacement. What is the probability of drawing two blue balls?	4/9
Two letters are chosen at random with replacement from the word BIBLE. What is the probability that they will both be vowels?	4/25

Lesson 156 – Probability of Compound Events

They should take the time to understand the examples at the top of the page. The formula is quicker, but only if you can quickly figure out the two probabilities. Sometimes it's easier just to list the actual outcomes than to figure out how to figure out the probability.

Here are the set ups for the first ones in each section.
1. 1/6 x 1/6
2. 1/5 x 1/5
3. 2/6 x 4/6

Review 156 – Subtracting Decimals

They will need to follow the directions laid out in Lesson 152. The difference is that they are subtracting.

Answers   3.27   4.36   1.93

Lesson 157

Day 157 Probability of Compound Events

A. Two events are **dependent** if the outcome of the first event affects the probability of the second event. Drawing cards without replacement is an example of dependent events. When events A and B are dependent, the probability of both occurring is the product of the probability of A and the probability of B after A occurs: P(A and B) = P(A) × P(B after A).

B. Let's see an example. Suppose you make a 2-digit number using the digits 1 to 4 and not allowing repetition of digits. What is the probability that both digits are odd?

Using the formula:
- P(first digit is odd) = 2 odds / 4 numbers = 1/2
- P(second digit is odd) = 1 odd / 3 numbers = 1/3
- P(both digits are odd)
  = P(first digit is odd) × P(second digit is odd)
  = 1/2 × 1/3 = 1/6

Using the sample space:
- There are 12 possible outcomes:
  12, 13, 14, 21, 23, 24, 31, 32, 34, 41, 42, 43
- There are 2 favorable outcomes:
  13, 31
- P(both digits are odd) = 2/12 = 1/6

C. The probability formulas are useful, but sometimes it is simpler and more straightforward to use sample spaces. Let's see another example. Suppose you roll two dice. What is the probability that the sum is 5?

Using the sample space:
- There are 36 possible outcomes:
  11, 12, 13, 14, 15, ..., 61, 62, 63, 64, 65, 66
- There are 4 favorable outcomes:
  14, 23, 32, 41
- P(sum of 5) = 4/36 = 1/9

D. Two cards are randomly selected from a stack of five cards numbered 1 to 5, without replacement. Find the probability of each event as a fraction.

Selecting 2 first and 4 second 1/20

Selecting an odd number first and an even number second 3/10

Selecting two numbers greater than 4 0

E. A bag contains 2 red balls and 4 blue balls. You randomly draw a ball from the bag two times, without replacement. Find the probability of each event as a fraction.

Selecting a red ball first and a blue ball second 4/15

Selecting two blue balls 2/5

Selecting at least one blue ball 14/15

F. A die is rolled twice. Find the probability of each event as a fraction.

Rolling two numbers that are the same 1/6

Rolling two numbers whose sum is exactly 10 .... 1/12

Rolling two numbers whose sum is at most 4 .... 1/6

Day 157 Practice

A. Determine whether the events are independent or dependent.

Tossing heads on a coin and rolling a 6 on a die .... Independent

Rolling an odd number on a die two consecutive times .... Independent

Choosing two even numbers from 1 to 9 without repetition .... Dependent

Selecting a 5 from a deck of cards, replacing it, and then selecting a queen as the second card .... Independent

Drawing a red marble from a jar containing some marbles and not replacing it, and then drawing a blue marble from the jar .... Dependent

B. A 2-digit number is formed from the digits 1 through 9 with repetition *not* allowed. Find each probability as a fraction.

P(number is 25) = 1/72

P(number is 88) = 0

P(number is even) = 4/9

P(number is less than 40) = 1/3

C. Find each probability as a fraction.

Two dice are rolled. What is the probability that the sum is 8? 5/36

Three coins are tossed. What is the probability of getting at least one heads? 7/8

A die is rolled twice. What is the probability that the second roll is greater than the first roll? 5/12

A jar contains 3 red marbles and 3 blue marbles. What is the probability of drawing two red marbles without replacing them back in the jar? 1/5

Two letters are chosen at random without replacement from the word BIBLE. What is the probability that they will both be vowels? 1/10

Cheyenne rolls a die and spins a spinner with four equal sections numbered 1 through 4. What is the probability of getting the same number? 1/6

Grace makes a 4-digit password using the digits 1 to 9 without repetition. What is the probability that all four digits are odd? 5/126

Lesson 157 – Probability of Compound Events

They are going to be practicing with probability again. The difference is that the second event is affected by the outcome of the first event. It depends on what happened before. That's why it's called a dependent event.

Here's an example. If there were ten kids getting picked for a team, the first kid has a one in ten chance of getting picked. The next kid has a one in nine chance of getting picked. The next kid has a one in eight chance of getting picked, and so on.

When you read something like P(A and B) = P(A) x P(B after A), read it in words. The probability of two events happening equals the probability of the first event times the probability of the second event after the first event has occurred.

Review 157 – Subtracting Decimals

They will need to follow the directions laid out in Lesson 152. The difference is that they are subtracting.

Answers   4.928   1.297   0.264

Lesson 158

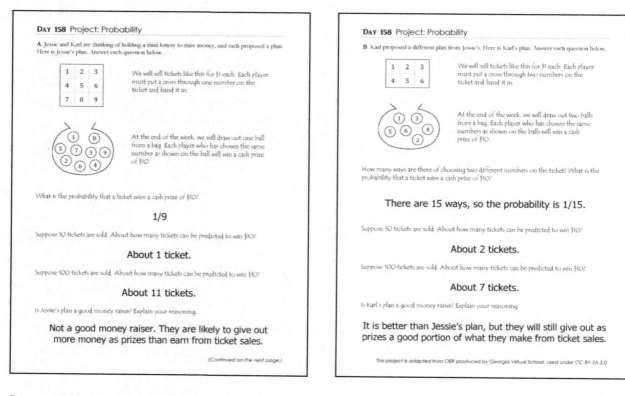

DAY 158 Project: Probability

A. Jessie and Karl are thinking of holding a mini lottery to raise money, and each proposed a plan. Here is Jessie's plan. Answer each question below.

1	2	3
4	5	6
7	8	9

We will sell tickets like this for $1 each. Each player must put a cross through one number on the ticket and hand it in.

At the end of the week, we will draw out one ball from a bag. Each player who has chosen the same number as shown on the ball will win a cash prize of $10.

What is the probability that a ticket wins a cash prize of $10?

1/9

Suppose 10 tickets are sold. About how many tickets can be predicted to win $10?

About 1 ticket.

Suppose 100 tickets are sold. About how many tickets can be predicted to win $10?

About 11 tickets.

Is Jessie's plan a good money raiser? Explain your reasoning.

Not a good money raiser. They are likely to give out more money as prizes than earn from ticket sales.

(Continued on the next page.)

DAY 158 Project: Probability

B. Karl proposed a different plan from Jessie's. Here is Karl's plan. Answer each question below.

| 1 | 2 | 3 |
| 4 | 5 | 6 |

We will sell tickets like this for $1 each. Each player must put a cross through two numbers on the ticket and hand it in.

At the end of the week, we will draw out two balls from a bag. Each player who has chosen the same numbers as shown on the balls will win a cash prize of $10.

How many ways are there of choosing two different numbers on the ticket? What is the probability that a ticket wins a cash prize of $10?

There are 15 ways, so the probability is 1/15.

Suppose 50 tickets are sold. About how many tickets can be predicted to win $10?

About 2 tickets.

Suppose 100 tickets are sold. About how many tickets can be predicted to win $10?

About 7 tickets.

Is Karl's plan a good money raiser? Explain your reasoning.

It is better than Jessie's plan, but they will still give out as prizes a good portion of what they make from ticket sales.

Lesson 158 – Project: Probability

There is a second page today! Make sure they continue. They are evaluating two different lotto plans to figure out which one is a good idea for raising money.

They should be able to explain their final conclusions to you.

No Review

Lesson 159

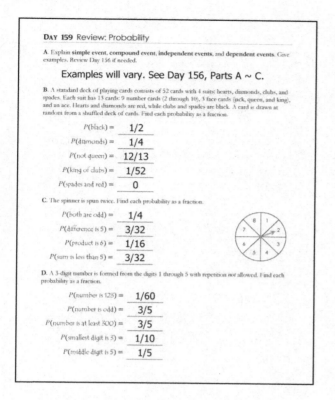

Lesson 159 – Review: Probability

This is a review. They can use previous pages for review. The top of the page lists how many cards are in each category, such as how many face cards, to help them find the probability.

In Part C they will need to think through a little math.

2nd one: 8 & 3, 3 & 8, 7 & 2, 2 & 7, 6 & 1, 1 & 6 (6) One spin can be any of 6 numbers, 3/4. The other spin has to be the one specific number that together with the first number has a difference of 5, 1/8. Probability = 1/8 x 3/4 = 3/32

3rd one: 1 x 6, 2 x 3, 3 x 2, 6 x 1 (4) One spin can be any of 4 numbers, ½. The other spin has to be the one specific number that multiplies to equal 6, 1/8. Probability = 1/8 x ½ = 1/16

Part D

2nd one: They can pick 3 out of the 5 for the last digit to make it odd. The other two don't matter, so their probability is 1 then, whatever it is works. 3/5 x 1 x 1. You can approach it other ways to get the answer. That's how I thought it through.

4th one: Smallest digit is 3 means that every choice has to be 3, 4, or 5. At first that's 3/5 then it's 2/4 then it's 1/3. The number of choices goes down by one each time and the number of odd choices left goes down each time. 3/5 x 2/4 x 1/3

No Review

Lesson 160

DAY 160 Catch up and Review!

A. Catch up if you are behind. You can go back and redo a lesson that caused you trouble.

B. Use the review problems below to make sure you're on track. If you get any problem wrong, go back and redo the corresponding day's lesson.

Day 141 Which box-and-whisker plot correctly shows the data set {1, 4, 2, 6, 2, 7, 6, 3, 4}?

Day 143 A survey of 1,000 U.S. households found that 680 of them own a pet. Identify the population and the sample.

P = All US households, S = 1000 US households

Day 146 What is the probability of picking a red marble from a bag containing 4 red marbles and 8 blue marbles?

1/3

Day 148 A coin is tossed 50 times and lands on heads 28 times. What is the experimental
Day 150 probability of tossing heads? What is the theoretical probability of tossing heads?

Experimental = 14/25   Theoretical = 1/2

Day 152 List all possible outcomes when you toss three coins.

HHH, HHT, HTH, HTT, THH, THT, TTH, TTT

Day 154 You roll a die 55 times. About how many times can you expect to roll a 6?

About 9 times.

Day 155 You roll two dice. What is the probability that the sum is 7?

1/6

C. Make sure you know the key terms. Can you explain each term in your own words?

☐ Probability   ☐ Simple event   ☐ Independent events
☐ Sample space   ☐ Compound event   ☐ Dependent events

DAY 160 Practice

A. Find the total number of possible outcomes in each situation.

Jacob rolls a die and selects a month of the year.	72
Cheryl selects an integer from 1 to 9 and a letter from the word SPACE.	45
Larry has a choice of ham, tuna, or turkey and a choice of white, wheat, or rye bread to make a sandwich.	9
Alison takes a multiple choice test which consists of 5 questions. Each question has 4 choices. You may use a calculator.	1,024
Karen makes a 4-letter password using the alphabet of 26 letters with repetition allowed. You may use a calculator.	456,976

B. Use the sample space above to find each probability as a fraction.

Jacob rolls an odd number and selects an even month.	1/4
Cheryl selects a multiple of 3 and a consonant.	1/5
Larry's sandwich has turkey.	1/3
Alison gets all questions correct.	1/1,024
Karen makes a 4-letter password starting with the letter K.	1/26

C. Solve each problem. Round your answers to whole numbers.

Aubrey tosses a coin 120 times. About how many times can she expect to get heads?	60 times
Max makes free throws with a probability of 65%. If Max takes 25 free throws, about how many will he make?	16 throws
Victoria rolls a die 80 times. About how many times can she expect to roll a number less than 3?	27 times
A spinner has six equal sections. One section is red, two sections are blue, and the rest are green. Luke spins the spinner 20 times. About how many times can he predict to land on red or green?	13 times
According to historical weather data, Levi's city had temperatures above 90 °F 16% of the time in August. About how many days can Levi predict temperatures above 90 °F this August?	5 days

Lesson 160 Catch Up and Review

Have your child check themselves using the lesson page and go back to work on problem areas. See if your child can explain the terms on the page. If they are doing well, have them use the practice page today to stay sharp.

No Review

Lesson 161

DAY 161 Writing and Evaluating Expressions

A. Describe the **order of operations**. Why do we use it? Show how order of operations affects the result when evaluating the expression $4 + 3 \times 5$. Review Day 18 if needed.

Add first = 35   Multiply first = 19

B. Explain how to find the value of the expression $2x + 5$ when $x = 3$. Review Day 20 if needed.

Substitute 3 for x. $2x + 5 = 2 \cdot 3 + 5 = 11$

C. Evaluate each expression.

$2^3 + 5 \times 4$ 28 $3 + 6 \times (8 - 2) - 4$ 35

$(5 - 4)^2 \times 3$ 3 $(4 + 6)^2 \div (7 - 2) + 8$ 28

D. Evaluate each expression when $x = 4, y = 2,$ and $z = 7$.

$2x + 5$ 13 $x^2 + 2xy + y^2$ 36

$5z - 3(x + y)$ 17 $4(x + z)^2/(9 + y)$ 44

E. Write an expression that answers each question.

Charlotte drove x miles in 4 hours. What was her average speed in miles per hour (mph)?   x/4

Ella had y apples. She used 8 apples to bake pies and 7 apples to make jam. How many apples does she have left?   y − 8 − 7

Cookies cost $0.90 each. Cupcakes cost $1.50 each. Justin bought m cookies and n cupcakes. How much did he pay in total?   0.9m + 1.5n

F. Evaluate your expression to answer each question above.

The average speed (mph) if Charlotte drove 240 miles   The number of apples left if Ella had 23 apples at first   The total cost Justin paid for 5 cookies and 8 cupcakes

60 mph   8 apples $16.50

DAY 161 Practice

A. Evaluate each expression.

$3^2 + 3 \times 2$ 15 $2^3 + (9 + 15) \div 6$ 12

$8^2 \div (9 - 5)^3$ 1 $4 + 2^4 \div 8 \times (8 - 4)^2$ 36

$4 + 5 \times 6 \div 5$ 10 $(7 \times 12 + 6)^2 \div (6 \times 5)$ 270

$(6^2 - 6) \div 2 \times 4$ 60 $(15 + (9 - 2) \times 9)^2 \div 6^2$ 169

B. Evaluate each expression for the given value(s) of the variable(s).

$7(x - 3); x = 9$ 42 $4a - 4b; a = 9, b = 6$ 12

$(k + 5)/3; k = 4$ 3 $7pq - p^2; p = 4, q = 2$ 40

$m(2 + m); m = 3$ 15 $h^2 + k^2 - 2; h = 3, k = 4$ 23

C. Write an expression that answers each question.

Kris paid $u for 6 donuts. What is the unit price per donut?   u/6

Tylor had n candies and ate 1/3 of them. How many candies does Tylor have left?   n − (1/3)n

A rectangular prism has a width of x cm. Its length and height are 4 cm shorter than its width. What is the volume of the prism?   x(x − 4)^2

D. Evaluate your expression to answer each question above.

The unit price per donut if Kris paid $7.50   The number of candies left if Tylor had 27 candies at first   The volume of the prism if it has a width of 6 cm

$1.25   18 candies   24 cm³

Lesson 161 – Writing and Evaluating Expressions

They are switching gears back to PEMDAS and expressions. If they think of all subtraction as adding a negative and all division as multiplying the reciprocal, then there's never confusion over what needs to happen first to get the correct answer.

When they need to explain, they can just tell you. They don't need to write it out, but they need to explain. If they can't explain it, they don't know it.

In Part C they are following the order of operations. They solve inside the parentheses, then the exponents. If the exponent is outside the parentheses, then they add or subtract whatever is in the parentheses and then that answer is raised to the exponent.

In Part D they substitute in the values and then solve. 5z means 5 times z.

In Part E they write expressions. In Part F they are told the answers. They will put an equals sign after the expression and then the answer given in F. They will solve for the variable.

Review 161 – Word Problems

These are word problems that are going to require arithmetic with decimals.

Answers   6.3 gallons, $6.88, $64.84

Lesson 162

Lesson 162 – Commutative and Associative Properties

Commutative is about moving around numbers. You can freely reorder numbers that are being added or multiplied. Associative is about combining certain numbers first. You can freely combine numbers that are multiplied or added. You can't do that with subtraction and division, but you can if you make those adding negatives and multiplying reciprocals.

In Part A adding 13 and 47 is 10 + 40 + 10(which is 3 + 7). 60 + 29 is then easy to do.

In Part B multiplying 2 x 5 makes 10, which makes it easy to multiply by 16.

Those are the things they are looking for, things that when combined end in zero, making the answers easier.

In Part F they are just rewriting the words as expressions.

Review 162 – Multiplying Decimals

To multiply the decimals, they just multiply the digits and then place the decimal correctly in the answer. The total number of decimal places in the question need to be in the answer. These only have decimal places in one number. 0.3 x 8 would have one decimal place in the answer.
Answers   2.4   0.28   0.056

Lesson 163

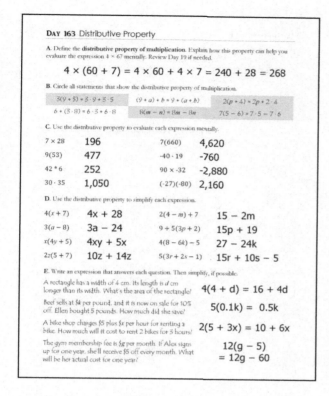

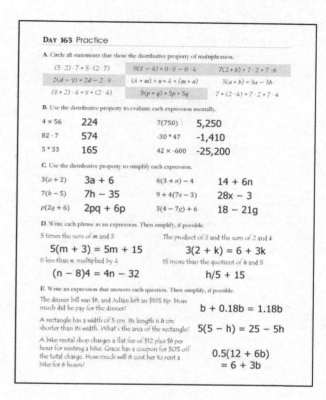

Lesson 163 – Distributive Property

In Part B only the middle top is not distributive. That one is associative.

In Part C they are to break apart the place values.

$$7 \times 28 = 7(20 + 8) = 140 + 56 \qquad 7(600 + 60) = 4200 + 420$$

In Part D they use the distributive property and then combine like terms (basically the numbers).

In Part E they are just writing the expressions. They should simplify the expression. Here are some set ups.

width times length = 4(d + 4) = area
amount times price times percent = 5k x .1 = amount off

Review 163 – Multiplying Decimals

This is the same thing except there are decimal places in each number. The answer needs to have the same total number of decimal places.   2.1 x 3.4 = 21 x 34 with two decimal places

Answers   3.45   1.53   2.12

Lesson 164

DAY 164 Using Formulas

A. A **formula** is a mathematical statement that shows the relationship between different variables. Formulas are used in many fields such as physics, biology, engineering, finance, medicine, and economics. Here are some real-world formulas.

Time-speed-distance formula

$$d = rt$$

where d = distance, r = rate (speed), and t = time.

Simple interest formula

$$I = Prt$$

where I = interest, p = principal, r = annual interest rate (as a decimal), t = time (year).

Pythagorean theorem

$$a^2 + b^2 = c^2$$

where a = base of a right triangle, b = its height, and c = its hypotenuse, or diagonal side.

Cylinder volume formula

$$V = \pi r^2 h$$

where V = volume, r = radius of a circle (base), and h = height of a cylinder.

B. While constructing a real-world formula is difficult because it has to be proved true in every case, using an already-found formula is simply a matter of evaluating an algebraic expression. Use the formulas above to solve each problem. Use 3.14 for π.

Tony drove for 3 hours at an average speed of 58 miles per hour (mph). How many miles did Tony drive? — **174 miles**

A train traveled 750 kilometers in 6 hours. What is the train's average speed in kilometers per hour (km/h)? — **125 km/h**

Sam put $3,000 in her savings account at a simple interest rate of 2% per year. How much interest will Sam earn in four years? — **$240**

Carol borrowed $1,500 from a bank and paid back $1,575 after one year. At what simple interest rate did Carol borrow the money? — **5%**

A right triangle has a base of 3 cm and a height of 4 cm. What is the hypotenuse of the triangle? — **5 cm**

A right triangle has a base of 5 inches and a height of 12 inches. What is the perimeter of the triangle? — **30 in**

A right triangle has a base of 8 cm and a hypotenuse of 10 cm. What is the area of the triangle? — **24 cm²**

A cylinder has a radius of 1 foot and a height of 2 feet. What is the volume of the cylinder? — **6.28 ft³**

A cylinder has a radius of 10 cm and a volume of 3,140 cm³. What is the height of the cylinder? — **10 cm**

DAY 164 Practice

A. You already know many important formulas in geometry. Below are the area formulas of common shapes you've learned so far. Use them to solve each problem. Use 3.14 for π.

Circle	Triangle	Rectangle	Parallelogram	Trapezoid
$A = \pi r^2$	$A = \frac{1}{2}bh$	$A = lw$	$A = bh$	$A = \frac{1}{2}h(b_1 + b_2)$
r = radius	b = base, h = height	l = length, w = width	b = base, h = height	b_1, b_2 = two bases, h = height

I am a circle with a diameter of 2 inches. What is my area? — **3.14 in²**

I am a square with an area of 36 square meters. What is my perimeter? — **24 m**

I am an equilateral triangle with a perimeter of 18 cm. My height is 5.2 cm. What is my area? — **15.6 cm²**

I am a rectangle with a length of 5 feet. My perimeter is 11.8 feet. What is my area? — **4.5 ft²**

I am a right triangle. The lengths of my sides are 10 cm, 24 cm, and 26 cm. What is my area? — **120 cm²**

I am a parallelogram with a base of 8 inches. The ratio of my base to height is 4.5. What is my area? — **80 in²**

I am a trapezoid with bases of 3 meters and 5 meters. My area is 16 square meters. What is my height? — **4 m**

B. Below are some geometry formulas you will learn in high school. Use them to solve each problem. Leave π in your calculations.

Pythagorean theorem	Volume of a sphere	Surface area of a sphere
$a^2 + b^2 = c^2$	$V = \frac{4}{3}\pi r^3$	$SA = 4\pi r^2$

I am a sphere with a radius of 3 inches. What is my volume? — **36π in³**

I am a sphere with a radius of 5 inches. What is my surface area? — **100π in²**

I am a right triangle with a base of 9 feet and a height of 12 feet. What is my perimeter? — **36 feet**

I am a prism with right triangles as bases. My base triangle has base 6 cm and height 8 cm. My height is 10 cm. What is my surface area? — **288 cm²**

Lesson 164 – Using Formulas

They can think of these formulas as expressions or equations that they need to solve. There will be variables given that they can just plug in.

Here are some word problem set ups. Make sure they label their answer. Going back to see what to label it may help them check to see if they are answering the question! It's up to you if you want to allow a calculator.

1. 3 x 58 = # of miles
2. 750/6 = average speed km/h
3. 3000 x 0.02 x 4 = interest earned over four years $
4. 1500 x ? = 75 (or 1500 x 1.? = 1575) Divide 75 by 1500. Answer in %.
5. $3^2 + 4^2 = c^2$

Review 164 – Multiplying Decimals

This is the same thing but with more decimal places. 0.08 x 0.5 = 0.040 = 0.04

Answers   0.504   23.52   20.15

Lesson 165

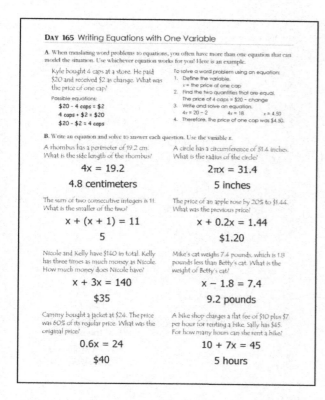

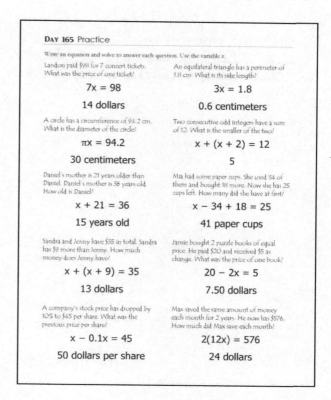

Lesson 165 – Writing Equations with One Variable

They are writing equations. This is just like writing expressions but they are equal something. There are some things they will need to know or realize.

C = two times pi times the radius

It would also help to know that a rhomus has four equal-length sides.

Consecutive integers come right after each other, so x and x + 1 are consecutive. Finding the next odd (or even) number would be x and x + 2.

To find the previous price, they need to multiply the percent and amount and then subtract that off the price.

Review 165 – Multiplying Decimals

This is the same thing but with more decimal places.

Answers   1.819   1.94   46.9872

Lesson 166

DAY 166 Addition and Subtraction Equations

A. Write a real-world problem that could be represented by the equation $x + 6 = 10$. Then solve the equation to find the answer to your problem. Show the steps. Review Day 24 if needed.

Answers will vary. See Days 24 and 28.

B. Solve each equation.

$x + 5 = 17$ $16 + x = 23$ $x - 4.2 = 0.9$
x = 12   x = 7   x = 5.1

$3 + x - 9 = 12$ $x + 0.7 = 4.5 - 1.2$ $2.5 = 0.4 + 1.27 + x$
x = 18   x = 2.6   x = 0.83

$x + \frac{1}{4} = \frac{1}{2}$ $x - \frac{2}{3} = \frac{1}{6}$ $x + 1\frac{2}{5} = 2\frac{3}{4}$
x = 1/4   x = 5/6   x = 1 7/20

$x - \frac{1}{3} = \frac{1}{2} + \frac{2}{3}$ $4\frac{1}{3} = 2 + x - \frac{1}{9}$ $x + 1\frac{3}{4} = 2\frac{1}{2} - \frac{3}{4}$
x = 1 1/2   x = 2 4/9   x = 0

C. Write an equation and solve to answer each question. Use the variable x.

The perimeter of a quadrilateral is 22 cm. Three of the sides are 5 cm, 5 cm, and 6 cm. What is the length of the fourth side? $5 + 5 + 6 + x = 22$ 6 centimeters

Claire found 87 seashells on the beach. Sam found 65 seashells. Thirty-four of them were broken. How many unbroken seashells did they find together? $x + 34 = 87 + 65$ 118 seashells

Tylor read 3/8 of a book yesterday. He read some more today. So far he has read 5/8 of the book. What fraction of the book did he read today? $3/8 + x = 5/8$ 1/4 of the book

DAY 166 Practice

A. Solve each equation.

$x + 18 = 35$ $27 + x = 49$ $x - 9 = 64$
x = 17   x = 22   x = 73

$5 + x - 7 = 16$ $2 + 9 + x = 25$ $x + 4 = 3 + 5 \times 2$
x = 18   x = 14   x = 9

$1.2 = 0.9 + x$ $x + 4.97 = 5.204$ $0.18 + x = 1.5 - 0.4$
x = 0.3   x = 0.234   x = 0.92

$x - \frac{5}{8} = \frac{3}{4}$ $x - \frac{1}{6} = \frac{3}{8}$ $x + 2\frac{1}{3} = 5$
x = 1 3/8   x = 13/24   x = 2 2/3

$x - \frac{1}{5} = \frac{1}{2} + \frac{3}{5}$ $2\frac{1}{6} = 2 + x - \frac{2}{3}$ $4\frac{1}{2} + x = 5\frac{2}{3} - \frac{3}{4}$
x = 1 3/10   x = 5/6   x = 5/12

B. Write an equation and solve to answer each question. Use the variable x.

There were some people in the auditorium. Thirty-five of them left, and 25 people entered. There were 52 people after that. How many people were there at first? $x - 35 + 23 = 52$ 64 people

Sarah has some red, blue, and yellow markers. Half of them are red and 3/10 are blue. What fraction of the markers are yellow? $1/2 + 3/10 + x = 1$ 1/5 of the markers

Ronald bought 5 notebooks and some colored pencils. Notebooks cost $2 each. He paid $20 and received $3 as change. How much did the colored pencils cost? $5 * 2 + x = 20 - 3$ 7 dollars

Lesson 166 – Addition and Subtraction Equations

An example for Part A would be that there are 6 people and another group showed up and then there were 10 people. How many were in the group?

Part B requires them to combine like terms, which is just numbers right now and just adding and subtracting. They will do the opposite to get the variable on its own.

First one: $x + 5 = 17$
        $x - 5 = 17 - 5$
        $x + 0 = 12$ which is just $x = 12$

Word problems:

1. $22 = 5 + 5 + 6 + x$
2. $87 + 65 - 34 = x$
3. $3/8 + x = 5/8$

Review 166 – Multiplying Decimals

This is the same thing.

Answers   13.2   22.25   0.81084

Lesson 167

DAY 167 Multiplication and Division Equations

A. Write a real-world problem that could be represented by the equation $5x = 20$. Then solve the equation to find the answer to your problem. Show the steps. Review Day 26 if needed.

Answers will vary. See Days 26 and 28.

B. Solve each equation.

$4x = 52$	$105 = 5x$	$1.4x = 9.8$
x = 13	x = 21	x = 7

$7x = 8 + 2 \times 3$	$x + 2x = 8 + 4^2$	$4.32 - 1.92 = 0.08x$
x = 2	x = 8	x = 30

$\frac{x}{5} = 17$	$0.32 = \frac{x}{7}$	$\frac{1}{3}x = \frac{2}{7}$
x = 85	x = 2.24	x = 6/7

$\frac{1}{4}x = 1\frac{3}{5}$	$\frac{x}{5} = \frac{1}{2} \times \frac{2}{3} \times 6$	$5\frac{1}{2} + \frac{3}{4} \times \frac{2}{3} = \frac{x}{4}$
x = 6 2/5	x = 10	x = 24

C. Write an equation and solve to answer each question. Use the variable x.

A rectangle with a width of 6 cm has an area of 54 cm². What is the length of the rectangle?	6x = 54	9 cm
Amy drove 140 miles at an average speed of 56 miles per hour. How many hours did she drive?	56x = 140	2.5 hrs
Max and Kris have $51 in total. Max has twice as much money as Kris. How much money …	x + 2x = 51	$17
Justin went for a movie. He spent ½ of his money on a ticket and ⅕ on snacks. In total, he spent $14. How much money did he have at first?	x/2 + x/5 = 14	$20

DAY 167 Practice

A. Solve each equation.

$9x = 108$	$78 = 5x$	$0.7x = 0.49$
x = 12	x = 15.6	x = 0.7

$19 + 13 = 4x$	$2^3 + 4 \times 7 = 6x$	$3x - x + 8x = 0.25 \times 4$
x = 8	x = 6	x = 0.1

$0.9x = 3.3 + 1.2$	$1.24 = 4x - 0.9x$	$0.5x = 25 - 3.5$
x = 5	x = 0.4	x = 43

$\frac{x}{8} = 15$	$0.9 = \frac{x}{4}$	$\frac{3}{4}x = \frac{3}{5}$
x = 120	x = 3.6	x = 4/5

$\frac{3}{5}x = 1\frac{1}{2}$	$\frac{x}{2} = \frac{3}{4} - \frac{1}{4} + 4$	$\frac{6}{7} \times 2\frac{4}{5} \times 1\frac{2}{3} = \frac{x}{2}$
x = 2 1/2	x = 9	x = 8

B. Write an equation and solve to answer each question. Use the variable x.

Jim scored 90% on his math test. He got 27 problems correct. How many problems …	0.9x = 27	30 problems
The volume of a prism is 125 cm³. Its square base has a side length of 5 cm. What's …	25x = 125	5 cm
Mark cut a 12-inch ribbon into ³⁄₄-inch pieces. How many pieces does he have …	(3/4)x = 12	16 pieces
Kim and Curtis have 9 coins in total. Curtis has half as many coins as Kim. How many …	x + x/2 = 9	6 coins

Lesson 167 – Multiplication and Division Equations

A Part A example could be that you need 20 apples and there are 5 in each little bushel, then how many bushels are needed.

In Part B they need to combine like terms. For example, $2 + 3$ would combine to 5 and $2x + 3x$ would combine to 5x. You can't combine $2 + 3x$. x and x^2 are also two different things. They are not alike. They shouldn't be combined.

$2x + 3x = 20$ (need to combine like terms)
$5x = 20$ (need to divide each side by 5 or multiply by one fifth)
$x = 4$

Word problems:
1. $6x = 54$
2. $140 = 56x$
3. $51 = 2x + x$
4. $½ x + 1/5 x = 14$

Review 167 – Word Problems

They are going to be multiplying decimals to solve these. Make sure they label their answers.

Answers $42.90, $29.85, 63 miles

Lesson 168

DAY 168 Two-Step Equations

A. Write a real-world problem that could be represented by the equation $4x + 7 = 15$. Then solve the equation to find the answer to your problem. Show the steps. Review Day 85 if needed.

Answers will vary. See Days 85 and 165.

B. Solve each equation.

$5x + 17 = 37$	$28 = 7(x - 2)$	$9(x + 0.2) - 5 = 3.1$
x = 4	x = 6	x = 0.7

$\frac{x}{9} + 15 = 18$	$17 - \frac{x}{8} = 15$	$\frac{x}{5} + 0.8 = 9.4$
x = 27	x = 16	x = 43

$\frac{2}{3}x + \frac{1}{4} = \frac{1}{3}$	$\frac{1}{6}x - \frac{2}{3} = \frac{5}{6}$	$1\frac{1}{5}x + 1\frac{4}{5} = 4\frac{1}{2}$
x = 1/8	x = 9	x = 2 1/4

C. Write an equation and solve to answer each question. Use the variable x.

The sum of three consecutive integers is 30. What is the smallest of the three?	$x + (x + 1) + (x + 2) = 30$	9
Ron had $15. After he bought pears at $1.50 each, he had $3 left. How many pears …	$15 - 1.5x = 3$	8 pears
The perimeter of a rectangular garden is 24 feet. Its length is 8 feet. What is the width …	$2 * 8 + 2x = 24$	4 feet
Larry has a 158-page reading assignment. So far he has read 83 pages. If he reads 25 pages …	$83 + 25x = 158$	3 days

DAY 168 Practice

A. Solve each equation.

$6x + 11 = 35$	$4(15 - x) = 16$	$9.4 = 1.8 + 0.8x$
x = 4	x = 11	x = 9.5

$24 = \frac{x}{5} + 19$	$\frac{x}{6} - 11 = 10$	$\frac{x}{3} + 4.2 = 15$
x = 25	x = 126	x = 32.4

$\frac{3}{5}x - \frac{1}{4} = \frac{1}{5}$	$\frac{1}{2}\left(x + \frac{1}{6}\right) = \frac{1}{4}$	$2\frac{3}{4}x + 1\frac{1}{6} = 5\frac{2}{3}$
x = 3/4	x = 1/3	x = 1 7/11

B. Write an equation and solve to answer each question. Use the variable x.

Ronald used half of his stamps, and bought 6 more. He now has 18. How …	$x/2 + 6 = 18$	24 stamps
Jack wants to save $76 in 4 weeks. He now has $8. How much should he …	$4x + 8 = 76$	$17
Danny had $40. After buying 3 concert tickets, he had $13. How much did it …	$3x + 13 = 40$	$9
The perimeter of a rectangle is 26 cm. The width of the rectangle is 5 cm shorter than its length. What is …	$2x + 2(x - 5) = 26$	9 cm
Melvin bought 4 notebooks and 6 pens. Notebooks cost $2 each. He paid $20 and received $3 as change. How much …	$4 * 2 + 6x = 20 - 3$	$1.50

Lesson 168 – Two-Step Equations

In Part A, one example would be if you had seven oranges and needed fifteen and each bag had four oranges, how many bags do you need to buy?

Here's an example of two-step equations.

$2 + 3 + 2x + 3x = 20$ (need to combine like terms)

$5 + 5x = 20$ (need to subtract five from each side or add negative five)

$5x = 15$ (need to divide each side by 5 or multiply by one fifth)

$x = 3$

Word problems:
1. $x + x + 1 + x + 2 = 30$
2. $15 - 1.5x = 3$
3. $8 + 8 + 2x = 24$
4. $158 = 83 + 25x$

Review 168 – Division

They are supposed to divide into decimals if necessary. Thirty-five divided by two. Two goes into three, one time. Two then goes into fifteen seven times. Then there is a remainder of one. They place a decimal point next to the five and add a zero. Now two goes into ten five times. The answer is 17.5. The decimal place goes straight up into the answer.

Answers   0.8   4.1   0.25

Lesson 169

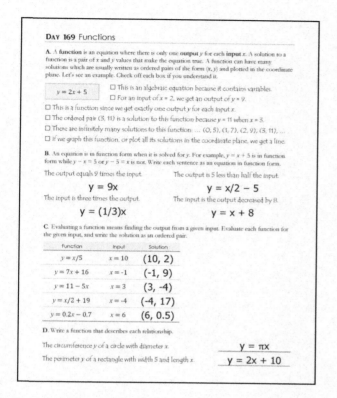

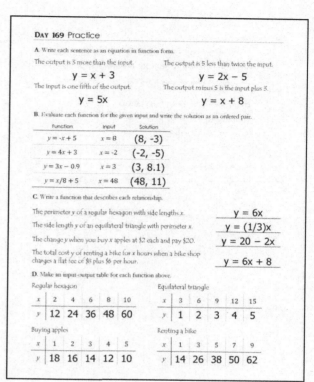

Lesson 169 – Functions

This is talking about "inputs," but this is really just substituting in a value for a variable like they've done many times before. They put in the value for X and solve. The answer is the Y. You can write the answer x = 1 y = 2 for instance or write them as an ordered pair (x, y) or (1, 2) from the example.

A function is when the equation is solved for Y. It has to look like $y =$ something.

In Part C the first number in each ordered pair will be the X given. The second number is the Y, the solution.

Review 169 – Dividing Decimals

If there is a decimal place in the divisor, the number on the left going into the other, they have to get rid of that. They multiply both by ten until there are no decimal places in the divisor.

Answers   0.9   20   300

Lesson 170

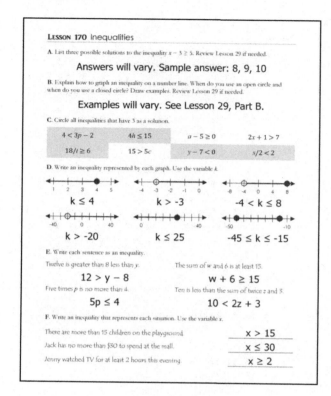

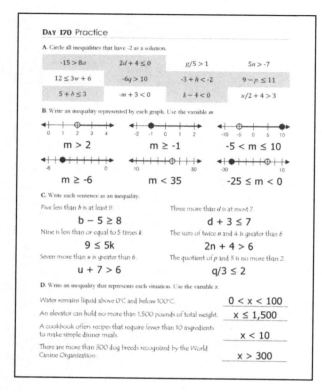

Lesson 170 – Inequalities

For Part B they can remember that an open circle shows that number is not part of the solution. A line with no dot at the end is considered to continue on. If there is a dot on each side, then the answer is greater than and equal to one number and less than and equal to the other.

Review 170 – Dividing Decimals

They will continue practicing dividing decimals.

Answers   8.3   2.6   14

Lesson 171

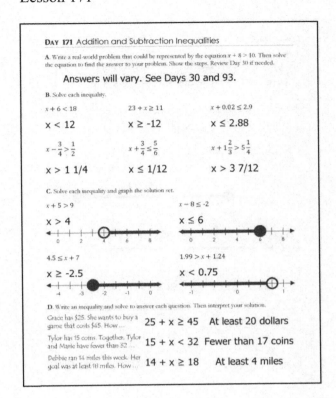

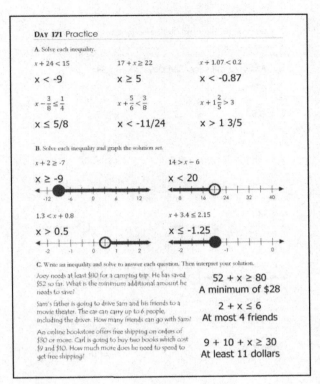

Lesson 171 – Addition and Subtraction Inequalities

For Part A one example might be that you need more than 10 eggs in order to make pound cake and you have 8, so how many more eggs do you need, at least?

They are going to solve these inequalities just like equations. The greater than/less than sign stays facing the same way. They have done these before.

Review 171 – Dividing Decimals

They will continue practicing dividing decimals.

Answers   590   13   180

Lesson 172

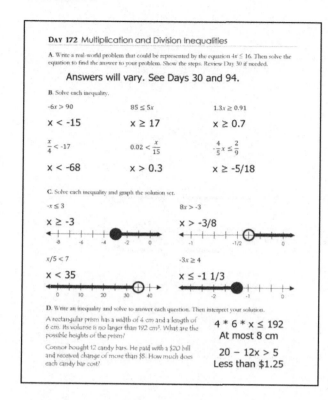

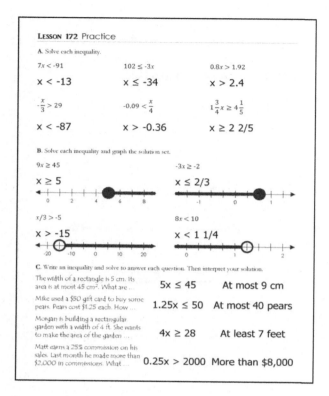

Lesson 172 – Multiplication and Division Inequalities

An example for Part A would be that you can't take more than sixteen people and each group will have four people in it, how many groups can you take?

They have done these before. They will multiply or multiply by the reciprocal in order to get the X, the variable, alone. This time, if they multiply by a negative number, the greater than/less than sign needs to flip.

Review 172 – Dividing Decimals

They will continue practicing dividing decimals.

Answers   268.9   11.54   44.25

Lesson 173

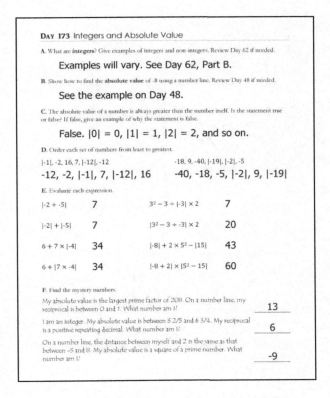

DAY 173 Integers and Absolute Value

A. What are **integers**? Give examples of integers and non-integers. Review Day 62 if needed.

Examples will vary. See Day 62, Part B.

B. Show how to find the **absolute value** of -8 using a number line. Review Day 48 if needed.

See the example on Day 48.

C. The absolute value of a number is always greater than the number itself. Is the statement true or false? If false, give an example of why the statement is false.

False. |0| = 0, |1| = 1, |2| = 2, and so on.

D. Order each set of numbers from least to greatest.

|-1|, -2, 16, 7, |-12|, -12   -18, 9, -40, |-19|, |-2|, -5

-12, -2, |-1|, 7, |-12|, 16   -40, -18, -5, |-2|, 9, |-19|

E. Evaluate each expression.

|-2 + -5| **7** $3^2 - 3 + |-3| \times 2$ **7**

|-2| + |-5| **7** $|3^2 - 3 + -3| \times 2$ **20**

6 + 7 × |-4| **34** $|-8| + 2 \times 5^2 - |15|$ **43**

6 + |7 × -4| **34** $|-8 + 2| \times |5^2 - 15|$ **60**

F. Find the mystery numbers.

My absolute value is the largest prime factor of 208. On a number line, my reciprocal is between 0 and 1. What number am I?   **13**

I am an integer. My absolute value is between 5 2/5 and 6 3/4. My reciprocal is a positive repeating decimal. What number am I?   **6**

On a number line, the distance between myself and 2 is the same as that between -5 and 8. My absolute value is a square of a prime number. What number am I?   **-9**

DAY 173 Practice

A. The absolute value of a sum is the sum of the absolute values of the addends. Is the statement true or false? If false, give an example of why the statement is false.

False. |4 + (-2)| is not equal to |4| + |-2|.

B. Order each set of numbers from least to greatest.

|-8|, 5, -2, -15, 10, |-15| 20, |-9|, -9, |-14|, -5, 0

-15, -2, 5, |-8|, 10, |-15| -9, -5, 0, |-9|, |-14|, 20

C. Evaluate each expression.

|-6| + 12   **18** $|2 - 2^3 + -4 \times 2|$ **14**

|-6 + 12| **6** $2 - 2^3 + |-4 \times 2|$ **2**

|-6| + |12| **18** $|2 - 2^3| + |-4| \times 2$ **14**

|-8 × 7 + 3| **53** $|3^2 - 7| + |5 \times -9|$ **47**

|-8| × 7 + 3   **59** $|7 - 3^2| + 5 \times |-9|$ **47**

D. Find the mystery numbers.

I am the opposite of the smallest positive integer. What is 8 less than the product of 6 and my absolute value?   **-2**

My absolute value equals the smaller of two consecutive integers whose sum is 5 squared. Zero is to my left on a number line. What number am I?   **12**

I am an even integer greater than or equal to 20% of 15 and less than the area of a triangle with base 3 and height 3. What number am I?   **4**

My absolute value is 9 less than the smallest two-digit prime number. If I double myself, I move to the left on a number line. What number am I?   **-2**

My absolute value is a factor of 120, and it is divisible by 3 but not by 6. I am greater than 18% of 5 and less than the ratio of the circumference of a circle to its diameter. What number am I?   **3**

Lesson 173 – Integers and Absolute Value

An integer is any number line number such as …-1, 0, 1…

The absolute value of any number is its distance from 0 on the number line.

In Part D they need to find the absolute value and then order them.

In order to evaluate the expressions in Part E, they should consider the absolute value lines like parentheses. They should do everything inside it in proper order and then work from there.

Review 173 – Dividing Decimals

They will continue practicing dividing decimals.

Answers   9.3   14   82.05

Lesson 174

DAY 174 Adding and Subtracting Integers

A. Explain how to add two integers with different signs. Give examples. Review Day 63 if needed.

Examples will vary. See Day 63, Part A.

B. Explain how to change subtraction into addition. Give examples. Review Day 63 if needed.

Examples will vary. See Day 63, Part A.

C. Here is a tip for you! There are many math strategies you can use. One strategy is to think of subtraction as addition and split a number into parts that make calculating easy. The first expression below, for example, can be thought as -5 + (5 + 3) + -17 = (-5 + 5) + (3 + -17). Evaluate each expression below. Use any strategy that works for you!

-5 + 8 - 17	-14	4 + 52 + -6 - -23	73
3 + -9 + 16	10	15 - 38 + 3 + -16	-36
2 - 4 + -12	-14	-7 + 14 + 35 - 49	-7
-10 + 7 - -5	2	6 + 17 - 22 - 5 + -4	-8
6 + -19 + -2	-15	-13 + 20 - 7 + -9 - 8	-17

D. Solve each problem.

The temperature yesterday was -3 °C. Today it was 5 degrees colder. What was the temperature today?   **-8 °C**

A submarine was 630 feet below sea level, then it ascended 325 feet. What is its new depth?   **-305 feet**

Joe had $508 in his bank account. He withdrew $86, wrote a check for $55, and deposited a check for $90. What is his final balance?   **$457**

The current temperature is -4°C in New York City, 2°C in Brooklyn, and 0°C in Buffalo. Which city is the warmest?   **Brooklyn**

The Dead Sea, the lowest elevation on Earth, is 1,312 feet below sea level. Mt. Everest, the highest elevation, is 29,028 feet above sea level. What is the difference in elevation between the two locations?   **30,340 feet**

DAY 174 Practice

A. Evaluate each expression.

3 + 17 - 15	5	9 + 22 + -6 + 13	38
2 + -14 - 7	-19	18 - 29 + 3 + 16	8
-5 + 9 + -16	-12	-25 + 4 + 16 - 39	-44
12 - 4 + -18	-10	46 - -12 + 4 - -17	79
4 + -19 - 35	-50	54 + -17 + 18 - 32	23
-14 - 9 + 17	-6	9 - 7 - 32 - 16 + 8	-38

B. Solve each problem.

An elevator was on the 12th floor of a building. It went up 3 floors and then down 9 floors. On what floor is the elevator now?   **6th floor**

The temperature in the morning was 6 °C, but it dropped to -5 °C in the evening. How much did it drop during the day?   **11 °C**

This year the city spent a total of $21,000,000, ending up with a deficit of $900,000. What was the city's budget this year?   **$20,100,000**

B.C. stands for "before Christ." A.D. stands for the Latin phrase *anno domini*, which means "in the year of our Lord." How many years apart are 150 BC and 235 AD?   **385 years**

In 260 BC Archimedes proved that the value of π lies between 3.1429 and 3.1408. In 2016 AD, Peter Trueb calculated π to 22.4 trillion digits. How many years passed between the two events?   **2,276 years**

C. Find the next two numbers in each integer sequence. Use the simplest rule you can find. (Hint: Check the sum or difference between two consecutive numbers.)

-5, -1, 3, 7, 11, **15, 19**   2, 5, 9, 14, 20, 27, **35, 44**

Lesson 174 – Adding and Subtracting Integers

When adding integers of separate signs:
1. If the signs are the same, you add them and keep the sign.
2. If the signs are opposite, you find the difference and use the sign of the larger number.
3. Subtracting a negative number is the same as just adding it. Take those two negative signs and combine them to make an addition sign. Change all subtraction into adding a negative.
4. When you are adding negative numbers, you can do it in any order because you are adding.

Review 174 – Word Problems

They will be dividing with decimals to solve the word problems.

Answers   230 square feet, 205 miles, 6.25 cups

Lesson 175

DAY 175 Multiplying and Dividing Integers

A. Explain how to determine the sign of the product or quotient of two integers. Give examples. Review Day 63 if needed.

Examples will vary. See Day 63, Part A.

B. Here is a tip for you! One strategy for multiplication is to use the distributive property, as introduced on Day 19. Another strategy is to split a number into factors and regroup the factors. For example, the first expression below can be thought as $5 \times 5 \times 4 \times 4 = (5 \times 4) \times (5 \times 4)$. Remember that division is just multiplication by the reciprocal. Evaluate each expression below. Use any strategy that works for you!

25×16	**400**	$25 \cdot 60$	**1,500**	$4(370)$	**1,480**
95×-3	**-285**	$-15 \cdot 12$	**-180**	$-14(35)$	**-490**
$84 \div -6$	**-14**	$-8 \cdot 6 \div 4$	**-12**	$9(-8)/18$	**-4**
$-51 \div -3$	**17**	$-9 \cdot 4 \div -6$	**6**	$5(6)/-15$	**-2**

C. Evaluate each expression when $x = -2$, $y = 6$, and $z = -5$.

xyz	**60**	$|xy| \cdot z$	**-60**	$-y/-x$	**-3**
$|xyz|$	**60**	$xy/-3$	**4**	$xyz/-4$	**-15**

D. Solve each problem.

A submarine was 1,430 feet below sea level, then it ascended at a rate of 75 feet per minute for 10 minutes. What is its new depth? **-680 feet**

Lynn withdrew $140 each week from her bank account for one year. Her final balance was $620. What was her starting balance? **$7,900**

The temperature at 9 a.m. was 5 °C. Since then, it has been dropping 1.5 degrees every hour. What will be the temperature at 4 p.m.? **-5.5 °C**

The population of a town this year is 56,200. It is expected to increase by 4,000 each year. What will be the population of the town in 3 years? **68,200**

DAY 175 Practice

A. Evaluate each expression.

15×-8	**-120**	$83 \cdot 60$	**4,980**	$7(-56)$	**-392**
$56 \div -4$	**-14**	$-48 \cdot 25$	**-1,200**	$-45(40)$	**-1,800**
$-84 \div -7$	**12**	$-6 \cdot -270$	**1,620**	$-6(15)/-9$	**10**
-24×-15	**360**	$-6 \cdot 6 \div 9$	**-4**	$21(-6)/14$	**-9**

B. Evaluate each expression when $x = -5$, $y = 4$, and $z = -8$.

xyz	**160**	xz/y	**10**	$xyz/-10$	**-16**
$|-xyz|$	**160**	$-z/-y$	**-2**	$(x/y) \cdot z$	**10**

C. Solve each problem.

A submarine was 120 feet below sea level, then it descended to 610 feet below sea level in 7 minutes. How many feet per minute did the submarine descend? **70 feet/min**

A mountain climber starts descending from 750 feet above sea level at an average speed of 30 feet per hour. How long will it take him to reach 40 feet above sea level? **23 hours**

Stacey had a lemonade stand for two weeks. For the first week, she had an average loss of $19 a day. For the second week, she had an average profit of $36 a day. What's her total profit? **$119**

Tom has $5,800 in his bank account. Every month, Tom's company deposits his salary of $2,100 and his rent of $670 is withdrawn automatically. What will be his balance in 6 month? **$12,380**

D. Find the next two numbers in each integer sequence. Use the simplest rule you can find.

2, 4, 8, 16, 32, 64, **128, 256**   1, 4, 9, 16, 25, 36, **49, 64**

Lesson 175 – Multiplying and Dividing Integers

When you multiply or divide by a negative, if the signs are the same, the answer is positive. If the signs are opposite, the answer is negative.

Division is the same as multiplying by the reciprocal. If you change all the division into multiplying by the recriprocal, then you can rearrange the multiplying however is easiest to combine them.

Review 175 – Adding Integers

They will add positive and negative numbers in the columns and rows to reach the target number.

Answers   11   -4   -1 | -10   2   14 | 5   8   -7

Lesson 176

DAY 176 Two-Step Equations

A. Explain **inverse operations**. How are they used to solve equations? How do you keep equations balanced when performing inverse operations? Review Day 28 if needed.

See Day 28, Parts A and B.

B. Solve each equation.

$2x + 4 = 10$

x = 3

$3 - 4x = -13$

x = 4

$29 = x - 6x + 4$

x = -5

$16 = -10 - 5.2x$

x = -5

$-0.5x - 7 = 9.4$

x = -32.8

$2.4x - 1.5 = 10.5$

x = 5

$\frac{x}{5} - 7 = -9$

x = -10

$2\frac{1}{4} = 6x - 1\frac{3}{4}$

x = 2/3

$\frac{1}{2}x - 2x = 1\frac{1}{2}$

x = -1

C. Use an equation to solve each problem.

Jessica put 22 feet of fencing around her rectangular garden with a width of 5 feet. What is the length of her garden?   6 feet

Maria bought some pencils at $0.30 each and 4 erasers at $0.15 each. The total cost was $3.30. How many pencils did Maria buy?   9 pencils

The perimeter of a rectangle is 22 cm. The width of the rectangle is 2 cm longer than its length. What is the length of the rectangle?   4.5 cm

The sum of three consecutive even integers is 24. What is 20 more than the product of the three numbers?   500

DAY 176 Practice

A. Solve each equation.

$5x - 4 = -9$

x = -1

$8 + 4x = -15$

x = -5.75

$19 = 2x - 7x + 7$

x = -2 2/5

$35 = -10 - 2.5x$

x = -18

$-0.4x + 9 = -5.2$

x = 35.5

$1.5x - 2.8x = 9.1$

x = -7

$\frac{x}{6} + 4 = -7$

x = -66

$\frac{2}{3}x + 4x = -\frac{1}{3}$

x = -1/14

$3\frac{1}{5} = \frac{2}{5}x - \frac{3}{5}$

x = 9 1/2

B. Use an equation to solve each problem.

Sam had $59. After buying some poster boards at $8 each, he has $11 left. How many boards did he buy?   6 posters

Jill bought some crayons. She lost one-fifth of them and now has only 16. How many crayons did Jill buy?   20 crayons

In 2 years Owen will be twice as old as his younger brother Larry. Owen is 14 years old now. How old is Larry?   6 years old

C. Use an equation to find the three numbers and answer the question for each case.

The sum of three consecutive integers is 39. What is 5 less than the smallest of the three?   12, 13, 14   7

The sum of three consecutive odd integers is 21. What is 15 more than the product of the three numbers?   5, 7, 9   330

The sum of three consecutive integers is 8 more than twice the largest number. What is ...   9, 10, 11   1000

Lesson 176 – Two-Step Equations

The inverse is the opposite. Examples are that 2 + (-2) = 0 and 2 x ½ = 1.

We use the inverse to isolate the variable, to get it alone.

Review 176 – Adding Positive and Negative Fractions

They will add positive and negative numbers in the columns and rows to reach the target number.

Answers   1/4   -2 7/8   -2 1/4 | -4 1/8   -1 5/8   7/8 | -1   - 3/8   -3 1/2

Lesson 177

DAY 177 Two-Step Inequalities

A. Explain the similarities and differences between solving equations and solving inequalities. Give examples. Review Days 24, 26, and 30 if needed.

Examples will vary. See Days 24, 26, and 30.

B. Solve each inequality.

$2(2x + 1) > 10$

x > 2

$9 \leq 2(8 - x)$

x ≤ 3 1/2

$2.7x - 4.2x \geq 4.5$

x ≤ -3

$9 \leq \frac{x - 7}{3}$

x ≥ 34

$\frac{x}{4} + 5 \leq 6$

x ≤ 4

$-1 \leq \frac{1}{5} - x$

x ≤ 1 1/5

$\frac{3 - x}{4} \leq -6$

x ≥ 27

$-6 < \frac{1}{2} - 2x$

x < 3 1/4

$-\frac{x}{3} - 2 \leq 7$

x ≥ -27

C. Use an inequality to solve each problem.

The sum of two consecutive integers is at most 31. What is the greatest possible value for the greater integer? — 16

A rectangle with a width of 4 cm has a perimeter of at most 24 cm. What is the largest possible length of the rectangle? — 8 cm

Joe wants to save at least $80 in 5 weeks. He now has $15. What is the minimum amount of money that he should save each week? — $13

Jessica has $8 more than Aubrey. Together, they have less than $24. How much money does Aubrey have? — Less than $8

DAY 177 Practice

A. Solve each inequality.

$x + 9 > 23$

x > 14

$-5x \leq 75$

x ≥ -15

$-15 < 8(x - 5) + 33$

x > -1

$1.5 > -6 - 2.5x$

x > -3

$-0.2x + 9 \geq -3.2$

x ≤ 61

$2.5x - 4(x - 2) < 3.8$

x > 2.8

$\frac{x}{3} - 2 < -4$

x < -6

$9 \geq \frac{x}{2} - 3x$

x ≥ -3 3/5

$-5 + \frac{4}{7}x < \frac{5}{7}$

x < 10

$\frac{x}{8} + 4 \geq 7$

x ≥ 24

$\frac{1}{2} > 5x - \frac{3}{4}$

x < 1/4

$\frac{2}{3}x - x \leq \frac{1}{4}$

x ≥ -3/4

B. Use an inequality to solve each problem.

A right triangle has a base of 8 cm. Its area is at least 16 cm² and at most 36 cm². What are the smallest possible height and largest possible height of the triangle? — 4 cm, 9 cm

Chris wants to buy some pencils and 5 pens. A pencil costs $0.80 and a pen costs $1.20. He has only $20 to spend. What is the maximum number of pencils Chris can buy? — 17 pencils

A cuboid has a width of 4 cm and a length of 6 cm. Its volume is at least 72 cm³ and at most 192 cm³. What is the difference between the largest possible height and the smallest possible height? — 5 cm

Lesson 177 – Two-Step Inequalities

They need to get the variable by itself. They start by simplifying and combining like terms.

They need to remember to flip the inequal sign when multiplying or dividing by a negative number.

Review 177 – Adding Positive and Negative Decimals

They will add positive and negative numbers in the columns and rows to reach the target number.

Answers   -0.42   1.28   0.94 | 1.96   0.6   -0.76 | 0.26   -0.08   1.62

Lesson 178

DAY 178 Ratios, Rates, and Unit Rates

A. Explain how to simplify the ratio 32/56. Show the steps. Review Day 11 if needed.

Divide 32 and 56 by GCF 8. (32 ÷ 8)/(56 ÷ 8)= 4/7

B. Explain the difference between a rate and a unit rate. Give examples. Review Day 11 if needed.

Examples will vary. See Day 11, Part C.

C. Simplify each ratio to lowest terms.

9 to 15   **3:5**   12:16   **3:4**   40/35   **8:7**

8 to 20   **2:5**   28:21   **4:3**   84/98   **6:7**

D. Find a unit rate that represents each situation. Be sure to include the units in your answers.

544 points in 8 games   90 children in 6 groups

43 points/game   **15 children/group**

$72 for 4.5 hours of work   270 miles in 4 1/2 hours

$16/hour   **60 miles/hour**

E. Solve each problem.

Emily bought 0.4 pounds of goat cheese and paid $5.80. What was the price of the cheese per pound?   **$14.50**

Store M sells a 2-kilogram bag of rice for $6.90. Store N sells a 5-kilogram bag of rice for $18.00. Which store offers the better deal?   **Store M**

Walter can type an average of 870 words in 15 minutes. Jamie can type an average of 312 words in 6 minutes. Who types faster?   **Walter**

Ana bought 5 concert tickets online. The shipping cost per order was $8, and she paid $93 in total. What was the price of one ticket?   **$17**

Joshua bought 8 apples at $9.60 and 6 melons at $16.80. Ariana bought 6 apples and 8 melons at the same prices as Joshua. How much did they spend in all?   **$56**

DAY 178 Practice

A. Simplify each ratio to lowest terms.

8 to 14   **4:7**   36:28   **9:7**   40/72   **5:9**

B. Find a unit rate that represents each situation.

1,505 words on 7 pages   217 miles in 3.5 hours

215 words/page   **62 miles/hour**

$72.80 for 4 tickets   132 pages in 5 1/2 days

$18.20/ticket   **24 pages/day**

C. Solve each problem.

Oliver ran 100 meters in 15 seconds. Carter ran 150 meters in 22 seconds. Who ran faster?   **Carter**

Store P sells 2 cucumbers for $1.10. Store Q sells 8 cucumbers for $4.20. Which store has the better buy?   **Store Q**

Rodney paid $9.20 for 8 candy bars. Max bought 10 candy bars at the same price as Rodney. How much did Max pay?   **$11.50**

A grocery store was offering a one-day BOGO (buy one get one free) sale on 10.75-ounce cans of tomato soup. Carl bought 8 cans and paid $5.96. What is the non-sale price per can?   **$0.99**

D. Find the mystery ratios. Write your answers using a colon.

I am equivalent to the ratio of vowels to consonants in the word "RATIO." The sum of my two numbers is the least common multiple of 4 and 10. What ratio am I?   **8:12**

I am equivalent to the ratio of the circumference to the area of a circle with a radius of 5 cm. The difference between my two numbers equals the number of faces in a rectangular prism. What ratio am I?   **4:10**

I am the simplest form of the ratio of the coefficient of x to the coefficient of y in the expression 5(2x + 4y) + x − 2xy − 9y + 7 when simplified. What ratio am I?   **7:3**

Lesson 178 – Ratios, Rates, and Unit Rates

To simplify a fraction, they need to divide the numerator and denominator by the same number.

A rate is a fraction, a unit rate is a fraction with the number 1 in the denominator.

They can treat the ratios just like fractions when simplifying.

Review 178 – Riddle

They need to read carefully to figure out the mystery number.

Answers   24/48   4/20   75/100

Lesson 179

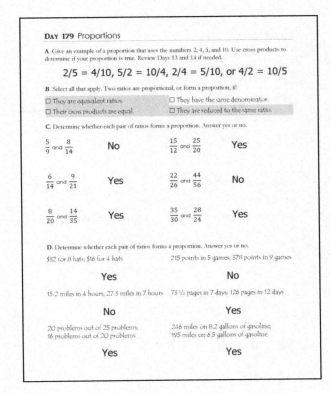

DAY 179 Proportions

A. Give an example of a proportion that uses the numbers 2, 4, 5, and 10. Use cross products to determine if your proportion is true. Review Days 13 and 14 if needed.

$$2/5 = 4/10, \ 5/2 = 10/4, \ 2/4 = 5/10, \text{ or } 4/2 = 10/5$$

B. Select all that apply. Two ratios are proportional, or form a proportion, if:

☐ They are equivalent ratios.   ☐ They have the same denominator.
☐ Their cross products are equal.   ☐ They are reduced to the same ratio.

C. Determine whether each pair of ratios forms a proportion. Answer yes or no.

$\frac{5}{9}$ and $\frac{8}{14}$ No $\frac{15}{12}$ and $\frac{25}{20}$ Yes

$\frac{6}{14}$ and $\frac{9}{21}$ Yes $\frac{22}{26}$ and $\frac{44}{56}$ No

$\frac{8}{20}$ and $\frac{14}{35}$ Yes $\frac{35}{30}$ and $\frac{28}{24}$ Yes

D. Determine whether each pair of ratios forms a proportion. Answer yes or no.

$32 for 8 hats; $16 for 4 hats   215 points in 5 games; 378 points in 9 games

Yes   No

15.2 miles in 4 hours; 27.3 miles in 7 hours   73 ½ pages in 7 days; 126 pages in 12 days

No   Yes

20 problems out of 25 problems;   246 miles on 8.2 gallons of gasoline;
16 problems out of 20 problems   195 miles on 6.5 gallons of gasoline

Yes   Yes

DAY 179 Practice

A. Simplify each ratio. Find all ratios that can form a proportion with each other.

15:18   25:30   90:105   175:210
 5:6   5:6   6:7   5:6

B. Determine whether each pair of ratios forms a proportion. Answer yes or no.

$\frac{4}{18}$ and $\frac{6}{24}$ No $\frac{18}{42}$ and $\frac{28}{35}$ No

$\frac{9}{16}$ and $\frac{3}{12}$ No $\frac{14}{36}$ and $\frac{21}{54}$ Yes

$\frac{6}{14}$ and $\frac{21}{49}$ Yes $\frac{36}{63}$ and $\frac{28}{49}$ Yes

C. Determine whether each pair of ratios forms a proportion. Answer yes or no.

$65 in 5 hours; $91 in 7 hours   50 m in 9 seconds; 120 m in 20 seconds

Yes   No

$30 for 4 tickets; $51 for 6 tickets $12.80 for 160 copies; $17.60 for 220 copies

No   Yes

56 balls in 14 bags; 72 balls in 18 bags   750 km in 6 ¼ hours; 570 km in 4 ¾ hours

Yes   Yes

154 words in 3 ½ minutes;   5 ¼ cups of beans for 6 servings of soup;
319 words in 7 ¼ minutes   3 ½ cups of beans for 4 servings of soup

Yes   Yes

Lesson 179 – Proportions

In Part A they can set it up anyway they like. It is true if they set it up 2/5 and 4/10. They can show it by multiplying 2 by 10 and 5 by 4. You can see that these are just equivalent fractions. If numbers are proportional, their ratios are equivalent fractions.

Review 179 – Riddle

They need to read carefully to figure out the mystery number.

Answers   2.5   2.35   -3.375

Lesson 180

DAY 180 Proportions

A. Explain how to solve the proportion $9/15 = x/5$ in two different ways: using equivalent ratios and using cross multiplication. Review Days 13 and 14 if needed.

Divide 9 and 15 by 3, or solve 15x = 45.

B. Write a real-world problem that could be solved using a proportion. Then solve the proportion to find the answer to your problem. Show the steps. Review Days 13 and 14 if needed.

Answers will vary. See Days 13 and 14.

C. Solve each proportion.

$\frac{6}{8} = \frac{x}{10}$ x = 7.5 $\frac{15}{x} = \frac{12}{20}$ x = 25

$\frac{x}{5} = \frac{48}{30}$ x = 8 $\frac{30}{35} = \frac{x}{84}$ x = 72

$\frac{36}{48} = \frac{9}{x}$ x = 12 $\frac{x}{54} = \frac{45}{50}$ x = 48.6

D. Write a proportion and solve to answer each question. Use the variable x.

Nathan bought a shirt for $35. The sales tax is 8% ($8 per $100). How much sales tax did Nathan pay?

Marie drew a rectangle whose length-to-width ratio was 4 to 5. If the length of the rectangle was 10 inches, what was its width?

$2.80   **12.5 inches**

Carter can paint 100 ft² in 0.5 hours. How many hours will it take him to paint 5 rectangular walls that are 10 feet wide and 8 feet tall?

The price of beef is $6.50 per pound, and pork is $5 per pound. Ariel bought 3 pounds of beef and 2.5 pounds of pork. How much did she pay in total?

2 hours   **$32**

DAY 180 Practice

A. Solve each proportion.

$\frac{7}{x} = \frac{28}{16}$ x = 4 $\frac{40}{25} = \frac{32}{x}$ x = 20

$\frac{24}{27} = \frac{x}{9}$ x = 8 $\frac{x}{35} = \frac{36}{60}$ x = 21

$\frac{x}{8} = \frac{36}{72}$ x = 4 $\frac{12}{16} = \frac{18}{x}$ x = 24

B. Write a proportion and solve to answer each question. Use the variable x.

A 10-foot flagpole casts an 18-foot shadow. A nearby building is 25 feet tall. How long is its shadow?

It took Grace 40 minutes to walk 2.5 miles. How long will it take her to walk 6 miles at the same speed?

45 feet   **1 hour 36 minutes**

Mason bought a hat at $9.90. The price was 40% off its regular price. What was the original price?

It takes about 5 seconds for sound to travel 5,300 feet in air. How long will it take to travel 1 mile? (1 mile = 5,280 feet)

$16.50   **4.8 seconds**

C. Here are some tricky proportions. See if you can solve them!

$\frac{27}{x+8} = \frac{3}{5}$ x = 37 $\frac{18}{21} = \frac{2x+3}{14}$ x = 4.5

$\frac{40}{24} = \frac{5}{x-9}$ x = 12 $\frac{4-5x}{50} = \frac{27}{30}$ x = -8.2

Lesson 180 – Proportions

In Part A they can use equivalent fractions to solve for X, but using cross multiplication in the long run will be the easiest way to solve for X.

In Part B an example could be that you need 2 eggs to make one batch of brownies. If you need to make 3 batches, how any eggs will you need? 2:1 as x:3. 3 x 2 = 1x   6 = x

They will cross multiply to solve by multiplying the one denominator by the other numerator. They can make this easier by reducing the fractions first.

Review 180 – Riddle

They need to read carefully to figure out the mystery number.

Answers   6   19/11   75.32

We hope you had a great year with EP Math 6/7.

EP provides free, complete, high quality online homeschool curriculum for children around the world. Find more of our courses and resources on our site, allinonehomeschool.com.

If you prefer offline materials, consider Genesis Curriculum which takes a book of the Bible and turns it into daily lessons in science, social studies, and language arts for your children to learn all together. The curriculum also includes learning Biblical languages. Genesis Curriculum offers Rainbow Readers and a new math curriculum, A Mind for Math, which is also done all together and is based on each day's Bible reading. GC Steps is an offline preschool and kindergarten program. Learn more about our expanding curriculum on our site, genesiscurriculum.com.

Made in the USA
Columbia, SC
23 September 2024

42848618R00102